WOMEN OF THE VALOIS COURT

FAMOUS WOMEN OF THE FRENCH COURT.

From the French of Imbert de Saint-Amand.

Each with Portrait, 12mo, $1.25.

THREE VOLUMES ON MARIE ANTOINETTE.

MARIE ANTOINETTE AND THE END OF THE OLD RÉGIME.
MARIE ANTOINETTE AT THE TUILERIES.
MARIE ANTOINETTE AND THE DOWNFALL OF ROYALTY.

THREE VOLUMES ON THE EMPRESS JOSEPHINE.

CITIZENESS BONAPARTE.
THE WIFE OF THE FIRST CONSUL.
THE COURT OF THE EMPRESS JOSEPHINE.

FOUR VOLUMES ON THE EMPRESS MARIE LOUISE.

THE HAPPY DAYS OF MARIE LOUISE.
MARIE LOUISE AND THE DECADENCE OF THE EMPIRE.
MARIE LOUISE AND THE INVASION OF 1814.
MARIE LOUISE, THE RETURN FROM ELBA, AND THE HUNDRED DAYS.

TWO VOLUMES ON THE DUCHESS OF ANGOULÊME.

THE YOUTH OF THE DUCHESS OF ANGOULÊME.
THE DUCHESS OF ANGOULÊME AND THE TWO RESTORATIONS.

THREE VOLUMES ON THE DUCHESS OF BERRY.

THE DUCHESS OF BERRY AND THE COURT OF LOUIS XVIII.
THE DUCHESS OF BERRY AND THE COURT OF CHARLES X.
THE DUCHESS OF BERRY AND THE REVOLUTION OF JULY, 1830.

MARGUERITE OF ANGOULÊME

Women of the Valois Court

BY

IMBERT DE SAINT-AMAND

TRANSLATED BY
ELIZABETH GILBERT MARTIN

WITH PORTRAITS

WILDSIDE PRESS

CONTENTS

FIRST PART

MARGUERITE, SISTER OF FRANCIS I.

CHAPTER		PAGE
I.	INTRODUCTION	3
II.	THE YOUTH OF MARGUERITE OF ANGOULÊME	17
III.	THE MADRID CAPTIVITY	26
IV.	THE BEGINNINGS OF THE REFORMATION	44
V.	THE LAST YEARS OF MARGUERITE OF ANGOULÊME	57
VI.	POEMS AND LETTERS OF MARGUERITE OF ANGOULÊME	74
VII.	THE HEPTAMERON	92
VIII.	CONCLUSION	108

SECOND PART

CATHERINE DE' MEDICI AND HER CONTEMPORARIES AT THE FRENCH COURT

I.	INTRODUCTION	123
II.	THE HISTORIANS OF CATHERINE DE' MEDICI	135
III.	THE CHILDHOOD, OF CATHERINE DE' MEDICI	149
IV.	CATHERINE DE' MEDICI AT THE COURT OF FRANCIS I.	161
V.	DIANA OF POITIERS	175

CHAPTER		PAGE
VI.	MARY STUART	190
VII.	CATHERINE DE' MEDICI REGENT	206
VIII.	ELISABETH OF FRANCE, WIFE OF PHILIP II	222
IX.	THE CHILDHOOD OF MARGUERITE DE VALOIS	235
X.	JEANNE D'ALBRET	248
XI.	THE MARRIAGE OF MARGUERITE DE VALOIS	261
XII.	CATHERINE DE' MEDICI AND THE SAINT BARTHOLOMEW	271
XIII.	ELISABETH OF AUSTRIA AND CHARLES IX	281
XIV.	LOUISE DE VAUDEMONT AND HENRY III	293
XV.	MARGUERITE OF VALOIS AND HENRY OF NAVARRE	304
XVI.	CATHERINE DE' MEDICI AND THE DAY OF THE BARRICADES	321
XVII.	THE DEATH OF CATHERINE DE' MEDICI	329
XVIII.	CONCLUSION	336

LIST OF PORTRAITS

MARGUERITE OF ANGOULÊME . . . Frontispiece

CATHERINE DE' MEDICI 128

DIANE DE POITIERS 175

MARIE STUART, WHEN DAUPHINESS OF FRANCE . 194

ELISABETH OF FRANCE 222

JEANNE D'ALBRET 248

First Part

Marguerite, Sister of Francis I.

MARGUERITE, SISTER OF FRANCIS I.

I

INTRODUCTION

FRANCIS I. had exclaimed that a court without women is a year without springtime, and a springtime without roses. Adieu dark dungeons, long ennuis of a sombre and solitary life! The châtelaines, hitherto relegated to the depths of their provinces, obey the summons of the knightly King; they come to adorn by their presence those fairy-like palaces where life glides by in never-ending festivities. Appearing on the political scene, they play a great rôle there from the very start. The women of the sixteenth century have an exceptional attraction. Christian in certain aspects of their character, Pagan in others, they confound the Gospel with mythology, and issue from the churches to go and consult fortune-tellers and astrologers. Taking an active part in every event of this epoch so full of contrasts and agitations, wherein, to use Montaigne's expression, human nature was shaken in every direction, they are amazons and poets, they brave fatigue and danger, they rule by wit and beauty, by knowledge and by courage; they have the seductions of Armida.

In this strange, brilliant society, where erudition gains admission as a luxury, and the audacities of thought are welcomed as a new enjoyment; where the most unalloyed expression of social maturity and the immortal blossom of art begin perceptibly to unfold, and yet where a depth of violence and roughness amounting to barbarism is hidden beneath a surface of exquisite politeness, one sometimes inhales a breath of poesy, both sentimental and sensual, and sometimes an odor of blood. This epoch which has so many sufferings and so many pleasures, so many tears and so many bursts of laughter, where the gaiety of Rabelais twinkles amidst paroxysms of fanaticism and cries of hatred, where the passions remain savage although the fashions have a subtile grace; this picturesque epoch, dramatic above all others, presents itself under aspects which are by turns grandiose and grotesque, alluring and horrible. What characterizes it is a blended elegance and cruelty. Christian mysticism is united with the love of form which is the cult of paganism; the grossest superstitions blend with the most daring scepticism. Religion and debauchery take possession of the same souls. Tormented, uneasy, inconsistent century, to which may be applied the verdict of La Bruyère on Rabelais: "'Tis a monstrous mingling of fire and ingenious morality and filthy corruption; where it is bad it goes far beyond the worst, it charms the scum of the people; where it is good, it is even exquisite and excellent, perhaps the most delicate of viands." In this social world of the Valois, so curious to observe from the point of view of ideas and manners, all the heroines who have made their mark are worthy of the profoundest study. What variety there is in these feminine types, where one discovers every shade of human passion, and where, amidst the most tragical events, vices and virtues are developed under the conditions best fitted to illustrate them. If the levity of many of the beauties who shone at the court made them deserve Brantôme for a biographer, there were also women in this century where good and evil elbow each other, who are, as the *Chronique d'Anjou* says of Claude of France, "a true mirror of chastity, sanctity, and innocence." There are noble Christian women, who, arrayed in their modesty, are the glory of their husbands, the ornaments of their families, and who shed around them a fragrance of grace and goodness; there are women of superior intelligence who, rising above the prejudices of their age, soar into the spheres where the soul is purified and made strong.

To the foremost rank of these elect women belongs the *Pearl of Valois*, the sister of Francis I., the mother of Jeanne d'Albret, the grandmother of Henry IV., the *Marguerite of Marguerites*, "fourth Grace, and tenth Muse," as her contemporaries called her. To Francis she was the most unwearied of servants, the noblest of friends, the most generous of sisters.

"In the family, as it is dreamed of by hearts enamoured of the ideal, there is one being who plays a wholly unique part, and whose influence upon the young man has somewhat charming in it: it is the sister. If she is younger than her brother, she is almost a daughter to him; if she is older, she is almost a mother. . . . When death snatches our parents from us, with whom does memory bid us seek them? With our sister. Communing with her we evoke the days that are no more, the beings for whom we weep, and, pressing her to our hearts, it seems to us that we embrace also our father and our mother and all our vanished youth. . . ."

The author of these touching lines, M. Legouvé,[1] adds as a confirmation of what he has just said: "Well, this portrait of the sister, with her train of delicate and beneficent influences, has once been realized in history under the form of Marguerite of Navarre, the sister of Francis I. Francis and Marguerite were brought up together by their mother, Louise of Savoy, at the castle of Etampes. They were united by similar tastes for poetry and science, and as she was by two years the elder, her tenderness was blended with that maternal solicitude which befits so well the youth of sisters."

History should not separate from each other two

---

[1] *Histoire morale des femmes.*

types which summarize a society of which they were the most brilliant personages. Francis I. marks the transition between the Middle Ages and the modern world; Marguerite is the genius of the future, the modern woman with her noblest attributes. To study these two characters, which have some points of similarity and many more of unlikeness, is to examine under its different phases an epoch which, in spite of all, has left a profound and durable impression upon France.

A nature full of vehemence both in good and evil, Francis I. is the hero of an age of moral and material unrest, wherein manners, ideas, and beliefs are all in a chaotic state, and where humanity after a gestation full of anguish is bringing forth modern society with cruel throes. A character versatile and various, as Montaigne would say, he has the impulses of generosity and the base designs of egotism; at once poetic and trivial, delicate and gross, chivalric and Machiavellian, he passes in his amours from a refined mysticism to the lewdness of a trooper. One day he is as fanatical as the most ignorant monk, and the next he has the sceptical bearing of a libertine. He wavers between Calvinism and the tendencies of an inquisitor; he protects Protestants in Germany and sends them to the block in France. The defender of the faith is the Mussulman's closest ally. To-day he shelters the art of printing, to-morrow he would like to destroy all books. "Under the guise of an irresistible charm, under an exterior rich in promise, we shall find a soul all instinct, inconstant passion, and caprice. The sensibility, the generosity, lie at the surface; underneath is an insatiable thirst for pleasure, and an absorbing selfishness. He will deceive, oppress, or abandon all that he may have loved. Even art, which wins his most constant affection, touches him by his imagination, not his soul; by voluptuous grace and outward show, not by the ideal and divine."[1]

We must regard with much suspicion the admiration inspired in certain panegyrists by what they have agreed to call the chivalrous sentiments of Francis I. The Middle Ages are past, and we are no longer in the days of the knights of Charlemagne and the heroes of the Round Table. The crowned paladin, the very Christian King, knighted by Bayard, evokes in vain the ancient legends, and enthuses over the Amadis of the Gauls. The sixteenth century is not the epoch of troubadours. When Francis I. and Charles V. challenge each other to single combat, and heralds at arms bear the cartels across France and Spain, blazon on breast, and gonfalon in hand, people smile at these reminiscences of the past. They are the last vestiges of a time which is disappearing. Whatever they may say about it, no one believes any longer in platonic loves and ideal adventures. Rabelais does

---

[1] Henri Martin, *Histoire de France*, t. viii.

justice to all these exaggerations, relegating them to Nonsense Island (*Île des Lanternes*). Blow a blast on Roland's horn; it will not awaken the dead generations; chivalry is but a memory. Yet a few years and Michael Cervantes will write *Don Quixote*.

It must be admitted, nevertheless, that the old customs about to sink into the gulf of oblivion had had their prestige, and the sovereign who, if not in reality, yet in appearance, was their brilliant representative, was bound to exercise a strong attraction over the minds of his contemporaries. In spite of his faults and vices, his inconsequent policy as versatile and violent as himself, his name calls up a world of alluring memories. At his voice a new civilization, dissolute, immoral, but embellished with every splendor, arises on the soil strewn with the refuse of the Middle Ages. Magnificent dwellings, pleasing manors, spring up as by enchantment: Fontainebleau, La Muette, Saint-Germain, Villers-Cotterets, Chantilly, Follembray, and that palace of fairies created in the depths of the forest of Sologne, the marvellous and fantastic Chambord.

Though one agrees with M. Henri Martin that "France and this man who represents it, not by his inmost qualities, but by his external gifts and his defects, failed together of a grand destiny," yet he must none the less declare that, in spite of everything, few kings have preserved so much prestige in the memory of peoples as the courtly and magnificent monarch of the Renaissance. Shall modern historians be more rigid towards him than the brethren of his victims? "O pious spectator," says Theodore de Beza, as he numbers him among the reformers, "shudder not at the sight of this adversary! Does he not merit this honor who, having driven barbarism from the world, put in its place the three tongues (Hebrew, Greek, and Latin), and good literature, in order to open the doors of the new edifice?" No one can judge Francis I. impartially who does not take into account the prejudices of his times; and it must not be forgotten that at their coronation the Kings of France swore to exterminate heretics. Men are weighted by the errors of their age, and many crimes must be ascribed, less to individual wickedness, than to general folly. Francis I. was, after all, neither worse nor better than his epoch, and his life summarizes its chief contrasts.

Marguerite of Angoulême, on the contrary, showed herself superior to her age. She had the presentiments, the intuitions of the future. As we have said already, she is a woman essentially modern in her aspirations, ideas, morals, and even by her sufferings, and it is fitting to regard her under this aspect. "The image of Marguerite remains engraven on the mind as the symbol of all that was noble, good, generous, and liberal in the sixteenth century, of all the graces which win for princes the hearts of their people, especially of those simple graces which seem to banish admiration so as to leave more room for sympathy, and the charm of which continues to allure even posterity throughout the centuries."[1] A loving, amiable, delicate spirit, she casts a glimmer of poetry over the court of her brother, of whom she was the good angel. As Sainte-Beuve has said so well: "She is a person of real piety of heart, of knowledge, and of humanity, who joins a cheerful enjoyment of humor to a serious life, forming a very sincere *ensemble* of the whole." She remains faithful to her duty in the midst of a voluptuous and corrupt society where everything concurs to over-excite the senses and imagination, and her contemporaries are unanimous in their recognition of her virtue. All the great minds of her century take pleasure in doing her justice. In dedicating to her the third book of *Pantagruel*, Rabelais attributes to her a "rapt, transported, and ecstatic spirit," and places her yet living in the celestial dwellings. Erasmus wrote to her, in 1525: "I have long admired in you many eminent gifts of God, a prudence worthy of a philosopher, chastity, moderation, piety, an invincible strength of soul, and a marvellous contempt of all perishable things. And who would not consider with admiration in the sister of so great a king, qualities which can hardly be found in priests and monks?" Dolet addressed her a Latin ode, of which the following is a translation —

---

[1] M. Luro, *Conférences sur Marguerite d'Angoulême*.

"*To the Queen of Navarre.*

"Minerva was alarmed for her children; she was disquieted by fear lest the stupid common people and men, strangers to the liberal arts, might treat roughly, and cause to suffer, the elegant minds polished and ennobled by literature, that she wished to send into France from the cave of the Muses. She offered thee to the men of letters — thee, whose protection and authority would cover them with a safe buckler from the violence of a blended populace, and the threats of furious enemies. Is it to be wondered at if, having taken the learned under thine ægis, at the prayer of Pallas, thou dost honor, love, and defend them, and employ thy power for their assistance? Let them tremble, let them burst with rage, those wretches covetous of the glory which thence accrues to thee, who seek to soil the splendor of thy famous name. Thou wilt be recommended to posterity by the praises of that illustrious band of Minerva's sons who have been sheltered beneath thy far-reaching protection."

Marguerite merits this dithyramb. Never, in fact, is she happier than when saving a victim from persecution, in recompensing a poor man of letters, in relieving an artist's discouragement, or giving an asylum to a proscript. As Brantôme says, she is "a princess of broad mind and great ability both by nature and acquirements," and the most learned men of the kingdom honor her so greatly that they style her their Mæcenas. Her influence is always good. Clemency is on her lips. The desire to do good animates all she does. In a depraved age she finds means to approach the ideal woman such as we dream of her to-day: gentle, sensible, enlightened, virtuous without prudery, religious without fanaticism, learned without pedantry. Erudition detracts nothing from the easy bearing and natural grace of her mind. She hides her knowledge instead of displaying it, and in her writings gives not a hint that she possesses it. Everywhere and always she has that indulgence, that amiability, that charm of benevolence and repose, which makes woman the consoler of our pains.

At first glance, Marguerite's life seems a series of joys and excitements. Sister of the King of France, and herself a queen, admired by courtiers justly enthusiastic for her merits and virtues, she appears brilliant and honored, whether in her brother's palaces or the picturesque château of Pau, fronting that splendid horizon and those mountains which appeal to the imagination of poets. On all sides of her resound music, verses, ingenious dialogues, and amusing gossip. Every one takes turns in rhyming, singing, story-telling. But how many griefs and pains, deceptions and anxieties, there are in the course of this existence, whose woof seems at first glance made of silk and gold! As a young girl, Marguerite is married against her will to the Duke of Alençon, and fails to find in her husband the moral qualities she had a right to expect. "Francis I. seizes her daughter by this marriage, and shuts the child up in the château of Plessis-lez-Tours, lest she should be espoused to some prince not of his choosing. When she attains her twelfth year, he promises her to the Prince of Cleves in spite of Marguerite's entreaties. Is Francis I. a monster, then? No; he is a feudal brother. A thousand facts prove that he loves his sister sincerely; but he loves her as an eldest son was able to love in such a constitution of the family. To appropriate all the common patrimony, to sequester his niece if she offends him, to interfere with violence in the child's marriage, — all this seems to him to belong to the rights and almost the duties of his position as head of the family and as sovereign."[1]

Marguerite is profoundly afflicted by the sad and odious spectacle of the vices, abuses, and crimes which unroll before her. Scaffolds whereon Protestants are burned by a slow fire while singing canticles, constantly meet her eyes. How can a woman full of pity for human suffering behold without indignation the horrible torture of the strappado with which the persecuting monarch edifies his court? She who esteems so highly the dignity of thought, the independence of opinions, and the liberty of faith, must be plunged into consternation by the sight of so many abominable cruelties!

---

[1] M. Legouvé, *Histoire morale des femmes.*

It is salutary to reflect on all that is vexatious in careers that are in appearance the most highly privileged, and to know what griefs and miseries are covered by the domes of splendid palaces. The melancholy so well described in our days by poets of the romantic school belongs to all countries and to every age. No woman ever felt its attacks more keenly than Marguerite. The gaiety in her stories lies on the surface only. Often the recital of an amusing or a gay adventure is followed by a sad reflection on the uncertainty surrounding the problems of human destiny, the suffering that is the inseparable comrade of delight, the dregs of bitterness in every cup of pleasure. Marguerite suffers through her imagination, her mind, and her heart. She is religious, yet troubled by disquietudes unknown to the generation of women who preceded her. There are moments when she is beset by doubt, and when she wavers thus between Catholicism and the new doctrines, her conscience is disturbed by interior conflicts. She is one of those women who gaze anxiously towards both life and death, and who are tormented by their excessive intelligence and susceptibility. Her passion for poetry affords her consolations, but it also develops in her delicate and impressionable soul the faculty of moral suffering. The life of such women is necessarily doomed to sadness. The woes of others pain them like their own. Their destiny is never to find repose but in the tomb.

If Marguerite was surrounded by homage, she had cruel enemies as well. Fanatics, exasperated by her display of tolerant sentiments, pursued her with implacable hatred, and, desiring to see her under a cloud of heresy, they neglected no means to bring about her ruin. But the woman whom the instincts of her heart led beyond her age in the path of progress, teaching her to understand tolerance like L'Hôpital, like Henry IV., like Bayle himself; the artist enamoured of the ideal, who turned away from an abyss of mire and blood to contemplate pure light, has a right to the respect of posterity. The more depraved and cruel that her contemporaries appear to us, the greater is the charm and prestige of her rare qualities. The *Pearl of the Valois* shines by contrast. She is a precious jewel set in iron.

II

THE YOUTH OF MARGUERITE OF ANGOULÊME

MARGUERITE of Valois, daughter of Charles of Orleans, Count of Angoulême, and of Louise of Savoy, was born in the old castle of the city of Angoulême, April 11, 1492. Two years later, September 12, 1494, "the town of Cognac finds itself in great jollity, and there is no vine-dresser so poor that he does not toss his cap in air in sign of welcome, and toast in his best wine and handsomest goblet the heir just born to the Count of Angoulême, the kindly lord of this little region renowned for the gaiety of its men and the beauty of its women."[1] The brother and sister were educated together with the utmost care at the side of their mother, who became a widow at eighteen. Marguerite was remarkable from her childhood, not only for her natural graces, but the distinction of her mind, and her taste for letters. She talked with equal facility in French, Italian, Spanish, English, and German. Later she learned Greek and Hebrew. In spite of her joyousness and gaiety, she preferred

---

[1] M. de Lescure, *Les Amours de François Ier*.

theology to all other studies, and had from childhood that propensity to mysticism which recurs even in the midst of her most trifling writings.

To acquire the taste for poetry, which was to be one of the greatest charms of her existence, she had only to read and re-read the verses of her great-uncle, Charles of Orleans, the author of the delightful strophes which commence thus: —

> "Le temps a laissé son manteau
> De vent, de froidure et de pluie;
> Il s'est vêtu de broderie,
> De soleil riant, clair et beau." [1]

Marguerite was twelve years old when she first appeared at the court of Louis XII. with her brother, who, young as he was, already gave promise of what he was to be. His mother, Louise of Savoy, had a boundless admiration and affection for him. On her knees before this son, destined one day to be her King, her protector, avenger, and her pride, she flattered him with a fervor resembling the ecstasy of devotion. But one sentiment, maternal love, is exhibited in her journal, which contains but few pages, and goes no further than the year 1522. The dangers which her son may incur are what chiefly occupy her. Her style, dry enough where it touches

---

[1] The weather has dropped its mantle
Of wind and cold and rain;
And dressed itself in broidery,
In radiant sunshine, clear and fair.

THE YOUTH OF MARGUERITE 19

other subjects, takes on here the most affecting tone. At the age of seven, the young Prince was run away with by a mettlesome horse. His mother relates the dangerous adventure as follows: "On the feast of the Conversion of St. Paul, January 25, 1501, at about half-past two in the afternoon, my king, my lord, my Cæsar, and my son, being near Amboise, was run away with across the fields by a hackney given him by Marshal de Gyé, and the danger was so great that those who were present esteemed it irreparable. Nevertheless, God, the protector of widows and defender of orphans, would not abandon me, knowing that if chance had so suddenly deprived me of my love, I would have been too unfortunate." In the same journal Louise of Savoy lets us know that her son's favorite little dog "Hapegay, who was loving and faithful to his master, died October 24, 1502." And she attaches more importance to this death than to the birth of Queen Anne's daughter, which she mentions at the same time.

Marguerite shared her mother's sentiments, and her affection for her young brother likewise partook of idolatry. Louis XII. married her to Charles III., Duke of Alençon, whom she did not love. The wedding was celebrated at Blois, December 1, 1509, "with as much pomp and state as if she had been the King's daughter." But Duke Charles was not the ideal his young wife had dreamed of. She found consolation in her affection for her brother, and when he ascended the throne, she more than shared the admiration which all France entertained for the young monarch.

M. Henri Martin has very well said: "There is a unique combination of antiquity and chivalry in the brilliant apparition of the King of the Renaissance which resembles the fusion of ancient and Middle Age art in the monuments of that period. His strength, address, and intrepidity correspond to a figure like that of a demigod or a hero of the Round Table. His large and pleasing features, his brilliant eyes, and charming smile; his ingenious, bright, and active mind, curious about everything, as ready as his century itself for every novelty; his vivid, glowing imagination; his ardently enthusiastic, frank, and generous heart, easily responsive to the gentler emotions, all add to the immense attraction exercised by this young man, trained by a tutor instructed in all the knowledge of Italy."

Italy is the land of his chivalric dreams, the land he points out to the Venetian ambassadors, saying: "I will either conquer or die there." He crosses the Alps and acquires the glory of a new Charlemagne by the battle of Marignan. Louise of Savoy and Marguerite tremble with pride. "On September 13, 1515," says Madame Louise in her journal, "my son vanquished and set at naught the Swiss near Milan, beginning the combat at five in the afternoon, and continuing it all night and until eleven o'clock next morning; and I start this very day from Amboise to go on foot to Our Lady of Fontaines, to recommend to her what I love better than myself, that is, my dear son, the glorious and triumphant Cæsar, the conqueror of the Helvetians. Item, on that very day of September 13, 1515, between seven and eight o'clock in the evening, at several places in Flanders there was seen a flambeau of fire the length of a lance, which seemed as if it must fall upon the houses; but it was so bright that a hundred torches could not shed so much light." Wholly given over to the intoxications of love and glory, handsome, witty, as ready for gallant speeches as sword-thrusts, believing nothing impossible to his audacity, the victor of Marignan awakened a cry of enthusiasm not from France alone, but from all Europe.

The magnificent opening of his reign is certainly one of the most brilliant epochs of our history. There are times in the life of peoples when they grow young again, one may say, by the youth of their masters, and when, full of illusions and self-confidence, they spring toward the future with a joyous ardor. A morning light seems to illumine the horizon, and the fires of dawn are reflected in the armor of the warriors. Francis I. had brought back with him from Italy an impression of dazzling splendor. It was the hour when old Leonardo da Vinci "was majestically ending his career like a star which slowly descends towards the west without having lost one of its beams"; when were triumphing in all their glory those incomparable geniuses, Michael Angelo and Raphael, "both of them so happily called by names borrowed from the celestial hierarchy by the prophetic instinct of their parents; one the terrible angel of the divine warfare, of the lightning clouds of Sinai; the other the spirit of gentleness, serene light, and harmony, the white vision of Tabor. When a picture by Raphael arrived in France, Francis I. gave it a reception as ceremonious as the kings of other days could have done to the holiest relics coming from the East. It was a mark of high favor to be admitted to behold the masterpiece before the day when it was unveiled to the hungry glances of the court in the richest gallery of the palace, and to the flourish of trumpets."[1]

A group of Italian artists came to establish themselves in France. Painting arrived there with Leonardo da Vinci, Rosso, Primaticcio, and carving and sculpture with Benvenuto Cellini and Bramante.

"It suffices to glance over the accounts of the royal treasury or the descriptions of fêtes as they are reproduced in the chronicles to get a just idea of the sumptuousness of apparel and the infinite art employed on ornaments and furniture. The armor of a knight, his cuirass, his arm-pieces, were covered with perfectly chiselled goldsmith's work; his steel helmet glittered with gold and silver wire, and was

---

[1] M. Henri Martin, *Histoire de France*, t. viii.

surmounted by waving plumes. In time of peace his velvet cap was fringed with pearls and rubies; his tunic of silk or fine Florence cloth was thrown across his shoulders. At the courts of Fontainebleau and Amboise the ornaments bore traces of this taste for the Florentine Renaissance; one saw nothing but tables of silver and ivory, pearls, chased cups, bronze statues scattered among clumps of trees."[1]

The most brilliant woman in this dazzling scene was she whom Francis I. called his *Mignonne, la Marguerite des Marguerites*. She not only protected learned and literary men and artists, but she took part also in affairs of state, and frequently gave the best of advice to her brother. "Her discourse was such," says Brantôme, "that the ambassadors who conversed with her were enraptured, and carried back great reports of it to their own country; herein she came to the aid of the King, her brother, for they always sought her after having accomplished their principal embassy; and frequently, when he had great affairs in hand, he referred them to her while awaiting his determination and final resolution." It was thus that "by the industry of her noble mind and by sweetness" she surpassed the finesse of the most consummate diplomatists. She had an equal aptitude for language and for style. There is nothing exaggerated about the eulogies given her by her valet-de-chambre, the poet, Clément Marot.

---

[1] M. Capefigue, *François Ier et la Renaissance*.

Her taste for letters and the arts was a real passion. Her contemporaries said she had made a Parnassus of her chamber. The little city of Alençon became another Athens. Although her own conduct was irreproachable, the Duchess had around her, according to the fashion of the times, a sort of court of love whose daily occupation it was to discuss questions of sentiment in subtle terms. These subtleties of thought and language on matters of the heart, these more or less ingenious discussions on love, concerning which one does not speak much when he truly feels it, this sentimental metaphysic, which is to real passion what shadow is to substance, all those fine conceits which afterwards became the fashion, were already in great esteem in the palaces of the sixteenth century. The poets who were in Marguerite's service as salaried valets-de-chambre incessantly treated questions of refined gallantry and amorous doctrine for her benefit. But such amusements satisfy neither mind nor heart; every well-ordered soul is quick to recognize their emptiness and vapidity. A factitious and indeterminate sentiment which is neither friendship nor love, having neither the sanctity of the one nor the charm of the other, cannot long please any but coquettish and worthless women. Even in the splendor of her youth, Marguerite had familiarized herself with lofty thoughts and austere meditations. She had already those fits of sadness from which those who reflect on human destiny must seek vainly to escape. Moreover, the moment was approaching when the horizon, so magnificent at first, would be overspread with clouds. Misfortune was soon to knock at the door of the amiable Princess, and the sensitive but courageous soul of this elect woman was destined by Providence to grow strong amid trials.

III

THE MADRID CAPTIVITY

ALL France was in mourning. Francis I. had just lost the battle of Pavia (February 24, 1525). Wounded in the leg and the face, the hero of Marignan had long defended himself with rare vigor, but after having his horse killed under him, and his armor all dented with gun-shots and lance-thrusts, he had been obliged to surrender his bloody sword to the Viceroy of Naples. The royal prisoner was at first taken to the fortress of Pizzighettone, on the Adda, between Lodi and Cremona. Subjécted to the closest vigilance, under the guard of Captain Alarcon and a chosen troop of Spanish arquebusiers, he sought in prayer consolations for his misfortune. "Religious sentiments habitually showed themselves in every difficult circumstance of his life; he seemed profoundly penetrated by them."[1]

It is curious to observe how, in the sixteenth century, corrupted souls returned quickly to God when attacked by suffering. This king, so irreligious in days of triumph and splendor, became devout

---

[1] M. Aimé Champollion-Figeac, *Captivité du roi François Ier*.

in adversity. His sister Marguerite wrote to him: "Monseigneur, if you wish your mother to remain in health, I entreat you to consider your own, for she has heard that you mean to keep this Lent without eating either flesh or eggs. As far as a very humble sister may supplicate you, I implore you not to do it, and to consider that fish does not agree with you: and believe that if you do so, she swears that she will likewise; and if that happens, I can see both of you lose strength."

Mingling gallantry with religion, according to his custom, from the depths of his melancholy solitude the captive sent chivalrous regrets and ardent effusions to the lady of his thoughts, Mademoiselle d'Heilly, afterwards Duchess d'Étampes, her "whose device he wore under his armor on the day of Pavia," the woman "whom he had promised not to flee, and to whom as well as to honor he had been obedient in fighting until he was taken."[1]

In imitation of his great-uncle, Charles of Orleans, he found a consolation for his ill-fortune in poetry. In honor of his mother, his sister, and his mistress, he composed epistles, rondeaux, and eclogues, and celebrated in touching verses the "pleasant region where courses the fair Loire." Inspired by a nobly patriotic impulse, he wrote a letter from his person to the parliaments of France, in which he said: "Since for my own honor and that of the nation I

---

[1] M. Mignet, *Rivalité de François Ier et de Charles-Quint*.

have preferred an honest prison to a shameful flight,
be assured that none shall ever say that, not fortunate enough to procure the welfare of my kingdom,
I may do it wrong through desire to escape, esteeming myself happy to dwell in prison all my life for
the freedom of my country."

It would be difficult to describe the sadness, pity,
devotion, and profound affection which France then
experienced for her King. "He is so wonderfully
loved," wrote an envoy to Charles V., "that if his
ransom were converted into money it could not be
made so excessive that it would not soon be ready."

If this was the sentiment of all France, one can
imagine what the tender heart of Marguerite must
have felt. She wrote to Marshal de Montmorency,
who shared the King's captivity: "True it is that
I shall envy you all my life because I cannot serve
him as you are doing; for though my will surpasses
any that is possible to you, fortune, which made me
a woman, wrongfully restrains me by rendering the
means difficult. But I hope that God who sees my
desire reserves for me an hour when I shall have
my turn; to which life, death, and all that can be
feared or desired will be voluntarily sacrificed for
him." At this very time, Marguerite lost her husband, the Duke of Alençon, who had been one of
the causes of the defeat of Pavia, and who was said
to have died of chagrin on that account (April,
1525). After sixteen years of marriage she remained
a widow and childless. She forced herself to hide

her grief, especially from her mother, then much occupied by the cares of the regency. Being unable to render any service, she said she would think herself too unhappy were she to trouble and disturb the mind of her who was performing such great ones. Seeking in religion the needful strength to overcome the most bitter trials, she addressed this admirable letter to her brother, at the time when he was about to be transferred from Pizzighettone to Spain: —

"Monseigneur, the further they remove you from us, the greater becomes my firm hope of your deliverance and speedy return, for the hour when men's minds are most troubled is the hour when God achieves His masterpiece. . . . And if He now gives you, on one hand, a share in the pains which He has borne for you, and on the other, the grace to bear them patiently, I entreat you, Monseigneur, to believe unfalteringly that it is only to try how much you love Him, and to give you leisure to think and understand how much He loves you; for He desires to have your heart entirely, as for love He has given you His own, in order, after having united you to Him by tribulation, to deliver you to His own glory, and your consolation by the merit of His victorious resurrection, so that through you His name may be known and sanctified, not in your kingdom only, but in all Christendom, and even to the conversion of the infidels. Oh! how blessed will be your brief captivity, by which God will deliver so many souls from that of infidelity and eternal damnation. Alas! Monseigneur, I know that you understand all this far better than I; but seeing that in other things I think only in you, as being all that God has left me in this world, father, brother, and husband, and not having the comfort of telling you so, I have not feared to weary you with a long letter, which to me is short, in order to console myself for my inability to talk to you."

June 10, 1525, Francis I., changing his prison, took ship for Spain. "What deeply afflicted him was to salute the distant shores of France from the deck of the vessel. Off the islands of Hyères, where the fleet remained for a moment, he could see the white standard with the lilies floating from the turrets; alas! the clarion did not sound, as in happier times, to announce the presence of the King. There were neither shouts of joy nor any movement on the strand."[1] Entering the port of Palermo June 17, he arrived at Barcelona June 19, and thence sailed again for Valencia. The Spaniards received him with great respect. "The people of the Cid and of Amadis ran eagerly to see a living hero. The women went crazy over him. A daughter of the Infantado, Doña Ximena, declared that as she could not marry the King of France, she would never take another husband, and so became a nun."[2]

---

[1] M. Capefigue, *François Ier et la Renaissance*.
[2] M. Michelet, *La Réforme*.

And yet, in spite of the admiration he inspired, the captive saw with grief that his situation became worse daily. It was in vain that he humbly entreated the Emperor to grant him an interview. Charles V. persisting in refusing to see him, sent him from Valencia to Madrid, where his imprisonment became still more rigorous. At first he was confined in the square tower of Los Lajunos, the strongest of the towers flanking the walls of Madrid, and later in the gloomy dungeon of the Alcazar. This dark cell could inspire none but gloomy thoughts. "But one entrance conducted thither, and the only window which admitted light opened toward the south, at about a hundred feet from the ground, not far from Manzanares. Glazed on the inside, it was closed on the outside by a double grating of iron bars fixed in the wall. . . . Alarcon, stationed in the King's vicinity, with a troop of arquebusiers who principally occupied the lower part of the tower, had no difficulty in guarding the prisoner confided to him."[1]

It is easy to imagine what a man like Francis I. must have suffered in this narrow dungeon, where he, the crowned paladin, the hero of chivalric romances, the lady-killer, and bold swordsman, found himself reduced to implore in vain the mercy of his young conqueror, and where he gave himself the name of slave. Overwhelmed with chagrin, he fell

---

[1] M. Mignet, *Rivalité de François Ier et de Charles-Quint.*

seriously ill, and believed that his prison was to be his tomb. It was then that he remembered his sister, and his thoughts turned to her as to his good angel. It seemed to him that she alone might be able to deliver him, and that the devotion of a woman so full of wit and courage would be able to accomplish prodigies. On July 2, 1525, he sent Marshal de Montmorency to the Emperor to ask for a safe-conduct for Marguerite. Charles V. was quite willing to grant this request, hoping that the Duchess would help him wrest the cession of Burgundy from the captive.

Marguerite embarked at Aigues-Mortes, August 27, 1525, with President de Selves, Gabriel de Grammont, Bishop of Tarbes, Georges d'Armagnac, Archbishop of Embrun, and a sufficiently numerous suite of women. The idea that she was going to sacrifice herself for her brother filled her with joy. "Whatever it may be," she wrote him, "even to giving my ashes to the winds to do you a service, nothing will be either strange, difficult, or painful to me, but only consolation, repose, and honor." Landing at Barcelona, she learned on her way to Madrid that her brother was at the last extremity, and in spite of the excessive heat, which made travelling very painful, she traversed the distance separating them with exceptional rapidity. In her impatience to be at the end of her journey, she tried to escape the tediousness of waiting by composing verses which indicated the trouble and anxiety of her soul: —

"Le désir du bien que j'attends
Me donne de travail matière,
Une heure me donne cent ans;
Et me semble que ma litière,
Ne bouge ou retourne en arrière,
Tant j'ai de m'avancer désir,
Oh! qu'elle est longue la carrière
Où git à la fin mon plaisir!

"Je regarde de tous côtés
Pour voir s'il n'arrive personne,
Priant sans cesse, n'en doutez,
Dieu que santé à mon roy donne.
Quand nul ne voit, l'œil j'abandonne
A pleurer; puis sur le papier
Un peu de ma douleur j'ordonne.
Voilà mon douloureux métier.

"Oh! qu'il sera le bien venu
Celui qui, frappant à ma porte,
Dira: le Roi est revenu
En sa santé tres bonne et forte.
Alors sa sœur, plus mal que morte,
Courra baiser le messager
Qui telles nouvelles apporte
Que son frère est hors de danger." [1]

---

[1] Desire for the good that I await
Gives me an occupation,
An hour is like a hundred years to me;
And it seems to me my litter
Either does not budge or is going back,
So greatly do I long to advance.
Oh! how long is the road
At the end of which my pleasure lies!

I look on every side
To see if some one is not coming,

The Cardinal Legate Salviati, whom Marguerite met and passed on the way, says that she went flying to Madrid. She arrived there September 20, 1525. Francis I. seemed to have only a few hours to live, and Charles V., fearing to lose the fruits of the victory with the person of the vanquished, had finally consented, only the day before, to make him a first visit.

On the arrival of the Duchess, Charles V. came down to the foot of the staircase of the Alcazar. Still in mourning for her husband, she was dressed entirely in white, and her face was bathed in tears. The Emperor embraced her, and after saying a few courteous words, he led her to the sick man's bed. One divines what must have been the prisoner's emotions, when, deserted by fortune, humiliated, crushed by moral and physical sufferings, he saw the woman who had always been his best friend and

> And doubt not that I pray incessantly
> That God will give health to my King.
> When none is looking, I abandon my eyes
> To weeping; then to the paper
> A little of my grief I transfer;
> That is my doleful occupation.
>
> Oh! how welcome will he be
> Who, knocking at my door,
> Shall say: "The King is restored
> To sound and excellent health."
> Then his sister, worse than dead,
> Will run to kiss the messenger
> Who brings the great news
> That her brother is out of danger.

most faithful consoler appear beside him like a messenger from God. He experienced a mingling of joy and sorrow which increased his fever, and three days later his state was alarmingly worse. On the following day, September 24, he fell into complete insensibility, "without speech, hearing, or sight." The physicians avowed that there was no more hope.

Relying no longer on any human remedies, Marguerite fervently implored the assistance of God, and God did not forsake her. She had an altar provided with all the religious emblems erected in the chamber of the fainting King. All the persons belonging to her suite and the companions of the unfortunate monarch being assembled, Mass was said by the Archbishop of Embrun, and solemn chants re-echoed in the dungeon. The sick man was aroused by the sound of this sweet harmony. His lethargy had ceased. Marguerite appeared to him like the image of his native land coming to console its King. Under the semblance of a woman, all France was watching at the bedside of the royal sufferer. The kneeling spectators were praying to God and weeping. When the Mass was ended, the Duchess had the Blessed Sacrament presented to the King that he might adore It. "It is my God," said he, "who will heal my soul and body; I beg you that I may receive Him." Then, the Host having been divided in two, the King received one half with the greatest devotion, and his sister, communicating with him, the other half. The sick man felt himself sustained by a supernatural force. A celestial consolation descended into his soul, just now despairing. Marguerite's prayer had not been unavailing. Francis I. was saved.

Marguerite left her convalescing brother, to seek Charles V., and try to carry on the great negotiation which had brought her to Spain. The cession of Burgundy was invariably the rock upon which this negotiation split. The Duchess arrived at Toledo with twenty of her women, all on horseback like herself, on October 3. The Emperor went to meet her, and gave her a gracious reception, taking pains to say, notwithstanding, that her journey was useless unless she brought with her the cession of Burgundy. Marguerite was not discouraged. According to Brantôme, she appeared before the Council of Spain, and "there she triumphed by making a good speech, and accomplished so much by her noble words that she rather made them agreeable than odious or displeased; all the more because she was beautiful, the widow of M. d'Alençon, and in the flower of her age. All that is very well adapted to move and influence persons who are hard and cruel." She went from Toledo to Madrid, from Madrid to Guadalaxara, the residence of the Duke de l'Infantado, who displayed so much interest for the cause of Francis I. that he and his son were officially notified from the court not to converse any more with the Duchess d'Alençon. "But the ladies were not interdicted," she writes, "and to them I shall talk twice as much." It was to the sister of Charles V. that she chiefly addressed herself, Eleanor, widow of the King of Portugal, who was then about to marry the Connétable de Bourbon. Marguerite, to use Sainte-Marthe's[1] expression, began to concoct a marriage between her brother and this princess. Eleanor's imagination became excited in favor of the prisoner whose wife she desired to become. The face of things became so changed by this means that although the negotiations had no result as yet, the situation of Francis I. gradually improved. Still, his choice was limited to perpetual imprisonment or a burdensome and shameful treaty.

In spite of all her efforts, Marguerite could not induce Charles V. to substitute anything for Burgundy as the price of his captive's ransom. On this point the Emperor remained inexorable. Marguerite, a thorough Frenchwoman at heart, would not pledge her brother to such conditions. Then Francis I. took a noble resolution. In presence of the Archbishop of Embrun, Marshal de Montmorency, and President de Selve, he abdicated in favor of the Dauphin, December, 1525. In the letters-patent which he signed before them, he said concerning Marguerite: "Our very dear and much loved only sister, the Duchess of Alençon and Berry, has taken the trouble and labor to come to

---

[1] Sainte-Marthe, *Oraison funèbre de Marguerite d'Angoulême.*

the Emperor across land and sea, and has sought by every fair and honest means she could think of to induce him to perform an act of honor and humanity."

Then recalling the severe conditions exacted by Charles V.: "We have resolved rather to endure such and so long an imprisonment as it may please God we shall bear. We offer it to Him together with our liberty for the welfare, union, peace, and preservation of our subjects and our realm, for which we would employ not only our own life, but that of our very dear children, who were born, not for us, but for the good of our realm, and true children of the commonwealth of France."

He prescribed, at the same time, that the Dauphin should be crowned, designated his mother, Louise of Savoy, as regent, and, in case of the death of that princess, the Duchess of Alençon. Finally, he reserved to himself the right to resume the throne if he should be delivered later on.

Meantime, the end of the truce was approaching, and Marguerite, whose safe-conduct Charles V. had refused to extend, started on her return to France, carrying with her the act of abdication, which still remained a secret. She travelled slowly, hoping constantly that some good news would stop her midway, and that the Emperor would decide to offer less severe conditions. By one of her letters it is evident that on December 3, she took from noon until seven o'clock to ride five leagues on horseback. She had reckoned on being at Narbonne for the

Christmas festivities. But she suddenly received a letter from her brother advising her to make all speed. Charles V. had just been informed of the act of abdication which would so greatly lessen the importance of his capture, and, to avenge himself, he intended to arrest Marguerite if she were found on Spanish soil at the expiration of the time fixed for the safe-conduct.

"Madame the Duchess, in the month of December," says a protest of the King, dated January 13, 1526, "was constrained in cold and snow and frost to pass and traverse the kingdoms of Castile and Arragon, the seigniories of Barcelona and Roussillon, in order to enter France before the truce ended, and was unable to obtain from the Emperor a safe-conduct to pass by way of the kingdom of Navarre, so as to be the sooner beyond the dominions of the Emperor, all of which were clear and evident signs of his wish to retain the said lady, Duchess of Alençon, a prisoner in case she were found in Spain after the truce."

Marguerite, by dint of great fatigue, accomplished four days' travel in one, and reached the French frontier an hour later than the time mentioned in her safe-conduct. She was inconsolable for having failed to bring back her brother. One of the many letters she wrote him at this period terminates as follows : " Still in my litter, which is more wretched than ever, since it has not had the good fortune to bring you back, and still more of keeping you company therein, I entreat Him alone who can and will bring all to a good end, which is firmly hoped for from His goodness by your very humble and very obedient subject and sister."

In this correspondence, which displays an affection and devotion equal to every trial, Marguerite forgets nothing which could console the heart of the royal captive; she delineates in affecting terms the love and fidelity of his people: —

"Whenever I speak of you to two or three," she writes him from Béziers, "as soon as I name the King, every one draws near to listen; so that I am constrained to give them tidings of you, and never end without an accompaniment of tears from people of all conditions, whose desires and prayers are so often present to God that I doubt not He who causes them is willing to grant them; for it is time, and He only knows that, unless we see you soon, the love we bear you is so great that to live will be impossible, especially to mother, who lives for you alone, as she has told me, and to her who was born for both of you, and who heartily desires ever to be your very humble and very obedient subject and sister, Marguerite."

Another time she addresses the father rather than the monarch, and, sketching a picture of the prisoner's family, she writes him about his five children: —

"And now they are all entirely recovered and very healthy. M. le Dauphin is studying wonderfully, and combining a thousand other occupations with school; there is no question of rage now, but of all the virtues. M. d'Orléans sticks fast to his book, and says he means to be good; but M. d'Angoulême knows more than the others, and does things which should rather be reckoned prophetic than childish, and which, Monseigneur, you would be amazed to hear. Little Margot[1] is like me, and doesn't wish to be ill; but they assure me here that she is very graceful, and will become more beautiful than Mademoiselle d'Angoulême was."[2]

Apparently, Marguerite had not succeeded in her mission, but in reality she had greatly forwarded the deliverance of her brother. It was owing to her that Charles V. did not follow the counsels of Chancellor Gattinara, who had desired Francis I. to be treated with the greatest rigor. By arranging a marriage between the prisoner and Queen Eleanor she had completely changed the conditions of his captivity. On recovering his health, he diverted himself by excursions, banquets at the houses of Spanish grandees, and visits to monasteries and convents, where he exercised his royal privilege of touching for scrofula. The Spanish, who from the time he fell ill had crowded the churches to entreat God to restore him, surrounded him with homage and kindly attentions.

He ended by sacrificing his parole to his liberty,

---

[1] Marguerite, second daughter of Francis I., who became Duchess of Savoy.

[2] That is to say, the author of the letter, Marguerite herself, who was born Mademoiselle d'Angoulême.

swearing as a king, a gentleman, and a Christian to keep promises which he was firmly resolved to break. As hostages he gave his two eldest sons, one of them eight years old, and the other seven. "These poor and charming children were to be taken beyond the Pyrenees, quickly separated from their attendants, shut up in the castle of Pedraza amidst the mountains, almost deprived of light and air as well as liberty, left in shameful poverty, with worn-out clothes, and a little dog as sole companion, without receiving any tidings from their family during three years and more of war, and even without hearing a single word of their own language, the use of which they lost so completely that, after the peace of Cambrai, they could not understand the messenger sent by their father to pay them a visit and apprise them in French of their deliverance."[1]

M. Mignet has described with the charm and precision that belongs to all his narratives, the exchange, which took place March 17, 1526. At seven o'clock in the morning, the Viceroy of Naples, accompanying Francis I., and Lautrec conducting the Dauphin and the Duke of Orleans, reached the desolate shores of the Bidassoa. "The exchange was made with the most minute and suspicious precautions. In the middle of the river, between Fontarabia and Hendaye, had been placed a pontoon in the form

---

[1] M. Mignet, *Rivalité de François Ier et de Charles-Quint*.

of an estrade, which was kept immovable by anchors at equal distances from either shore, and which it had been agreed that the King and his children should mount together, so that he should pass into France and his children into Spain at the same moment. Two boats of the same size, manned by an equal number of rowers, had been prepared on each bank. Lannoy entered one of them with Francis I., Lautrec the other with the two young princes. The boats, starting together, reached the pontoon at the same time. The King embraced his children, and, descending into the boat which had brought them, was rowed ashore. 'Here I am King again!' he cried, as his foot touched the soil of France; 'I am King, I am King again!'"

Then he sprang on a horse, and spurring it, rode at full speed as far as Bayonne, where he was greeted with transports of joy and homage by his mother and his courtiers. He could not forget that if he were still alive and at liberty, it was to his sister, his *mignonne*, that he owed his safety. Brantôme reports him as often saying, "that without her he would have died, for which he was under obligations to her that he would ever recognize, and would love her as he had always done, until his death. And she did the same for him."

Marguerite's devotion was more useful than an army to Francis I. A woman's heart had found more resources than the skill of diplomatists and the knowledge of statesmen.

IV

THE BEGINNINGS OF THE REFORMATION

SOME have sought to represent Marguerite as Catholic in name but Protestant in fact, and this accusation, brought against her by implacable enemies during her life, has not ceased to be aimed against her memory. That the sister of Francis I. was made indignant by certain abuses, the sale of indulgences, for instance; that she wished to resist pagan tendencies and appeal from mythology to the Gospel; that she had a horror of ignorance, fanaticism, persecution, and the impious and cruel doctrine which consisted in enlightening souls by the fires of the stake; that she granted her sympathy, protection, and assistance to the victims of liberty of conscience, is incontestable. But what is not less true is, that she remained loyal to the faith of her fathers all her life.

The Reformation, like the French Revolution, had its golden age, its period of noble enthusiasms and generous illusions. There was then no question either of impairing the force or the unity of dogma, of bringing the religious passions into the service of ambition and cupidity, of troubling men's souls, or of provoking civil wars. Luther repelled the name of heretic with horror and recognized the Church's right to proscribe schisms. The time had not yet come when Henry VIII. would transform himself into the pope of England, and Calvin dishonor Geneva by kindling the faggot of Michael Servetus. All that men wanted was to reform morals, by bringing back to earth the purity and ideal simplicity of the first Christian ages.

Knowledge and virtue promised to unite for the triumph of justice and truth. A breath of liberty rejuvenated men, and at this solemn moment, when the conscience of the human race seemed presently about to rise against abuses, vice, and scandals, the innovators no more dreamed of the religious wars than the men of 1789 foresaw the scaffolds of 1793.

Marguerite, whose mind was open to all things noble, could not remain unmoved by what was legitimate in such an intellectual and religious movement. But she was unwilling to see any blow aimed at dogma. It was precisely because she remained true to the faith of her childhood that she felt a righteous wrath on beholding the crimes of every kind by which the persecutors defiled religion. She suffered at beholding the sword substituted for the Word, and was never more afflicted than when obliged to contemplate her beloved brother under the aspect of a torturer. In the heart of this generous woman, irritated by injustice and exasperated by cruelty, there were treasures of gentleness and truly Christian charity for the victims of these abominable persecutions. The greater the danger incurred by defending the martyrs of liberty, the more did she feel that honor obliged her to give them a helping hand. Not sharing their errors, she yet desired to ameliorate their lot. She seemed like an image of mercy. The condemned invoked her name amid the flames of the scaffold. As is said of her in the funeral oration of which Sainte-Marthe is the author: "She made herself the port and refuge of all the disconsolate. Thou shouldst have seen them at this port, some to raise their heads from beggary, others coming as from a shipwreck to embrace a long-desired tranquillity, still others to cover themselves with her favor as with the shield of Ajax against those who persecuted them. In fine, seeing them around this good lady, thou wouldst have called her a hen who carefully calls and gathers her little chicks and covers them with her wings." Marguerite devoted herself neither to the interests of Luther nor those of Calvin. The cause of which she was the eloquent, courageous, and convinced advocate was that of humanity.

The ideas that gave birth to the Reformation had begun to show themselves in France before causing an explosion on the other bank of the Rhine. Even in the time of Louis XII., Lefèvre d'Étaples, who taught theology and belles-lettres in Paris, had announced to his disciples that God would renew the world. In the first years of the reign of Francis I. a sort of little congregation had grown up about this savant. Guillaume Briçonnet, Bishop of Meaux, son of the minister of Charles VIII., kept up a religious correspondence with Marguerite in 1521. He called around him Lefèvre d'Étaples and his disciples, Farel, Gérard, Roussel, d'Arande. The King's reader, Duchâtel, his confessor, the Dominican Guillaume Petit, Bishop of Troyes and Senlis, were then on good terms with these innovators, who announced their intention of touching nothing but abuses, and Marguerite wrote to Briçonnet: "The King and Madame are more than ever inclined toward the reformation of the Church, being resolved to let it be known that the truth of God is not heresy." In 1552, Lefèvre published his French translation of the New Testament, with Commentaries. Holy Scripture was in fashion at court. In vain did the reactionary party maintain that Greek is the language of heresies, that whoever dared even to spell it would become a schismatic, that to open the Greek text of the New Testament, a book full of thorns and vipers, was to devote one's self voluntarily to certain death, and that as for Hebrew, one could not try to read it without becoming a Jew. Francis I. smiled at such exaggerations, and the religious movement, which showed itself at first under a scientific and literary aspect, was, if not encouraged, at least tolerated by the court.

This situation was somewhat modified by the King's captivity. The regent thought she saw a chance for her son's deliverance in a close alliance with the court of Rome. She desired the support of the Sorbonne also, and to satisfy public opinion, which regarded the disaster of Pavia as a chastisement from heaven, irritated by the progress of the heretics. An extraordinary commission was appointed by parliament. This was an inquisition partly religious and partly laic and Gallican. Imprisonments, confiscations, and punishments began. Emboldened by the absence of Marguerite, who was in Spain near her brother, the persecutors set to work with a sort of fury. Lefèvre d'Étaples, whose translation of the New Testament had just been prohibited, was obliged to quit the kingdom and went to rejoin Farel at Strasburg. Briçonnet retracted. Two of Marguerite's protégés, Clément Marot, the poet, and the gentleman Louis de Berquin, were arrested.

The innovators awaited the King's return with impatience. But on reaching France he displayed both in religion and politics the inconsequence and contradictions which were the basis of his character. At first he manifested indignation at the persecutions that had taken place in his absence, and was much impressed by a letter in which Erasmus had written him concerning the fanatics: "It is the faith which they allege, but they aspire to tyranny, even with princes. They march with a secure step, though underground. If the prince takes a notion not to submit to them in all things, they will declare at once, that he may be removed by the Church, that is, by certain insincere monks and theologians leagued together against the public peace." Francis I. announced his intention of protecting the men "of excellent learning" who were under the stroke of persecution. He sent an order from Bayonne for the release of Clément Marot and Berquin. Lefèvre d'Étaples was recalled from exile, and became the preceptor of the King's youngest son. In spite of the censures of the Sorbonne, the government authorized the reprinting of twenty-four thousand copies of the Colloquies of Erasmus. Marguerite, who married Henri d'Albret at the beginning of the year 1527, had Berquin enter her husband's service. The party of toleration seemed about to be victorious when the imprudences committed by the reformers induced a complete alteration in the state of affairs.

During Monday night in Whitsun week, June 1, 1528, a statue of the Virgin which was at the corner formed by the rue des Rosiers and the rue des Juifs, in the Faubourg Saint-Antoine, was thrown down and mutilated by unknown hands. The people uttered a cry of wrath. Processions starting from every parish went to the scene of the sacrilege to recite prayers and utter menaces. The entire University, doctors, licentiates, bachelors, masters of arts, students, all went thither under the leadership of their rector. Swept along by public sentiment, the King repaired to the place of the crime, bareheaded and carrying a candle in his hand. The parliament, flattering him so as to rule him with greater ease, declared itself "as greatly consoled and rejoiced by his presence as the apostles were when they beheld God after the Resurrection," and, uniting with the Sorbonne and the clergy, it persuaded him to become "the peculiar protector and defender of religion," and not to suffer in his kingdom "any errors, heresies, or false doctrines."

The persecution began anew. Marguerite, in spite of all her efforts, could not save the unfortunate Berquin, who again fell into the hands of the executioners.[1] He was burned on the Place de Grève, April 17, 1529. "When the cord that fastened him to the stake stifled his voice," says Theodore de Beza in the *Histoire Ecclésiastique,* "no one in the crowd called on the name of Jesus, whom it is customary to invoke in favor even of parricides and sacrilegious persons, so greatly had the multitude been excited against him by those men who are found everywhere and who can do what they like with the minds of simple and ignorant people."

Encouraged by their success, the persecutors pursued Marguerite with desperate fury, constantly aiming at her the most violent attacks. But they were striking at a woman who had as much intelligence as courage. Instead of buying repose at the cost of abandoning the unfortunates she had taken under her protection, she accepted the struggle with energy,

---

[1] See concerning Louis de Berquin, the excellent article published by M. Haureau in the *Revue des Deux-Mondes,* January 15, 1869.

and vigorously withstood all enmities. In 1532, at the very moment when the monks, treating her as a heretic, said from the pulpit that she ought to be "put in a sack and thrown into the Seine," she employed the King's confessor, Guillaume Petit, Bishop of Senlis, to translate the canonical prayer-book into French, suppressing all passages which she considered tainted with superstition.

At the same epoch she had published a little religious poem under the title of *Miroir de l'âme pécheresse*. It was merely a paraphrase, in verse, of several passages of Scripture. Yet the man who had placed himself at the head of the enemies of the Queen of Navarre, the savage Beda, found means to incriminate this innocent performance. Marguerite had not mentioned in it either the saints or purgatory. "Then," cried the accuser, "she believes neither in purgatory nor the saints!" He caused the book to be condemned by the Sorbonne, and at his instigation the principal of the College of Navarre ordered the pupils to perform a morality, or allegorical drama, in which Marguerite was represented under the character of a woman quitting her distaff for a French translation of the Gospels, presented to her by a Fury. Here the enemies of the Queen had overstepped their bounds. Francis I. was irritated. The principal and his actors were arrested. The ever-generous Marguerite asked pardon for them, and only obtained it by throwing herself at her brother's feet. There came a momentary respite in the persecutions. At the initiative of Nicolas Cox, rector of the University of Paris, the assembled Faculties disavowed the censure passed by the Sorbonne against the *Miroir de l'âme pécheresse.* Gérard Roussel, the Queen of Navarre's chaplain, was authorized to preach in Paris, and the diatribes of Beda against these sermons displeased Francis I. so much that Marguerite's savage enemy ended by being sent to the prison of Saint-Michel.

The reformers were at rest, when some among them were foolish enough to defy the King and thus to renew the era of persecution. October 18, 1534, Francis I. being then at Blois, on rising in the morning and leaving his room, found a placard against the Mass affixed to his own door. Beside himself, he broke into a rage, finding in the audacious poster an outrage directed at both the majesty of God and the majesty of kings. This was the moment when the Anabaptists were filling Germany with their crimes, and the rumor of the massacres of Münster had reached even to the court of France. The King, whose imagination was easily impressed, and whose sister was no longer at hand to inspire him with ideas of tolerance and moderation, resolved to treat heresy with inflexible severity. An expiatory procession took place January 21, 1535. It issued in great pomp from the church of Saint-Germain-l'Auxerrois. The relics of all the martyrs preserved in the sanctuaries of Paris were carried in it. The King marched bareheaded with a wax candle in his hand. Theodore de Beza says that there had been erected "a scaffold and a pile of faggots on which six persons were burned alive amid wonderful shouting from the people, so much excited that they were very near snatching them from the hands of the executioners and tearing them to pieces." The unhappy victims were bound fast to a tall machine. It was a piece of timber balanced on a fulcrum, which in descending plunged them into the flames of the burning faggots, but rose again immediately so as to prolong their agony until the flame should consume the cords that bound them and they fell into the middle of the fire.

The procession terminated at the church of Sainte-Geneviève. The King and the princes dined afterward at the house of the Bishop of Paris. After dinner, the court, the parliament, and the ambassadors assembled in the great hall of the bishopric. There Francis I. ascended a pulpit. He expressed his grief "that persons could be found in his realm so wicked and wretched as to wish to sully its fair name by sowing in it damnable and execrable opinions." He required of all the spectators, and through them of all his subjects, that each of them should denounce all "whom they knew to be adherents or accomplices of heresy 'without regard to alliance, lineage, or friendship.'" The royal orator added that for his own part, "were his arm infected with such gangrene, he would separate it from his body; that is to say, if his own children were so wretched as to fall into such execrable and accursed opinions, he would give them as a sacrifice to God."

Francis I. was so exasperated against the innovators that, including heretics, men of letters, and savants in the same condemnation, he signed, in that fatal year 1535, letters-patent ordering the suppression of printing. The "Father of Letters" soon revoked this barbarous ordinance. Nevertheless, it demonstrates the pitch of fury at which he had arrived. At this period Marguerite needed a real force of soul to continue playing her part of protectress of the victims. Her little court of Nérac always remained their asylum. But her enemies daily redoubled their fury against her. One of her letters, written in 1541, at the period when she had to struggle against the violent opposition of the Bishop of Condom, shows the fears she entertained for her life. She had been told she would be poisoned by the incense burned before her in church, and there was a time when she felt obliged to have Mass said in her own room.

No effort was spared to irritate her brother against her. Nevertheless this justice must be done to Francis I. that he always defended his sister from the calumnies perpetually devised against her. "I have heard a veracious person say," says Brantôme, " that the Connétable de Montmorency, who was in the greatest favor with him, discussing one day with the King, made neither difficulty nor scruple in telling him that if he really desired to exterminate heretics in his kingdom he must begin at court with his nearest kindred, naming the Queen his sister. To which the King replied: 'We will not speak of her. She loves me too much. She will never believe anything but what I believe and will never adopt a religion prejudicial to my state.'"

In the latter years of her life, Marguerite, while continuing to protect the martyrs of Protestantism as she had done in the past, attached herself more and more to Catholicism. Her rare intelligence had perfectly well noted the weak sides of a reform which forgot to reform itself, and whose leaders, seeking liberty only for themselves and not for others, had the singular pretension to construct a creed to their own liking and to confine free examination within limits traced merely by their own caprice.

The vital wound of Protestantism, which recoiled from its own principles and did not clearly know either what it wanted to destroy or what it wanted to preserve, that inconsequence which could not fail to strike all reflective minds, dispelled many illusions, and prevented the yielding of blind faith to the semi-audacities of the innovators. As Michelet has said: "The human soul, almost on the point of launching forth into the infinity of the unknown, glanced backward again, interrogated its ancient path, asked if it were not enough to return to the days of old." Marguerite was unwilling to separate herself from the religion which had blessed her cradle and was to consecrate her tomb. Her historians agree in recognizing that at every epoch of her life she scrupulously observed all the religious practices of Catholicism. She loved its consoling poetry and found there a living source wherein to quench that thirst for love and hope which is the torment and the joy of certain souls. Her ardent and glowing imagination was not made for the cold abstractions and sombre rigorism of Calvin.

In the various practices of Catholicism there were some which met a want in her tender and somewhat mystical nature. I will cite only the veneration of the dead. She who had loved so much in this life would never admit that our prayers, our suppliant aspirations, could be useless or indifferent to these beloved dead who, for her, were not the absent, but only the invisible.[1] She founded nunneries, honored the relics of the saints, and had a veritable devotion toward the Blessed Virgin. At Paris she went to confession to François le Picard, dean of Saint-Germain-l'Auxerrois, and received communion from the hands of this virtuous person at the church of the Blancs-Manteaux, where her piety edified the faithful. The protectress of liberty of conscience remained a good Catholic. On her deathbed she had a right to say to the Franciscan who gave her the last sacraments, that she had never separated from the Church, and that what she had done for the reformed had proceeded solely from compassion.

---

[1] *Conférences* of M. Luro.

V

THE LAST YEARS OF MARGUERITE. OF ANGOULÊME

MARGUERITE, already so afflicted by the persecutions that sullied her brother's reign, found her sorrows still further increased by the family troubles which cast a sombre veil over the latter years of her life. January 24, 1527, at Saint-Germain-en-Laye, she had married her second husband, Henri d'Albret, King of Navarre, eldest son of Jean d'Albret and Catherine de Foix, from whom Ferdinand of Arragon had taken part of their dominions under the reign of Louis XII. This prince was only nominally King of Navarre. Béarn still belonged to him; but far from possessing a sovereign's fortune, his modest resources came from Francis I., who subsidized him in order to prevent his attaching himself to Charles V. Henri d'Albret was only twenty-four at the time of his marriage, while Marguerite was in her thirty-sixth year. She seems to have made a love-match, but everything inclines one to believe that her young husband, who did not make her happy according to the testimony of his contemporaries, was moved rather by ambition than inclination.

Francis I. covered the newly-married pair with promises. He renounced in their favor all claims on the county of Armagnac, and pledged himself to have the kingdom of Navarre restored to his brother-in-law, but he did not keep this engagement. In a word, as M. Michelet says, Marguerite espoused poverty and ruin.[1] Her brother indemnified her in a measure by endowing her with the duchies of Alençon and Berry, the counties of Armagnac and Perche, and in general all the seigniories which she held from her first husband, or rather, by right of appanage. In reality, Marguerite remained dependent on Francis I. whose assistance she was many times obliged to seek.

She had two children by her second marriage, — a daughter born January 7, 1528, who was the famous Jeanne d'Albret, mother of Henry IV., and a son, born in 1530, who only lived two months. On the day of the little prince's death, his mother, who was then at Alençon, had this great passage from the Book of Job posted on the city walls: " The Lord gave him to me, the Lord hath taken him away. May His holy name be blessed." It was reserved for Jeanne d'Albret to become the object of Marguerite's greatest sorrows. She was only two years old when Francis I., who wished to dispose of her as he pleased, and especially to prevent any scheme for uniting her to the son of Charles V., withdrew her

---

[1] In his remarkable *Histoire des Peuples et des États pyrénéens*, M. Cénac-Moncaut has given some interesting details concerning Henri d'Albret.

from the direction of her parents, and caused her to be brought up in the castle of Plessis-lez-Tours. Marguerite was profoundly afflicted by this despotic action, but she was obliged to submit. If Jeanne had married the prince, who was to become Philip II., the usurpation of the kingdom of Navarre by the Spanish would have been legitimatized. They might even have acquired important possessions on this side of the Pyrenees. This idea became a source of anxiety to Francis I. He knew the marriage was greatly desired by many subjects of his brother-in-law, who hoped in this wise to recover their estates in Navarre. Cardinal de Gramont, Archbishop of Bordeaux and Lieutenant-Governor of Guyenne, surprised a correspondence between Henri d'Albret and Charles V. and sent it to the King. The little princess was then twelve years old. Francis I. was at this time desirous to gain William de la Marck, Duke of Cleves, who was on the point of giving his adhesion to the Emperor. More royal than brotherly, Francis I., without troubling himself about his sister's opposition, resolved that his niece should be affianced to the Duke of Cleves. From her infancy Jeanne had that firmness of character and force of will which was her characteristic trait through life. The heaviest threats were necessary to induce her to accept a betrothal which was not according to her mind. Francis I., more and more alarmed by the prospect of a union between his niece and the son of Charles V., sent for the Duke of Cleves to come to Châtellerault. All that Marguerite could obtain for her daughter, who was then but twelve and a half years old, was that the pretended consummation of Jeanne's marriage with the Duke should be nothing but an empty ceremony. Francis I. had required that the pair should enter the marriage-bed in the presence of witnesses, but it was surrounded by matrons as long as they remained together, and the Duke of Cleves, after signing a treaty of alliance with Francis I., returned alone to Germany. Abandoned in 1543 by the French troops, which left him at the Emperor's mercy, he sent a herald-at-arms to the King to demand his wife. Francis I. replied that he had nothing to do with that affair, and that the Duke must ask the King and Queen of Navarre for their daughter. Marguerite and her husband were delighted to find a pretext against a union which had never pleased them, and relying on a change of inclination in Francis I., they succeeded in obtaining from the Pope an annulment of the marriage concluded three years before.[1]

In a book which happily combines erudition with a charming style, Count Hector de La Ferrière-Percy[2] has drawn a curious picture of Marguerite's latter years. By the aid of the Queen's account-book he has very exactly indicated the nature of her occu-

---

[1] Jeanne d'Albret married Antoine de Bourbon in 1548.
[2] Marguerite d'Angoulême. Her book of expenses from 1540 to 1549: *Études sur ses dernières années*, par le Comte Hector de La Ferrière-Percy.

pations and her daily life. He shows her presiding with exquisite affability over her little court at Béarn, where, dressed "*comme une simple demoiselle*," and having none of the externals of royalty save the majesty of her form and bearing, she mingled with her subjects, spoke their language, visited the poor, and gave asylum to the proscribed.

At Pau, where she found an old feudal dwelling, she caused those magnificent terraces to be constructed from which may be seen the summits of the Pyrenees, and those beautiful buildings which bear the imprint of the Renaissance. But Marguerite was not happy in this beautiful abode. Her husband's disposition was very trying, and he did not live harmoniously with her. Melancholy had displaced gaiety. The diversions which had once amused that wittiest of women who wrote the *Heptameron* now seemed to her dull and lifeless. Worldly conversations upon love no longer pleased her, and it was she wrote these verses stamped with sadness : —

> "Mes cinquante ans, ma vertu affaiblie,
> Le temps passé, commandent que j'oublie,
> Pour mieux penser à la prochaine mort,
> Sans plus avoir mémoire ni remords,
> Si en amour a douleur ou plaisir." [1]

---

[1] My fifty years, my failing powers,
Time past, command that I forget,
To think the better of approaching death,
No more to have or memory or remorse,
If in love is either pain or pleasure.

At the time when shadows were thus creeping over Marguerite's last years, her brother, exhausted by an incurable disease, was the painful survivor of his own faculties, and the once-radiant sun was setting amidst clouds. It is the destiny of all men whose career has been brilliant, to expiate their days of triumph by painful trials. "The most lamentable spectacle, the one most productive of serious reflections, is the last period of life in any man or thing which has had any grandeur. When the existence has been commonplace, it resembles a smooth mirror on which the breath leaves hardly any trace. But when a man has been great, brilliant, and beautiful, and when one sees him broken down by sickness and death, when a vast intelligence is crushed and blighted, when striking beauty is effaced, when a voice sweet as an angel's changes and is lost, the soul experiences an ineffable sadness."[1] Marguerite, whose affection for her brother was profound, could not be consoled when she knew that he was suffering and unhappy. In vain the aging monarch redoubled his expenses.

"This court, always on the go, resembled a moving romance, a Pantagruelic pilgrimage, all along the Loire, from castle to castle, from forest to forest. Everywhere the hunting of stags and boars and stunning bugle blasts. Everywhere great banquets, and tables spread under the greenwood-tree for

---

[1] M. Capefigue, *François Ier et la Renaissance*.

thousands of guests. Then all this disappeared."[1] These pomps, these amusements, had no longer any attraction for a man whose imagination and character were alike deadened. A heart at peace may find happiness in the obscurest village.

"Est Ulubris, animus si te non deficit æquus."

But a heart which is not at peace finds it nowhere, not even in the most splendid palaces. By the beginning of the year 1547, the strength of Francis I. was visibly declining. Some time before that he had desired to summon his sister, who was always his most faithful comforter. It was under a dull wintry sky that the two saw once more the park of Chambord. "Leaning on the arm of his gentle Marguerite, his enfeebled glance wandered from the high painted window over those great woods stripped of their foliage, beneath which he had chased the deer, to that bleak horizon, faithful image of his present fortune. It was then, under the influence of one of those fits of sadness not to be shaken off at the sight of Nature's desolation, that he traced the words that Brantôme has preserved."

"Souvent femme varie,
Mal habil qui s'y fie."[2]

---

[1] Michelet, *La Réforme.*
[2] Count Hector de La Ferrière-Percy.
Woman often changes;
Foolish he who trusts her.

What he might well say of his mistresses and favorites, Francis I. did not apply to his sister, whose devotion and goodness had never failed for an instant. She left him with regret, as if she foreboded an approaching calamity. In February, 1547, the condition of Francis I. altered for the worse. A continual fever gradually undermined his strength. He tried in vain to struggle against the malady. "As if he hoped to escape, by activity, from the death that was on his track, he went from Saint-Germain to La Muette, Villepreux, Dampierre, and Loches; but the illness outstripped him. Worn out with fatigue, he arrived at Rambouillet, intending to stay there only one night; he was not to go any further; he took to his bed, and never left it again." March 31, 1547, the knightly King, the father of letters, the hero of Marignan, ceased to live.

Marguerite was then at the monastery of Tusson in Angoumois, where she went from time to time to meditate in the religious silence of the cloister, and to make retreats which lasted for several weeks. Dark presentiments had taken possession of her impressionable soul. "In the season which despoils nature there is not a breeze, not a breath, so light that it is not strong enough to detach the leaf from the tree that bears it. In the autumn of the heart there is not a movement which does not take away a happiness or a hope."[1] Marguerite suffered, but

---

[1] *Pensées*, de Madame Swetchine.

so long as she had her brother she did not complain. The whole strength of her affection was, one might say, concentrated on this friend of her infancy, this perpetual object of her respect, devotion, admiration, and tenderness.

A few days before the death of this beloved brother, she dreamed that he appeared to her, his face pallid, depressed, and that he called her in a plaintive voice. She at once sent several couriers to Paris to calm the anxiety inspired by this presage. In her anguished impatience she exclaimed: "Whoever shall come to my door to announce the recovery of the King, however tired, harassed, filthy, or dirty that courier may be, I will run to kiss and embrace him as if he were the finest gentleman in the kingdom, and if he needs a bed I will give him mine, and lie on the bare ground." The nuns were already acquainted with the fatal tidings, but had not the courage to announce them to the Queen. One of them was weeping and lamenting. The noise of her sobs could be heard throughout the cloister. It was a poor insane sister who was left at liberty because her madness was not dangerous.

"What are you groaning about, sister?" Marguerite said to her. "Alas! Madame, it is your ill-fortune that I deplore!" At these words, the Queen comprehended all. "You are hiding my brother's death from me," cried she, "but the spirit of God has revealed it to me by the mouth of this lunatic."

Then, falling on her knees and weeping, she began to pray. Marguerite spent the first forty days of her mourning in the monastery. Brantôme says her "regrets were so poignant that she could never after recover from them. She composed several pieces of verse on the death of her brother. They were her farewell to poetry which she had so much loved."

> "Je n'ai plus ni père ni mère,
> Ni sœur ni frère,
> Sinon Dieu seul auquel j'espère,
> Qui sur le ciel et terre impère.
> J'ai mis du tout en oubliance,
> Le monde, et parents, et amis;
> Biens et honneurs en abondance,
> Je les tiens pour mes ennemis." [1]

Never had Marguerite been inspired better than by sorrow: —

> "Les plus désespérés sont les chants les plus beaux.
> J'en connais d'immortels qui sont de purs sanglots." [2]

Yes, it is nothing but a sob, this sorrowful lay of the Queen of Navarre, who would not be consoled: —

---

[1] I have no longer either father or mother,
Neither sister nor brother,
Save God alone in whom I trust,
Who hath empery over heaven and earth.
All have I offered to oblivion,
World, parents, friends;
Possessions, honors in abundance,
I hold them for my enemies.

[2] The most beautiful songs are the most despairing.
I know immortal ones that are but mere sobs.
— ALFRED DE MUSSET.

"Las! tant malheureuse je suis,
Que mon malheur dire ne puis
Sinon qu'il est sans espérance . . .
Tant de larmes jettent mes yeux,
Qu'ils ne voient ni terre ni cieux,
Telle est de leurs pleurs abondance.
Ma bouche se plaint en tous lieux ;
De mon cœur ne peut saillir mieux
Que soupirs sans nulle allégeance.
Mort qui m'as fait ce mauvais tour
D'abattre ma force et ma tour,
Tout mon refuge et ma défense,
N'a su ruiner mon amour
Que je sens croître chaque jour.
Que ma douleur croit et avance.
O mort, qui le frère as dompté,
Viens doncques par ta grande bonté
Transpercer la sœur de ta lance . . ."[1]

---

[1] Alas! so unfortunate am I,
That my woe can say no more,
Save that it is hopeless . . .
So many tears escape my eyes
That they see neither earth nor skies,
So abundant are their tears.
My mouth complains in every place ;
From my heart nothing better can gush out
Than sighs without alleviation.
Death which has done me this ill turn
To batter down my strength and tower,
All my refuge and defence,
Has not been able to destroy my love,
Which I feel increasing every day
That my woe increases and advances.
O death, who hast conquered the brother,
Come then by thy great bounty,
Transfix the sister with thy lance.

68   MARGUERITE, SISTER OF FRANCIS I.

The manuscripts in the Imperial Library have preserved this eight-line stanza composed by Marguerite at the same period: —

> "Je cherche autant la croix et la désire
> Comme autrefois je l'ai voulu fuir;
> Je cherche autant par tourment d'en jouir,
> Comme autrefois j'ai craint son dur martyre.
> Car cette croix mon âme à Dieu attire;
> C'est le chemin très sûr pour l'aller voir.
> Par quoi les biens qu'au monde puis avoir
> Quitter je veux : la croix me doit suffire." [1]

After her brother's death she lived only for heaven. Abandoning the administration of all her possessions to her husband, she occupied herself with nothing but good works and prayers. She no longer worked at that famous collection of tales which she was in the habit of composing in her litter, as she travelled about, and dictating to one of her maids of honor. So the *Heptameron* remained unfinished, containing only seventy-two tales, instead of the hundred at first intended by Marguerite. The time for joyous diversions had passed away, and the Queen of Navarre no longer contemplated

---

[1] As much I seek the cross and it desire,
As formerly I wished from it to flee ;
So much by torments tow'rd it I aspire,
As once I feared its heavy martyry.
Because this cross doth draw my soul to God ;
To go to see Him 'tis the most sure road,
Whereby all goods that in the world may be,
Forsake will I : the cross shall suffice me.

anything but eternity. Her inquiring mind sought to penetrate the secrets of the tomb. Resigned as she was to the will of God, Brantôme tells us that she had moments of perplexity and uneasiness concerning the mysteries of the future life.

One day, when some one was speaking to her of the splendors of heaven and the joys of the elect, "All that is true," said she, "but we lie so long dead in the ground before arriving there!" Brantôme also relates that, being present while one of her chambermaids was in her death agony, she watched the last moments of the dying woman with anxiety, and looked fixedly at the already icy visage. One of her maids of honor having asked her why, she replied "that having heard many learned doctors say that the soul and spirit left the body as soon as it died, she wanted to see if there came from it any noise or the least echo in the world of their removal and departure, but that she had perceived nothing." She added that "if her faith were not very firm, she would not know what to think of this dislodgment and disrupture of the soul and the body: but that she wished to believe what her God and her Church enjoined without carrying her curiosity any further."

The hour when she was to sound the great mystery was at hand. According to Sainte-Marthe, the presentiments which had announced the death of Francis to Marguerite were renewed to warn her of her own. A woman dressed in white appeared to her in a dream, and showing her a crown of flowers said in a low voice: "À bientôt."[1] On awaking, Marguerite comprehended that God was recalling her to Himself. She fell sick a few days later, and after three weeks of suffering, endured in a Christian spirit, she died at Odos-en-Bigorre, December 21, 1549, in her fifty-eighth year. Her last word was "Jesus!"

Few queens have been so much regretted by their subjects as the woman who had been "the help and protector of good literature, and the defence, shelter, and consolation of the distressed." The historian of Béarn exclaims, when speaking of this death: "It seems to me that the sun hides itself, that day becomes night, that the Muses depart with her, that the learned, tired of living, sink down at this one stroke." The poor were overwhelmed with grief. "How many widows are there," says Sainte-Marthe, "how many orphans, how many afflicted, how many old persons whom she pensioned every year, and who now, like sheep whose shepherd is dead, wander hither and thither, seeking to whom to go, crying in the ears of wealthy people, and deploring their miserable fate!"

The learned and the poets made it a duty to celebrate their protectress in funeral orations and in poems. To the tenth Muse, the fourth of the Graces, to the illustrious sister and wife of kings: —

---

[1] Till very soon.

"Musarum decima et Charitum quarta, inclyta regum
Et soror et conjux, Margaris illa jacet."

Ronsard dedicated to her a lyric poem worthy of the woman of whom he sang: —

> " Comme les herbes fleuries
> Sont les honneurs des prairies,
> Et des prés les ruisselets,
> De l'orme la oigne aimée,
> Des bocages la ramée,
> Des champs les blés nouvelets ;
>
> " Ainsi tu fus, ô princesse,
> (Ainçois plutôt, ô déesse !)
> Tu fus la perle et l'honneur
> Des princesses de notre âge,
> Soit en splendeur de lignage,
> Soit en biens, soit en bonheur.
>
> " Il ne faut point qu'on te fasse
> Un sépulcre qui embrasse
> Mille termes en un rond,
> Pompeux d'ouvrages antiques,
> Et brave en piliers doriques
> Élevés à double front.
>
> " L'airain, le marbre et le cuivre
> Font tant seulement revivre
> Ceux qui meurent sans renom,
> Et desquels la sépulture
> Presse sous même culture
> Le corps, la vie et le nom.
>
> " Mais toi dont la renommée
> Porte d'une aile animée

Par le monde tes valeurs,
Mieux que ces pointes superbes,
Te plaisent les douces herbes
Les fontaines et les fleurs."[1]

---

[1] As flowering herbs
Are the glory of meadows,
And rivulets of meads,
The beloved vine of the elm,
Green boughs of the shady wood,
And sprouting grain of fields;

So thou, O princess,
(Say rather, O goddess!)
Wert the pearl and the glory
Of the princesses of our age,
Whether in splendor of lineage,
Of possessions, or of happiness.

We must not make for thee
A sepulchre which should embrace,
A myriad statues in one round,
Pompous with antique works,
And brave in Doric pillars
Reared up in double rows.

Bronze, marble, and copper
Can do so much but to revive
Those who die without renown,
And whose sepulture
Weighs down beneath the same pressure
The body, the life, and the name.

But thou, of whom the renown
A living pen
Bears through the world the worth,
Better than those proud peaks,
Thou art pleased with gentle shrubs,
With fountains, and with flowers.

M. Nisard has said with exquisite grace: "The poets called the marguerite the queen of flowers, and what would most often be an insipid flattery was then an expression of sentiment. The gentle spirit of this princess, this perfume of delicacy and goodness in writings more amiable than brilliant, these pleasingly blended rather than vivid colors, these charming perfections of a secondary order, are they not of the marguerite species?"

We have studied the moral qualities of the Queen of Navarre. It remains to glance rapidly over her writings, and to prove that in her case the style was the woman.

VI

POEMS AND LETTERS OF MARGUERITE D'ANGOULÊME

THE Queen of Navarre owes her celebrity as much to her writings as to her actions. The qualities of mind and heart which made of her an elect lady are found in her poems, her letters, and her tales. Placing the protégé and the protectress in the same rank, an eminent critic [1] has observed: "Marguerite and Marot are not writers of genius; they perfect the French spirit within the somewhat narrow circle in which it remained enclosed during the Middle Ages rather than add to its ideas or widen its horizon. The truths they express are most frequently those which art neglects, so familiar and present with us are they. Without our knowing it, a great many please us on account of the period of the language, and the idea that they were novelties to our fathers. But the progress of the French mind throws off at length the rust of the Middle Ages, and this very state of the language assures to Marguerite and to Marot a durable place

---

[1] M. Désiré Nisard, *Histoire de la Littérature*.

in that fecund sixteenth century whose dawn is in a measure announced by the soft and pleasing lustre of their writings."

No one can appreciate an author rightly without knowing the century in which he lived. The literary defects of the Queen of Navarre are those of her epoch, while the merits of her writings are wholly her own. The French lyre had not been tuned, and French poetry was more like a chrysalis than like a butterfly floating in an azure sky. As M. Georges Guiffrey[1] has said so well: "They were looking for the road then, and only advanced by dint of long groping and heavy labor. . . . The expeditions of Louis XII. and Francis I. into the country of Dante and Petrarch revealed unknown treasures. Our tongue essayed these ornaments which could not be mastered at the first trial; they had to be cut to fit; our language itself had need of being improved and polished. At the beginning of the sixteenth century this labor exhausted the efforts and the talents of our authors. It was an ungrateful task, but one worthy of gratitude, for it provided the riches of the future."

The verses composed at this period of transition often resemble prose, and are rather to be called versification than poetry. At every step they are hindered in their course by the obstacles of the

---

[1] Preface to an unpublished poem by Jehan Marot, published by M. Guiffrey, 1 vol. Renouard.

language. Hardly do we find a few good grains amidst the tares, a few particles of gold among the artificial gems and vulgar ornaments. Unskilful imitations of antiquity, exaggerated and pretentious metaphors, prolixities, and harsh accents abound in all these pieces of verse, wherein the art of making melody is usually more apparent than the melody itself. The Muse, somewhat barbarous still, does not yet know how to wear her chlamys. Her gait is awkward. Her voice, harmonious at moments, quickly relapses into monotony and hoarseness. "The best poets of the time, to begin with Marot, often made detestable verses, just as the worst rhymsters sometimes hit upon very pretty chances. In this respect the entire sixteenth century affords something like a continual and confused effort at extrication. Francis I., from the day he ascended the throne, gave the signal for this puissant labor which was to aid in expanding and definitely polishing the French language. Thanks to the impulse given by him from above, there was soon a universal clearing of the ground all around him."[1] A poet himself, he served as an example to his court. In default of a great talent, he had a real passion for poetry, and, like the trouvères, he liked to make use of the lyre and the sword by turns.[2] His verses, too celebrated in his lifetime, and too

---

[1] M. Sainte-Beuve, *Portraits littéraires*, t. iii.
[2] *François Ier, poète*, poems and correspondence collected and published by M. Aimé Champollion-Figeac, 1 vol. 1837.

quickly forgotten afterwards, have happily been brought to light again. They show, in spite of all their imperfections, that the king had not stifled the poet, and that a heart, sensitive to art, beat underneath the lily-embroidered mantle. In the sorrowful epochs of his career, Francis I. always recurred to poetry. It is a proof that he loved it sincerely. It served him to formulate one of the most melancholy and most striking judgments that ever monarch pronounced on the nothingness of the grandeurs of this lower world: —

> "Plus j'ai de biens, plus ma douleur augmente;
> Plus j'ai d'honneur et moins je me contente,
> Car un reçu m'en fait cent désirer.
> Quand rien je n'ai, de rien ne me lamente,
> Mais ayant tout, la crainte me tourmente
> Ou de le perdre, ou bien de l'empirer.
> Las, je dois bien mon malheur soupirer,
> Vu que d'avoir un bien je meurs d'envie,
> Qui est ma mort, et je l'estime vie."[1]

Marguerite was doubly the sister of Francis I., by nature and by poetry. It pleased her to write

---

[1] The more my goods, the more my sorrow grows;
The more my honors, less is my content;
For one I gain, a hundred I desire.
When nought I have, for nothing I lament;
But having all, the fear doth me torment,
Either to lose it or to make it worse.
Tired, full well may I my misery mourn,
Seeing I die of envy but to have a good,
Which is my death, and I esteem it life.

in verse to this brother, so much admired and loved, for whom all the treasures of lyrical language seemed to her not rich enough.[1] M. Sainte-Beuve, who has made a profound study of the poetry of the sixteenth century, finds that "the talent of the illustrious sister is of an incomparably different order from that of the King; every time she takes the pen, the reader feels it in the firmness of tone, and a certain elevation of thought. Yet we must not expect, even from her, a delicacy of taste which did not then exist, nor a long succession of good verses such as at this date it was not given to any but the fluent vein of Marot to produce."

The poetry of the Queen of Navarre appeared in Lyons, in 1547, under the title: *Les Marguerites de la Marguerite des Princesses*. It is a collection of little poems, fugitive pieces, epistles, chansons, and ballads. The mystical element stands for much in it. The *Miroir de l'âme pécheresse*, for example, which brought down on the Queen the wrath of Noël Beda, the syndic of the Theological Faculty, is merely a commentary on various passages of Scripture. The history of the *Satyres et des Nymphes de Diane* imitate, but ungracefully, the style of Ovid. The *Coche*, or the *Débat d'Amour*, is a versified thesis on matters of gallantry more insipid than attractive. There is nothing very

---

[1] Marguerite's poems occupy much space in M. Champollion-Figeac's collection.

remarkable in any of the productions we have just mentioned. But beside these attempts there are verses truly poetic: they are those in which the Queen, no longer inspired by her wit, but by her heart, seeks neither literary effect nor parasitic ornaments, but obeys the impulse of a profoundly sensitive soul. Sensibility is the distinctive character of the poems in which she is really moving, because she is really moved. Does she speak of her inner life, her sorrows, her vexations? she becomes eloquent:—

"Rien ne nous rend si grands qu'une grande douleur."[1]

At her brother's death she was reminded of Dante:—

"Douleur n'y a qu'au temps de la misère
Se recorder de l'heureux et prospère,
Comme autrefois en Dante j'ai trouvé:
Mais le sais mieux pour avoir éprouvé,
Félicité et infortune austère.
Prospérité m'a fait trop bonne chère,
Pour tôt après me la rendre si chère:
Hélas! mon Dieu, que m'est-il arrivé?
Douleur!

"Voire en façon que presque en désespére
D'avoir perdu tant d'amis et mon frère
Que tant valait! il est assez prouvé!

---

[1] Nothing makes us so great as a great sorrow.
—Alfred de Musset.

> Or, quelque ennui qu'un cœur est aggravé
> vous remets ma perte aigre et amère
> Douleur !" [1]

Poetry and religion were her two consolers. As she says so well: —

> " Un mal va toujours empirant,
> Et s'il est tel qu'il ne puisse être pire
> Il s'amoindrit quelquefois à le dire." [2]

Looking at her crucifix, she exclaims: —

> " C'est mon vouloir et propos arrêté
> De n'être plus celle-là qu'ai été,
> Ni m'amuser du misérable monde,

---

[1] No grief is like that which in time of wretchedness,
Recalls to mind times prosperous and happy,
As formerly I learned in Dante's page,
Yet know still better now from having proved
Felicity and most austere misfortune.
Prosperity hath feasted me too well
To rate good cheer so soon at such high price:
Alas! my God, what has happened to me?
    Anguish!

Indeed, since I am almost in despair,
At having lost so many friends and my brother,
Whose worth was great! the case is well made out.
Now, whatsoever grief weighs down my heart,
In you recalls my piercing loss, and bitter
    Anguish!

[2] An evil ever goes from bad to worse,
  And if it be one that can be no worse,
  Sometimes it lessens it to tell it.

Vu la douleur qui y règne et abonde,
Dont jour et nuit mon cœur est tourmenté."[1]

In a burst of piety worthy of a Saint Theresa, she composes this religious chant, wherein love divine utters a cry reaching even unto death: —

> " Seigneur, quand viendra le jour
> Tant désiré,
> Que je serai par amour
> A vous tiré.
> Ce jour de noces, Seigneur,
> Me tarde tant!
> Que de nul bien ni honneur
> Ne suis content.
> Essuyer des tristes yeux
> Le long gémir,
> Et me donnez pour le mieux
> Un doux dormir."[2]

---

[1] It is my will and firm intent
To be no more what I have been,
Nor to amuse myself in this poor world,
Seeing the griefs that reign there and abound,
And which by day and night torment my heart.

[2] Lord, when shall come the day
I long to see,
When by pure love I shall
Be drawn to Thee.
That nuptial day, O Lord,
So long delays,
That no content I find
In wealth or praise.
Wipe from these sorrowing eyes
The tear that flows,
And grant me Thy best gift,
A sweet repose.

Is not that fitting language for a woman who said she "had borne more than her load of the ennui common to every well-born creature"? Every time that she abandons artificial commonplaces then in fashion, and suffers her soul alone to speak, Marguerite utters strains that are really inspired. The verses dedicated to her brother are always noble and pathetic because they issue from her heart; her style gains in strength and ardor. The portrait she traces of her king is magnificent. The odes of Pindar are not inspired by a more exalted influence.

> " C'est lui que ciel et terre et mer contemple,
> La terre a joie, le voyant revêtu
> D'une beauté qui n'a point de semblable,
> Auprès duquel tous beaux sont un fétu.
> La mer, devant son pouvoir redoutable,
> Douce se rend, connaissant sa bonté,
> Et est pour lui contre tous secourable.
> Le ciel s'abaisse et, par amour dompté,
> Vient admirer et voir le personnage
> Dont on lui a tant de vertu conté.
> C'est lui qui a grâce et parler de maître,
> Digne d'avoir sur tous grâce et puissance,
> Qui, sans nommer, se peut assez connaître.
> C'est lui de tout qui a la connaissance
> Et un savoir qui n'a point de pareil.
> Il n'y a rien dont il ait ignorance.
> De sa beauté il est blanc et vermeil,
> Les cheveux bruns, de grande et belle taille;
> En terre il est comme au ciel le soleil
> Hardi, vaillant, sage et pieux en bataille;

Fort et puissant, qui ne peut avoir peur
Que prince nul tant soit puissant l'assaille.
Il est bénin, doux, humble en sa grandeur,
Fort et puissant, et plein de patience,
Soit en prison, en tristesse et malheur.
Il a de Dieu la parfaite science
Que doit avoir un roi tout plein de foi,
Bon jugement et bonne conscience;
De son Dieu garde l'honneur et la loi;
A ses sujets doux support et justice;
Bref, lui tout seul est digne d'être roi."[1]

---

[1] 'Tis he whom sky and earth and sea contemplate,
The earth is joyous, seeing him invested
With beauty passing all comparison,
Near which all else that's fair's not worth a farthing.
The sea before his formidable power
Becometh gentle, knowing all his goodness,
And against all men ready is to help him.
The sky bends down and by love over-mastered,
Comes to admire and see the personage
Of whom so much that's good hath been recounted.
'Tis he hath grace, and like a master speaketh,
Who, without naming, knows himself most fully.
He that of all things hath the cognizance
And knowledge that hath nowhere any peer.
Nor is there aught of which he knoweth nothing.
As for his beauty, he is white and ruddy,
Brown are his locks, and tall and fine his figure;
He is on earth most like the sun in heaven,
Bold, valiant, wise and doughty he in battle;
Mighty and strong, who never could be frightened,
What prince however powerful assail him.
He is benign, sweet, humble in his grandeur,
Mighty and strong, replenished too with patience,
Whether in prison, or in woe and sorrow.
He hath of God the full and perfect science,
Fitting a king whose faith is nowhere lacking,

Apparent as it is, the exaggeration in this does not shock because it proceeds from a sincere sentiment, a real admiration, and not from a base and fawning spirit. Marguerite's affection for her brother is a cult. It is this pure and noble passion which imparts a penetrating charm to her correspondence. Michelet has very well said: "The volume of letters addressed to the King amazes and perplexes one, not by the vehemence, but the invariable permanence of a sentiment which is always the same, which has neither phrases nor crises of diminution or increase, which has neither heights nor depths. The whole life of this *infinitely pure* person was replenished by a single sentiment. The immense and charming collection of Madame de Sévigné's letters alone remind us of these. Marguerite's sometimes have their charm (for example when she writes the captive King what his children are doing), and they have above all their passion and inexhaustible emotion." Their style is firm and concise; the Queen of Navarre says clearly what she desires to say. There is a perfect agreement between her expression and her thought.

One is all the more grateful to Marguerite for this excellent diction, seeing that the bad taste of the period furnished her with quite different models. M.

Nor yet his judgment nor his healthy conscience;
He heedeth of his God the law and honor;
Is to his subjects sweet support and justice;
In brief, to be a king he sole is worthy.

Génin has justly remarked that "Marguerite must have been gifted by nature with great solidity of judgment and exquisite good sense, or she would have been entirely spoiled by her frequent intercourse with a mystic so forcible as Bishop Briçonnet." The manuscript of this religious correspondence, which belongs to the Imperial Library, contains not less than eight hundred pages, and it is difficult to give a notion of such a medley of inflated metaphors and mystic enigmas. "Oh! how blessed is the faithful soul," exclaims the bishop on the subject of the Incarnation, "who, through union with the bullet of the double cannon cast in the virginal furnace, full primed with powder, is enkindled by charity to take by force the kingdom of heaven, until then impregnable! O resonant abyss, and infinite mine of annihilating powder, and furnace of inextinguishable love, attracting all, attracting everywhere!" Intoxicated by the jargon of mysticism, as Don Quixote was by the romances of chivalry, the same prelate writes to Marguerite: "Madame, he who is desert is swallowed up in desert; seeking the desert and not able to find it; and when he finds it is yet more perplexed, is a bad guide to guide another out of the desert and lead him into the desert desired. Desert and hungered with death-producing hunger, how long till it be crowded to the eyes!" And so on through an interminable series of phrases in the same style. Everything about this correspondence is ridiculous.

Marguerite was only thirty years old, Briçonnet fifty-five. And in writing to him she signs herself: "Your useless mother." Another time she signs: "Your freezing, thirsty, and hungry daughter, worse than dead, the living dead, Marguerite."

It is a singular thing that the century which enjoyed Erasmus admired Bishop Briçonnet. Twice he was Ambassador Extraordinary at Rome. He represented France in the councils of Pisa and of Lateran. He was considered a thunderbolt of religious eloquence. But Marguerite, who had at least as much good sense as wit, at last wearied of this worse than idle nonsense.

She humbly entreated the prelate to employ fewer metaphors. "The poor wandering sheep," she wrote to him, "cannot understand what good there is in the desert for lack of knowing that she is deserted; she prays you, by your affection, not to run so fast in this desert that no one can follow you, and so the abyss called on by the abyss, may end by engulfing the poor wandering sheep." The correspondence with Briçonnet ended in 1525. Freed from this direction which, applied to another woman, might have made her the author of ridiculous affectations, Marguerite wrote with the naturalness, simplicity, and lofty charm which thenceforward characterized her style.

"Marguerite's letters, nearly all of them addressed to her brother, although less lively in manner than her tales, on account of the respectful formalities she observed toward the king even when expressing the tenderest attachment for the brother, are full of the same gentleness, address, and suggestiveness which one admires in the conversation of Dame Oisille. The diction is the same, abundant, facile, free from strong expressions or audacities, save in some passages on God, where Marguerite, moved sometimes by faith, and again by sentiment, rises to those thoughts which can only be translated by expressions created for them."[1] The style is at once noble and familiar. Every line displays profound affection and a devotion equal to all proof. The reader is convinced that for this brother so much beloved, the woman who is the model of sisters would sacrifice even the last drop of her blood.

Marguerite is truly eloquent in her letters. How moved she is, and how easily she communicates her emotion when, on the road to Madrid, she writes to the royal captive: "Monseigneur, I know well the force of that love which our Lord has put into us three,[2] for what I thought impossible when considering only myself, is easy when I remember you. Supplicating Him who gave me being not to leave it so useless that it may not serve for that deliverance for which I could account all servitude

---

[1] M. Désiré Nisard, *Histoire de la littérature française.*
[2] Francis I., Louise of Savoy, and Marguerite. Cardinal Bibiena called them the Trinity. *Che scrivere a Luisa di Savoia era come scrivere alla stessa Trinità.*

a gracious freedom!" How one feels her sincerity when she writes again, December 2, 1525: "To serve you is the only reason that makes me desire life, strength, and health, for death, after having done something toward that good which I desire, could be so joyful to me that I would esteem it a redoubled life!" How she consoles the prisoner! "God is for you, seeing that His word is true, which promises that He will be with those who are in tribulation, whereby I see you surrounded on every side." And when she comes back alone from Spain, how she considers "more than ever wretched" her litter, which has not had the good fortune to bring back the King!

In 1536, Charles V. in a discourse pronounced at Rome in full consistory, before the Pope and the cardinals, had insulted Francis I. Marguerite, indignant, writes to her brother: "All women long to be men to aid you in bringing down his pride."

The Imperialists had invaded the south of France. To serve her country and her king, Marguerite feels the courage of an Amazon. After having visited the French camp at Avignon, she writes to Francis I.: "Monseigneur, although it is not for me to praise a thing of which my condition makes me ignorant, yet I cannot help writing you that all the captains have assured me they have never seen a camp so strong and suitable as this one." This valiant army electrifies her. "I would be too happy," she says, "to die with so many virtuous persons. . . . Please God, the Emperor may try to cross the Rhone while I am here. All woman as I am, I would undertake to prevent him from passing it at the risk of my life." Every time that Francis I. goes to war, she longs to have the right to follow him. "I would renounce my royal blood," she writes to him in 1537, "to be chambermaid to your washerwoman, and I give you my faith, Monseigneur, that far from regretting my robe of cloth of gold, I greatly long to be of service to you in disguise." With what effusion she thanks him, in November, 1542, for a visit he had paid her at Nérac! "Monseigneur, the honor of having received you in this poor house, and regret at not having been able to welcome you according to my desire and resolution, have so much amazed me, that, but for the joy of seeing you in such health as all your family must desire, I should have been unable to bear this sudden glimpse of so great a good so ill received." Her gratitude, which exaggerates the least benefits received from her brother, is expressed in the most ardent terms: "I remain the most indebted creature to you that ever was, seeing that it pleases you to do so much for me as King, master, father, brother, and true friend, that I can never consider you under any of these aspects without finding myself astonished by the love you are pleased to display for me, so great that if Almighty God does not repay you this charity, I shall complain of the severity of His bounty."

Among all Marguerite's letters, that which has most affected us, that which seems to show her tender and sympathetic character the best, is dated in January, 1543. After ten years of marriage, Catherine de' Medici, who had been considered barren, had just given birth to a son, the future Francis II. Marguerite, who was then ill, learned the happy tidings. She trembled with joy. "Monseigneur," she wrote to Francis I., "this is the most beautiful, the most desired, and most necessary day that ever your eyes and those of your realm have seen; it is a day worthy to drive away from you the night of all the vexations of the past year; it is a day so efficacious, that, in bringing you the title of grandfather, it makes you fifty years younger. Your new successor prolongs the pleasure of your possession; his new nativity renews your own." Her patriotism as a Frenchwoman, and her tenderness as a sister are alike excited. "What more," she says, "could you ask of God in this world? All this last year you have felt His mighty hand battling for you against your enemies visible and invisible, so that neither their forces nor their intentions have been able to injure either your kingdom or your person; but you have remained a victorious, wise, and conquering King. All these beautiful titles are crowned by that God has now given you, of grandfather." She imagines her brother so happy! "I see in spirit all those whom you love rejoice even to weeping, and I behold the tears which, I am sure, spring to your eyes from a greater joy than I saw you experience at the birth of your first born." Happiness cured Marguerite. "The malady would be very great which could not be converted into health, or which would prevent me from going in procession with the people to make bonfires." The letter ends with a Christian thought, an acknowledgment, a sort of canticle of thanksgiving to God, the author of all joy. Happy or unhappy, Marguerite's heart always beats for heaven. *Non inferiora secutus.*

VII

THE HEPTAMERON

FROM the literary point of view, Marguerite's principal title to fame is the *Heptameron*.[1] Not many works have represented a society more faithfully. One feels that, according to the author's programme, there is "none of its tales which is not a true history." The gentlemen set on the stage by the Queen of Navarre have lived. I seem to meet them when I pass through the galleries of Fontainebleau or Chambord. The echo of their shouts of laughter and their gallant speeches comes to my ear. I think of their sword-thrusts, their gallant adventures, their loves and their troubles. I love the Gallic frankness of this work where sadness blends with gaiety; where the divine follows the profane; where the words of Holy Writ alternate with phrases in the manner of Brantôme; where all unites and is amalgamated as in human life; where a whole epoch is resuscitated.

What animation there is in these piquant conversations between gentlemen who rebel against the

---

[1] See the excellent edition published by M. Le Roux de Lincy, and the remarkable introduction which precedes it.

metaphysics of sentiment, and women who are witty but somewhat coquettish, who protest as well as they can against the non-Platonic principles of their *serviteurs!* "Thence arise a quantity of delicate ideas, refined observations, and many charming creations in the language of sentiment, heart, and politeness. One feels that the social spirit, the taste for the pleasures of intelligence, have penetrated into the French higher classes; that people reflect, analyze, and study themselves more." [1]

With the sixteenth century begins what is later called fashionable life (*la vie de salon*). The French mind acquires the charm of elegance. People begin to learn how to treat questions gracefully without going into them profoundly; to pass rapidly from one subject to another; to run over the whole gamut of sentiments and ideas with the light hand of a lute-player. The *Contes de la reine de Navarre* give us a curious specimen of the conversations *à la mode* under the reign of Francis I. The women, who, until then had been relegated to the depths of feudal dungeons, had now come to enliven the court by their presence. An habitual visiting was established between the two sexes, and "in this first contact, the instincts of reserve and delicacy, which are woman's natural attribute, began to feel, though not without resistance, the influence of the grosser tastes of man." As has been extremely well remarked by M. de

---

[1] M. Désiré Nisard, *Histoire de la littérature française.*

Loménie, it is this combat between two contrary tendencies which is painted to the life in the *Heptameron*. " Then although the feminine mind, with its refinements, triumphs where the matter of questions is concerned, it yields more or less in manner to the impulse given by the stronger sex. It is not until the following century that the feminine mind, more inured to warfare, will take its revenge, and, before equilibrium is re-established, will obtrude itself even to excess." Like nearly all productions of the sixteenth century, *les Contes de la reine de Navarre* are full of contrasts, the brutalities of the Middle Ages being on an equal footing with all that is most graceful and refined in the modern spirit.

Marguerite had not invented this species of literature. She imitated Boccaccio, whose immortal *Decameron*, the masterpiece of Italian prose, had produced works modelled on the same plan in every European language. In the soirées of that epoch, when cards and dancing took no such preeminence as at present, the ladies took pleasure in listening to the reading of tales which were sometimes interesting and tragic, and nearly always gallant and licentious. It was one of the fashionable diversions of high society in those days. The Queen of Navarre, incited by a sort of literary ambition, wished to emulate an author who provided the entertainment of the court. She was a Boccaccio of the female sex, with less genius but perhaps more sensibility, and, in any case, with more edifying conclusions.

Marguerite has placed the scene of the *Heptameron* in a picturesque part of the Pyrenees, in the midst of torrents, rocks, and mountains, opposite the beautiful Aspe valley, a setting both charming and magnificent. Several persons of quality, both French and Spanish, have assembled in September at the baths of Cauterets. After a few weeks the Spaniards have been able to return to their own country; but the French have been stopped on the road by the rise of the streams.

The Béarnais Gave having overflowed its banks, they have been obliged to seek refuge in the monastery of Our Lady of Servance, until the inundation should cease. What are they to do until the roads become passable? How occupy the interminable days? How succeed in being patient? They consult Dame Oisille, a widow famous for her wisdom: "My children," she responds, "you ask me a very difficult thing, to teach you a pastime which shall free you from weariness, for, having sought the remedy all my life, I have never found but one, which is the reading of the Sacred Writings (the Old and New Testaments), in which is found the true and perfect joy of the spirit, from whence proceeds the repose and health of the body." A younger and less austere woman than Dame Oisille, Parlamente, then makes a motion which is well received. "I think," she says, "that there is none of us who has not read the Hundred tales of Boccaccio, newly translated from Italian into French, and so highly spoken of by King Francis, the first of his name, and by Monseigneur the Dauphin, Madame the Dauphiness, and Madame Marguerite, that if Boccaccio could hear them where he now is, he would come to life again at the praise of such persons." Then, after proposing to follow the example of the illustrious story-teller, "If it pleases you," she adds, "we might go every day, from noon to four o'clock, into that beautiful meadow beside the Gave, where the trees are so thick that the sun cannot dispel the shade nor overheat the cool air; there, sitting at our ease, each of us might relate some history we have known or else heard from some one worthy of credence. We might finish the Hundred by the end of ten days."

Parlamente's remarks are applauded. Then it is agreed that the time shall be divided between sacred and profane things. In the mornings the company shall assemble in the room of Dame Oisille to be present at her moral readings. From there they will go to hear Mass. The venerable matron has said: "It seems to me that if you would give an hour every morning to reading the Bible, and then pray devoutly during Mass, you would find in this desert the beauty which may be in all cities, because he who knows God sees all things fair in Him and all ugly without Him." After Mass came dinner. Then, at noon, they repair to the meadow, "So beautiful and pleasant that a Boccaccio would be needed to describe it." And there each relates his story, and chooses the narrator who shall follow him. Each story is followed by a conversation in which the whole company takes part.

Some approve the conduct of the hero or the heroine. Others condemn it severely. There are paradoxical opinions and judicious ones. The gentlemen often hold morality very cheap, but the ladies protest in the name of virtue. Oisille, the experienced widow, is the soul of the reunion. She regulates the order of the Tales; she is the court of last resort in delicate questions and the most arduous problems of sentimental casuistry; she formulates the most serious reflections on human frailty, the bitterness of the passions, the inconsiderate ardor of youth and the illusions of hope. At four o'clock the monastery bell rings for Vespers. The company repair thither, not without making the good monks wait for them occasionally. However, they do not complain, but sometimes hide behind the hedge to overhear the stories.

Dame Oisille, the woman whom every one respects, Dame Oisille who is witty without malice, virtuous without prudery, religious without affectation, is she not Marguerite herself? In the gentlemen who are her interlocutors, does not one recognize masculine fatuity, and the favorite notion of men, that, after having had one successful siege there is no place which will not surrender? Now, as in the sixteenth century, who has not heard the same imprecations against the so-called weaker sex, the same medley of anathemas and thanksgivings on the subject of Eve's daughters? Do we not know that race of husbands who disbelieve in the virtue of all wives except their own, and who are so often deceived in both judgments? In the surface of things there are changes from age to age. The foundation is always the same. People discuss intrigues in our existing salons as they did in the palace of the Queen of Navarre. Only, are there many of our fashionable women who do so with as much wit as Marguerite?

She knew what opinion to hold concerning the egotism of men who always have the word love in their mouths, but who so rarely have the thing itself in their hearts. "Do not think," says Guébron, one of the speakers in Tale XIV., "that those who pursue ladies take so much pains for love of them; no, no; for it is solely for love of themselves and their own pleasure." — "My faith," says Longarine, "I believe you; for, to tell you the truth, all my servitors have invariably begun by talking about me, and showing their desire for my life, welfare, and honor; but they end with themselves, desiring their own pleasure and glory. Wherefore, the best way is to dismiss them after the first part of their sermon."
— "Then," asks Emarsuite, "must we refuse a man as soon as he opens his mouth, without knowing what he meant to say?"— Parlamente answers: "My opinion is that at the start a woman ought never to seem to understand what the man is coming to, nor yet, when he declares himself, to be able to

believe him; but when he comes to swearing it very strongly, it appears to me it would be more honest for ladies to leave him in that good road rather than to go down as far as the valley." — " But, Nomerfide, ought we to believe from that they love us from bad reasons? Isn't it forbidden to judge our neighbor?" — "You can believe what you like about it," says Oisille, "but you must fear lest it may be true, and from the moment that you perceive the least spark of it, you ought to fly; this fire burns the heart all the sooner when it is not perceived."

How well the Queen of Navarre understood the tricks, the deceits, and dangers of what we nowadays call flirtation. How well she knew how to discern the real sentiments of these professional lovers who mistake self-love for love, and who, in boasting that they adore such or such a beauty, have never worshipped anything but their personal ease and convenience! How wisely she estimated those sham attentions which cease when pleasure ends and devotion begins! These brilliant seducers, who, like the Roman augurs, cannot look each other in the face without laughing, how well she knew how to make them speak in their own language! Hircan swears in Tale XII. "that he has never known any woman, except his own wife, whom he did not wish to cause to offend God very grossly." Simonbault says as much, and adds that he had wished all women wicked except his own. — Guébron says to him: " Truly! You deserve that your own should be such as you would like to have the others; but for my part I can swear that I have loved a woman so much that I would far rather die than have her do for me anything which would cause me to esteem her less; because my love was so founded on her virtues, that I would not have been willing to see a spot upon them for any good I might have known thereby." — Saffredant beginning to laugh, says to him: "I thought, Guébron, that the love of your wife and your own good sense had cured you of being amorous; but I see they have not, for you are still employing the expressions with which we are accustomed to deceive the sharpest and gain the attention of the wisest; for what woman will close her ears when we commence at honor and virtue? But if we should show them our hearts just as they are, there are many of us who are welcomed among ladies of whom they would make small account."

It was all very well for the gentlemen of the *Heptameron* never to miss Mass or Vespers, but they were hardened sinners all the same. Oisille and Parlamente have their hands full to moralize them. In one of the tales a prince (who is none other than Francis I.), on his return from a gallant adventure, stops at a convent of religious and performs his devotions. "Do you think," asks a lady of the company, "that these prayers were well-founded?" — "I suppose we ought not to judge," replies Parlamente, "because it may be that on returning the repentance was such that the sin was forgiven him." —

"It is very difficult," says Hircan, "to repent of anything so pleasant. For my part, I have often confessed it but hardly ever repented."—"It would be better," says Oisille, "not to confess if one has not true repentance."—"Pray, Madame," replies Hircan, "I am grieved to have offended God; but the sin itself always pleases me."—"You and your like," says Parlamente, "would be glad if there were neither God nor law except such as your affection should ordain."—"I own to you," returns Hircan, "that I would like it if God took as great pleasure in my pleasures as I do, for I would often give Him matter for rejoicing."

It is to these sensual, frankly corrupted men that Parlamente displays, at the end of Tale XIX., the ideal purity of real love. Emarsuite has just related the history of a gentleman and a young girl who, being unable to be united, had both embraced the religious life. When the story is ended, Hircan, instead of showing himself affected, cries: "Then there are more fools and mad women than there ever were!"—"Do you call it folly," says Oisille, "to love honestly in youth and then to turn all this love to God?"—"And yet I have an opinion," says Parlamente, "that no man will ever love God perfectly who has not perfectly loved some creature in this world."—"What do you mean by loving perfectly?" asks Saffredant. "Do you call those perfect lovers who are bashful and adore ladies from a distance, without daring to display their wishes?"—"I call those perfect lovers," replies Parlamente, "who seek some perfection in what they love, whether goodness, beauty, or kindness, and whose hearts are so lofty and honest, that they would rather die than perform those base deeds which honor and conscience forbid; for the soul, which was only created to return to its Sovereign Good, cannot, while it is in the body, do otherwise than desire to win thither. But because the senses by which they can have tidings of it are dull and carnal on account of the sin of our first parent, they can show it only those visible things which most nearly approach perfection, and the soul runs after them, believing that in visible grace and moral virtues it may find the sovereign beauty, grace, and virtue. But when it has sought and experienced them without finding whom it loves, it passes on like the child who, according to his littleness, loves apples, pears, dolls, and other little things the most beautiful that his eyes can see, and thinks it riches to heap little stones together; but on growing larger, loves living things, and therefore amasses the goods necessary for human life; but he knows, by the greatest experiences, that in things one may possess there is neither perfection nor felicity, and he desires true felicity and the Maker and Source thereof."

Amidst these light tales, after gay anecdotes and remarks which are often indecent, how many touching words occur on the sorrows of the heart, the unhappiness of those who love and are not loved, on the chagrin of souls which, after dreaming of the

ideal, are crushed beneath the weight of the reality!
" There is no burden so heavy," says Longarine in
Tale XXI., "that the love of two persons truly united
cannot endure it; but when one of them neglects his
duty, and allows it all to fall upon the other, the
weight is insupportable."—"Then," says Guébron,
"you should have pity on us, who carry all the love
without your deigning to lighten it with the tip of a
finger."—"Ah! Guébron," says Parlamente, "the
burdens of the man and those of the woman are often
very different, because the love of woman, well
founded and resting upon God and His honor, is so
just and reasonable that he who would abandon such
an affection ought to be esteemed recreant and perverse toward God and all honest men. But the love
of the majority of men being entirely based on pleasure, ignorant women, always the dupes of their evil
will, sometimes engage themselves too deeply in
tender commerce; but when God makes them understand the malicious heart of him whom they thought
good, they can withdraw with honor and good repute,
for the shortest follies are always the best."

In the *Heptameron* the truest and most profound
philosophical reflections often follow a merry tale.
Marguerite, who had seen human grandeurs and
pettinesses so close at hand, knew by experience that
grief is at least as much at home beneath the domes
of palaces as under roofs of straw; that a robe of gold
brocade or a splendid jewel has never consoled a real
sorrow; that Providence dispenses goods and ills here

below with a less partial hand than people think; and that the poor would be in the wrong to cast envious glances at the ostentatious dwellings of the powerful. "For although poor people," it is said in Tale XXIX., "have neither goods nor honors like us, yet they have more of the commodities of nature than we do. Their viands are not savory, but their appetites are better than ours, and they nourish themselves better with coarse bread than we with rich soups. Their beds are not so handsome and well-made as ours, but they sleep better and rest more. They have not the painted and bedizened dames that we idolize; but they enjoy their pleasures oftener than we, and without fearing gossip, unless that of the beasts and birds that see them. In brief, what we have they lack, and in what we have not they abound."

With what noble firmness the Queen of Navarre vindicates the rights of woman! "It is right," says Parlamente, "that man should govern us as our head, but not that he should abandon us or treat us ill." In the midst of this society where adultery is all the fashion, what fine thoughts on the sanctity and dignity of marriage! "God," says Oisille in Tale XXXVII., "has so well ordered both man and woman, that, if it is not abused, I think marriage one of the most beautiful and secure estates that can be in this world, and I am sure that all who are here, no matter what pretence they make, think as much or more; and as much as man calls himself wiser than woman, so much the more grievously will he be punished if the fault is on his side." It is Oisille again who makes this remark whose profundity experience must vouch for: "I am of the opinion that there is no perfect pleasure when the conscience is not at rest." Could the most eloquent preacher say anything better about the duties of women than Parlamente in what follows? "Those who are overcome by pleasure ought not to call themselves women any longer but men, whose honor is augmented by fury and concupiscence; for a man who revenges himself on his enemy, and slays him for a contradiction, is esteemed a better companion for it; and the same is true if he loves a dozen other women with his wife; but the honor of women has another foundation: it is gentleness, patience, chastity."

What does it matter after that, if one does find indecent expressions and indelicate details in the *Heptameron?* The form is licentious, but the foundation is moral. The contrary is true of many productions of our own epoch. We must not forget how difficult it is for a writer to detach himself from the milieu in which he lives. What really appertains to him is not the spectacle he is present at, but the conclusion he draws from it. From the moment when Marguerite undertook to draw a picture of the society that lay before her eyes, the first merit must be the resemblance between the portraits and the models. For the artist and the philosopher, as well as for the historian, is anything better than the truth? The types of the *Heptameron* interest us because they are real. Marguerite paints her contemporaries as they are, not as they ought to be. In the sixteenth century familiar conversation between well-bred persons had a freedom of expression and manners which no one thought of criticising.

The books in vogue were the romances of chivalry in which love is so often described with naïve brutality. Even in the Christian pulpit the preachers, and especially the monks, made coarse jokes with the intention of turning them to the glory of God and the confusion of the devil. Who does not recall the licentious subjects sculptured in wood or stone in certain cathedrals? If the element of indecency insinuated itself even into churches, can one be surprised at the immodest expressions which came — I admit it — so easily to the end of Marguerite's pen? Let us not, moreover, be too severe on the crudities of our ancestors' speech, nor scandalized by their good Gallic laughter, their free and easy gaiety.

Do not trumpet so loudly the prudery of our times. No one who is in the habit of listening to the conversations in certain fashionable salons will go into ecstasies over their purity. The broad jests of our ancestors were possibly less dangerous to morals than the shady sentimentalities of many romancers and poets of our epoch. To call things by their own names, to say aloud what every one is secretly thinking, is not an actual crime. It is not by ribald tales and jests, *à la Rabelais*, that one could succeed in corrupting delicate souls. In order that vice may be attractive, it must soften its voice, cover itself with a rich mantle, and have the language of devotion, sympathy, and fidelity ever on its tongue.

Women have nothing to fear from a book like the *Heptameron*. What they ought to suspect is much rather that immoral literature, cloaked under the guise of prudery, which, confounding the alcove and the oratory, applies to guilty passions the language of divine love. The mystical rakes are probably the worst corruptors, and voluptuous pleasure has never so many seductions for souls endowed with the poetic instinct as when it is enveloped in a cloud of incense. The moments when the demon is to be most dreaded are those when he recalls the time when he was an angel.

VIII

CONCLUSION

WHEN one has studied a historic figure for some time, he feels affection for the heart he has endeavored to revivify, for the soul which, in some other abode, perhaps follows the thoughts of those who perpetuate its memory. He feels himself contemporaneous with the persons whom he has, so to say, entered into communication with, although they have been lying in their graves for centuries, and by interesting himself in their joys and sorrows, he becomes, through force of imagination, their guest and friend. Hence, when on the point of leaving them, he experiences an involuntary sadness. He would gladly prolong his farewells. It is such a sentiment as this which inclines us to ask the reader's permission to add somewhat more to a notice perhaps too long already, and to sum up, in a few words, the impression left on our own mind by the career of the sister of Francis I.

One of the customary faults of biographers is that of overrating the historical importance of those whose lives they narrate. We would not commit this fault, nor exaggerate the part played by the

Queen of Navarre. She was less remarkable for her deeds than for her intentions, and if she gave her brother lofty counsels, it must be admitted that she usually did so utterly in vain. Invoking against the vices and prejudices of her epoch those principles of morality and justice, of tolerance and humanity which must be the very foundation of all stable society, she had dreamed that the most Christian King might exert a tutelary and civilizing influence. She would have wished him to be everywhere the protector of the oppressed, the support of the learned, the crowned apostle of the Renaissance; that, while respecting dogmas, he should promote salutary reforms in the morals of the clergy, prevent religious wars by providing remedies for the abuses which were their cause or occasion, and direct, while confining within just limits, the movement which was spreading from one end of Europe to the other, and to which it was necessary to give satisfaction in some measure. In politics she would have desired that her brother, instead of wavering between all alliances, between all contradictions, should follow a straight line and methodically pursue the accomplishment of the legitimate ambitions of France. Francis I. preferred a perpetual change of ideas and systems, and by the fluctuations in his policy, he prepared the way for the disasters reserved for his race. Yet can it be said that Marguerite exerted no influence? Such an assertion would certainly be an error. Marguerite did not destroy the evil, but she lessened it. She did not succeed, in spite of all her efforts, in completely extinguishing the flames of the scaffolds, but she made them less frequent. She did not save all the literary men, all the savants, but she snatched more than one of them from the hands of their persecutors. She did not inspire great virtues in Francis I., but she softened his fierce nature, she gave him a taste for letters and the arts, she developed religious sentiments in him which became sincere, and caused the monarch whose life had been so dissolute to repent, and to die like a good Christian.

From the literary point of view, Marguerite is not a superior genius. She did not invent a style, she has not written a masterpiece. And yet she has rendered a real service to the French language. As M. Nisard has remarked: "The *Heptameron* is the first prose work that one can read without the aid of a vocabulary. Permanent forms of expression already form the substance of its style; superannuated modes are the exception." As a poet, the Queen of Navarre has added no new chords to the French lyre, but she has made those it already possessed vibrate with emotion, and, side by side with formless and defective attempts, she has strophes which are worthy to survive. When she is inspired by her heart, as often happens, her whole soul passes into her poetry; one finds ardor in her thought, lyricism in her images. As Count Hector de la Ferrière has said so well: "It is no longer an inert instrument which obeys a given impulse, but a voice which complains, a heart which suffers and which tells us so. In such moments she surpasses the poets of her time; she is, perhaps, the only one of her epoch who is inspired by her own sentiments, by her inner life, and who has spoken in that simple language which is the only one that befits great sorrows." For epistolary style she has given a true model, and her letters are as interesting for the precision and purity of their language, as for the noble simplicity of the ideas they express. The publication of Marguerite's letters has illustrated her character most completely. "The half smile which might be granted to fancy, when naming the author of the *Heptameron*, has gradually been displaced by a more serious and better founded appreciation. Hereafter, even through the lewd and unrestrained talk which was considered good manners in her day, it will be impossible not to recognize in her that lofty religious character, more and more mystical as it advances, that faculty of enthusiasm and of sacrifice for her brother which breaks out at every decisive moment, and which is like the star of her existence."[1]

The novel has laid hold of Marguerite's history, and instead of representing the Queen of Navarre as she really was, fantastic portraits have been drawn of her whose least defect is that of not resem-

---

[1] M. Sainte-Beuve, *François Ier, poète*.

bling their model. The Madrid captivity has been made the pretext for a host of more or less happy inventions. These fancies have had no result save that of substituting for the truth, which is more beautiful and striking than any falsehoods, be they what they may, conventional types which are never more than moderately interesting because they are not real.

The historical novel has the great fault of obstructing the memory with a mass of false notions which create in the mind a deplorable confusion. Each time that a souvenir recurs to the memory, one asks whether it is a fable or a reality. The novel and the history, contradicting each other every instant, end by mutual destruction, leaving in the memory a sort of spurious knowledge to which blank ignorance might be preferable. This factitious species will disappear, overcome by the analytical and patiently investigating methods which are now the order of the day, and which open inexhaustible treasures to modern erudition. We are convinced that every historical personage conscientiously studied necessarily fixes the attention, and that there is more interest, charm, and movement in reality than in the most skilful fictions. It is unnecessary to attribute to Marguerite, romantic adventures, to invent love affairs with the Connétable de Bourbon, with Clement Marot, the poet, in order to give her originality and prominence. The Madrid negotiation, described in its simplicity, interests me more vividly than all the incidents which could be invented at will to adorn this theme, and no romancer could image a scene more impressive than the Mass where the brother and sister shared the Sacred Host in the dungeon of the Alcazar.

Marguerite's career, in spite of certain contradictions more apparent than real, presents itself, in fine, under conditions of harmonious unity and perfect moral beauty. Her life, beginning with all the illusions of hope to end in the austere meditations of mature years, is the history of a noble, delicate, and generous soul. No doubt religion and the profane element clash with each other in her destiny. Her eyes are by turns raised to heaven and lowered to earth. But perhaps this is but a charm the more. Is not the contrast between the love of the world and the love of God the very heart of poetry? Every one who has both imagination and feeling has experienced the effects of these two sentiments, the strife between which is a grand spectacle, especially when it is God who comes off conqueror, as in the soul of Marguerite.

If I felt capable of drawing the moral portrait of the Queen of Navarre, I would choose the year 1531 to describe its physiognomy. Her hour of sadness has arrived. Marguerite has endured the greatest grief which can smite a loving soul. She had just lost her mother. That trinity of affections which united Louise of Savoy, her son, and her daughter, is now disrupted by death. The flowers have become less fair, the streams less limpid, the fields less gay. Everything begins to fade. Fortune has no longer the same smiles for the King of France as on the day of Marignan. As a young girl, Marguerite had dreamed of pure joys, of enchanting views, and each year has stolen from her an illusion and a hope. She has found cruelty where she hoped for gentleness, unthankfulness where she expected gratitude, crime where she looked for virtue. She cannot contemplate without fear that Reformation which, after proclaiming itself under favorable colors, has so quickly become threatening to religion and to politics as well. A mind profoundly sagacious and investigating, she becomes increasingly sad as she understands better the plague spots which afflict French society. Her delicate nature is vividly impressed by them. The diversions of intelligence cannot soothe the sorrows of her heart. Ideas, however grand and lofty they may be, do not take the place of sentiments. Science, in spite of its prodigious power, has never been able to satisfy a soul, and literature is a consolation only for those who are easily consoled.

Marguerite can soothe her troubles for the moment by her writings, but sorrow is not slow to resume its rights, and after a passing radiance the shadows of melancholy grow longer, and overcloud her heart. After the death of her son, she resolves never to wear anything but black for the rest of her life.

She has never liked splendid stuffs, or robes of gold brocade. What other princesses devote to their dress, she spends on the poor. Renouncing all ideas of coquetry, she chooses the most simple garb. Her Béarnais hood, surrounding her forehead and the upper part of her face, scarcely allows one to see the hair beside her temples. The expression of her countenance is subtlety on a base of kindness. Marguerite employs the greater part of the day in good works. She visits the sick and the indigent, consoles them by Christian exhortations, and after leaving them sends them money or other assistance secretly, so that her left hand may not know what her right hand does.

Having reached the summit of her spiritual and mental development, she enters that period of life which to ordinary women is dangerous, and to superior ones a time of moral progress and of edification. To know how to grow old is still more meritorious than to know how to die. To renounce the successes of youth without unhappiness is for flattered beauties the greatest proof of strength of character. After having climbed the mountain to that summit where one must begin to go down, she looks backward with regret to the road she has traversed, and forward with anxiety to that which must yet be trodden. But there is ·nothing severe or haughty in her sorrow. Instead of reproaching Providence, she filially bows her head beneath the hand of God which strikes her. She learns from suffering to be better, more charitable, and how to compassionate more truly the woes of others.

I see her in her little court of Béarn surrounded by the veneration of her subjects. The royal virtues of kindness, generosity, clemency, devotion to the public good, shine in her with all their brilliancy. It is known that the most powerful princes, the Connétable de Bourbon, Henry VIII., Charles V., himself, have thought of seeking her hand. Her renown has spread into every court of Europe. She is surrounded by a constellation of artists and literary men who find in her a protectress and an example. No one approaches her without a respectful emotion. Instead of clinging by a taste for pleasure to her vanishing youth, she withdraws from, and gives up the world. She is not ignorant that the last effect of sensual pleasure is the physical remorse of fatigue, and the moral fatigue of remorse. She knows what bitter dregs are in the bottom of the cup of sensual joys, and her soul, athirst for noble emotions, seeks elsewhere her desired ideal. Contemplation of divine things alone affords repose to her imagination, mind, and heart. She has seen the world close at hand, she has shone in it more brilliantly than any woman of her time, and the world has neither charmed nor given her consolation. Hence the conclusion of her existence will be one of profound piety. Her latter years will be truly edifying, and in her retreat at the Abbey of Tusson she will be more honored than in the midst of her court of great nobles, artists, and poets. Her reputation for science, wit, and intelligence will give all the more authority to her words and actions.

Between the splendor of her rank and the humility of her soul there is a contrast which renders her virtue all the more affecting. The woman who rates earthly grandeurs so justly is she who has known them best. She turns away her eyes from the crown and sceptre to look upon the crucifix. Sorrow, which embitters inferior souls, exalts great ones, and gives them real majesty. Marguerite's sadness, like her character, always retains somewhat of calmness and benignity. Religion and poetry unite to embellish even her griefs. As I think of the conclusion of a career so noble, a phrase of Madame Swetchine's recurs to my mind: "I commune with myself, O my God! at the end of my life, as at the close of a day, in order to bring Thee the thoughts of my faith and love. The last thought of a heart that loves Thee is like the last rays of the sun, more intense and more brilliant before they disappear. Thou hast willed, O my God! that life should be fair to its very end."

To sum up, what is it in the Queen of Navarre that most attracts our sympathy? Is it the keen and perspicacious intelligence which makes sport of difficulties? Is it the science which, ever on the outlook for new information, devotes itself to the most serious studies? Is it that political tact which transforms a woman into the rival of the most astute diplomatists? Is it the literary sentiment which makes of Marguerite not merely the enlightened protectress, the feminine Mæcenas of men of letters, savants, and artists, but also the remarkable writer whose poetry and prose alike entitle her to an honorable place in the constellation of the sixteenth century? What moves us above all is none of the things we have just enumerated. Far rather is it that exquisite sensibility, that gift of tears, that suave melancholy, that benevolent, affectionate, wide sympathy for all the afflictions of humanity, that bounty toward the living, that cult for the dead, those noble attributes of a good and beautiful nature which cause Marguerite to appear to us only under the aspect of a comforter.

Brantôme, who never mentions her but with veneration, tells the following anecdote about her: "The brother of the author of the *Dames galantes*, Captain Bourdeille, had known at the court of the Duchess of Ferrara, daughter of Louis XII., a Frenchwoman, Mademoiselle de La Roche, whom he had induced to love him; afterwards he brought her to the court of the Queen of Navarre, where she died. Three months later, Captain Bourdeille, being near Pau, went to pay his respects to Marguerite. The Queen met him just as she was coming out from Vespers, gave him a gracious reception, and led him, talking all the while, to the cemetery beside the church, which contained the tomb of her whom he had perhaps already forgotten. 'Cousin,' she said to him, 'do you not feel something stirring under your feet?'—'No, Madame,' he answered. 'But pay good attention, Cousin,' she returned. 'Madame, I have paid good attention, but I feel no motion, for I am standing on a solid stone.'—'Then I must tell you,' said the Queen, not to keep him longer in suspense, 'that you are standing on the tomb and the body of poor Mademoiselle de La Roche, who is buried underneath you, and whom you have loved so much; and since souls are still conscious after death, it cannot be doubted that this gentle creature, so lately dead, was agitated as soon as you were above her; and if you did not feel it, on account of the thickness of her tomb, do not doubt that she felt and knew it; and, seeing that it is a pious duty to remember the departed, and chiefly those whom one has loved, I beg you to say an Our Father, Hail Mary, and *De Profundis* for her, and sprinkle her with holy-water; and so you will acquire the title of a very faithful lover and good Christian.'"

Brantôme, ordinarily so light and superficial, is affected in relating this anecdote. Does it not sum up, in a few words, all there was of tenderness and charity, of poetry and the ideal, in that choice soul, the fulness of whose charm we have sought to comprehend?

Second Part

CATHERINE DE' MEDICI AND HER CONTEMPO-
RARIES AT THE FRENCH COURT

CATHERINE DE' MEDICI

CATHERINE DE' MEDICI

I

INTRODUCTION

AT no epoch in French history have women played a greater part than under the reigns of the later Valois. Their influence pervades politics, letters, and the arts. They direct public affairs, make and break treaties, share in every intrigue, hazard, and danger of the civil wars. The sovereigns are ruled by women: Francis I. by the Duchess d'Étampes, Henry II. by Diana of Poitiers, Francis II. by Mary Stuart, Charles IX. by Catherine de' Medici. Mingling in all the pleasures of the court, passionately fond of hunting, riding like intrepid amazons, assisting at tourneys and even duels, chiefly as the occasion of them, plunging headlong into the most audacious enterprises, the women throughout this dramatic and picturesque period, lead a brilliant, unquiet life, full of passions, adventures, and perils.

What singular types! what varied figures! 'Tis Catherine de' Medici, the cold, astute, cunning Florentine, "an Etrurian woman," as a Venetian ambassador said, "in whom the famous temporizer, Fabius, that great Roman, would have recognized his daughter." 'Tis Diana of Poitiers, the beautiful huntress, she whom Jean Goujon sculptured, nude and triumphant, embracing with marble arms a mysterious stag, enamoured like Leda's swan; Diana of Poitiers, the wondrous woman, the woman of eternal youth, the elderly Alcina who, to charm a youthful Roger, has discovered the fountain of youth; Diana of Poitiers, whom Primaticio's frescos at Fontainebleau sometimes represent as the luminous Queen of Night, and sometimes as a sombre Hecate surrounded by infernal fires. 'Tis Mary Stuart, the tragic heroine. 'Tis Marie Touchet, of whom Michelet has said: "Two things had power over Charles IX.; music, and this calm Flemish woman." 'Tis Jeanne d'Albret, "a Queen in whom nothing was woman but her sex," as d'Aubigné expresses it, "a soul wholly given to manly things, a mind capable of great affairs, a heart invincible by adversities." Jeanne d'Albret, who reared her son, the future Henry IV., "in rugged places, bareheaded and barefooted." 'Tis Marguerite de Valois, the famous Queen Margot, Brantôme's ideal, Marguerite de Valois, a marvel of grace and beauty, but also a finished model of libertinage of soul and body. 'Tis the Duchess de Montpensier, the frantic enemy of Henry III., the furious woman who pushes hatred even to frenzy, and who arms the hand of Jacques Clément.

In all the principal events of this age, so fertile in catastrophes, the women make their appearance on the scene. At Amboise, after the conspiracy, the court ladies witness the executions from the upper part of the castle terrace, "and thus give themselves a pastime precisely as if it were an affair of looking at a masquerade," without feeling an emotion of pity or compassion.[1] The only one of them who is troubled and melted into tears by the spectacle is the Duchess of Guise, the daughter of the Duke of Ferrara and Renée of France. At the siege of Rouen, Catherine de' Medici behaved like a warrior. "Cannon-balls and musket-shots rained about her, which she minded less than nothing. Still, there were women and girls in her company who did not like the sport, and when the Constable and M. de Guise remonstrated that some ill chance would befall her, she only laughed and asked why she should spare herself more than they did; that her courage was as good as theirs though not her strength, her sex forbidding that; as for the fatigue, she bore it very well, both on foot and on horseback, keeping her seat with the best grace, and not appearing masculine in her strange riding-habit, but a pretty princess, fair, very agreeable, and mild."[2] It is a marriage, that of Marguerite de Valois, which leads to St. Bartholomew's, the "red nuptials." It is a woman, Catherine de' Medici, who decided and

---

[1] *Mémoires*, de la Planche. [2] Brantôme, *Dames illustres*.

organized the massacre. On the day of the Barricades, it is she who, beguiling the Duke de Guise with false negotiations, gives Henry III. time to escape. Some months later, the Duke leaves the arms of a woman, the Marquise de Noirmoutiers, to fall under the poniard of *the forty-five,* and appear before the tribunal of God; then, when Henry III. is assassinated in his turn, a woman, the Duchess de Montpensier, exclaims, in a delirium of joy and vengeance: "I am sorry for only one thing — that he did not know before dying that 'twas I who struck the blow."

The heroines of the sixteenth century like still better to be feared than to be loved. We recognize their power at every moment. We know that to gratify a spite or heal a wound to their self-love, they do not recoil even from murder, and that in their view crime has a prestige and poetry of its own. "The Demoiselle de Châteauneuf, one of the king's favorites before he went to Poland, becoming enamoured of a Florentine and marrying, killed him like a man with her own hands on finding him a rake."[1] These women, voluptuous and cruel at the same time, inspired mad passions, insensate devotions, ecstatic admirations. D'Aubiac, who said of Marguerite de Valois, "I would like to have been loved by her, on penalty of being hanged not long afterwards," d'Aubiac, going to his death, "instead

---

[1] *Mémoires,* de l'Estoile.

of thinking of his soul and his salvation, kisses a blue velvet muff he retains from the favors of his lady." For these dangerous sirens, there are men who would deliver themselves up to ferocious beasts, who would plunge into the burning abysses of hell, without ruffling an eyebrow. Nothing is so much despised as life. Blood is shed like water. Even amidst the most frightful tragedies, and scenes of horror and carnage, the French character retains its gaiety, its carelessness, its liking for witticisms and chansons. The more precarious life becomes, the greater is the charm of gallantry. Balls alternate with massacres. Between two formidable tempests comes a clearing when the sky is blue, and spring smiles amid lilacs and roses. At this strange epoch, when elegance and barbarism unite, when the handles of stilettos are ornamented with real pearls, one listens in turn, and often simultaneously, to cries of fury and voluptuous melodies. Meyerbeer showed a just appreciation of this contrast, by making the savage tones of the benediction of poniards in the chorus of bathing women succeed the harmonious chants of Chenonceaux. Never has such another medley of material beauty and moral ugliness been seen. When vice, like Cleopatra's asp, is hidden in a basket of flowers; when religion itself becomes the accomplice of voluptuous pleasure; when the ceremonies of worship, instead of elevating and fortifying souls, are mere occasions for worldly pomp and extravagant luxury; when people are at the same time incredulous and superstitious; when public opinion, instead of being the guide of conscience, renders unjust, odious, and cruel verdicts, the human heart, having no longer either rule or compass, drifts from passion to passion, from one reef to another. A singular confusion reigns in the minds of men. Law and morality being both eclipsed at once, bewildered souls end by losing even the notion of remorse. As M. Mérimée has so well observed in the preface to his picturesque *Chronique du temps de Charles IX.* : "What is crime in a state of perfect civilization is considered merely an audacious action in a state of civilization less advanced."

How could virtues be found in a society where vice is not simply excused, but glorified; where fidelity in adultery is celebrated as the utmost height of the soul's grandeur; where in a jargon half chivalrous, half mystic, family disorders and social infamies are lauded to the skies? Brantôme is the image of his times. He admires rakishness as much as courage. There is something naïve and sincerely convinced in his respect for vice and elegant debauchery. According to him, virtue befits no women but those who are lowly born or ugly. As to beauties and great ladies, he recommends them to be inconstant in their love affairs, because "they should resemble the sun which sheds its light and heat on everybody in the world so well that everybody feels it." In this perverted century, religion is so distorted, so badly understood, that it ceases to be a check and safeguard. The whimsical Christianity of which the great lords and ladies then professed themselves adepts, bears no resemblance, great or small, to that of the Gospels; it is a sophisticated Christianity, which proscribes neither pride, hatred, luxury, nor the thirst for blood, and which transforms abominable crimes into acts of faith and meritorious works. The thought of death is only a contrast intended to enhance the charm of pleasure. From Christian pulpits preachers teach the spirit of vengeance and of cruelty. In their sermons they recoil neither from indecencies and buffooneries nor from appeals to popular excesses and the most savage passions. One might say that humanity, instead of kneeling before Christ, had mistaken the cross and was adoring the impenitent thief.

The great moralist of the period, the profound thinker whose book is the breviary of statesmen and political women, the most admired of all writers, whose ideas on government are regarded as axioms, and followed to the letter, is Machiavelli. "In the actions of men, and especially of princes, who cannot be examined before tribunal, what is to be considered is the result. Let the prince then think of nothing but how to preserve his life and his dominions; if he succeeds, all means he may have taken will be esteemed honorable, and lauded by everybody. . . . It is always good for the prince to appear clement, faithful, humane, religious, and sincere; it is so, likewise, to be all this in reality; but, at the same time, he should be sufficiently master of himself to be able, and to know how, if need be, to display the opposite qualities." Catherine de' Medici is a Machiavellian woman. The heroines bred in her school imitate the examples she gives them with docility. They reign by the defects, not the qualities, of their sex; they have wit and no feeling, charms and no morality, vices and not virtues; they deprave their minds and debase their characters. Their power, which is immense, is never exerted but for evil. More like devils than like angels, they persecute instead of consoling.

These women whose influence has in it nothing that is delicate, suave, or pure, produce a decidedly unpleasant impression. Doubtless, they are still encircled by a trace of the chivalric spirit, vitiated, and corrupted, but still bold, and madly adventurous. For these Armidas, these enchantresses who are more akin to the courtesan than to the great lady, the descendants of the knights of the Middle Ages, mock at death with a sort of frenzy. Assuredly these splendid women, sparkling with luxury, glowing with beauty, fascinate the eyes at once. One admires with Brantôme Catherine's female squadron. "You should have seen forty or fifty dames or demoiselles following her, mounted on beautifully accoutred hackneys, their hats adorned with feathers which increased their charm, so well

did the flying plumes represent the demand for love
or war. Virgil, who undertook to describe the fine
apparel of Queen Dido when she went hunting, has
by no means equalled that of our Queen with her
ladies." We repeat with Catherine de' Medici,
apropos of Mary Stuart: "Our little Scottish Queen
has only to smile to turn all Frenchmen's heads."
At sight of Marguerite de Valois we confess
with Ronsard that the beautiful goddess Aurora herself is overcome, and at Blois, one Palm Sunday,
when Brantôme shows us the charming princess in
the procession, her hair dressed and, as it were,
starred with diamonds, in a shaggy robe of cloth-of-gold from Constantinople, whose weight would
have crushed another woman, but which her large
and ample figure supports so well, we also admire
"her royal majesty, her grace half haughty and half
gentle."

But all this pomp, this brilliancy, cannot long
beguile us. Beauty cannot dispense with virtue.
The court festivities of the Valois no more conceal
their depravities than the statues and artistic objects
of Nero's Golden House conceal its shames. Vainly
does vice adorn itself with splendid vestments.
Vainly a fairy-like luxury spreads its marvels above
the ignominies of a dishonored society. One thinks
of Lady Macbeth: "All the perfumes of Arabia
cannot sweeten this little hand."

Nearly always the victims of their own passions,
the heroines of the sixteenth century find within

themselves their chastisement and torture. Pleasures how great soever, emotions no matter how violent, do not shelter them from the evils of every sort which are inseparable from all existences which lack peace of heart. Dissatisfied with themselves, in spite of their efforts to stifle remorse, they display, when one studies them at close quarters, an abyss of weaknesses and sufferings. In spite of hyperbolical praises and enthusiastic adulation, they end by being objects of contempt for their contemporaries, as well as for history. Under these costly laces, these robes of velvet or cloth-of-gold, hearts are beating which harbor every torment, every anguish. And yet, here and there in the midst of this corrupt society, there are some truly sympathetic types. As in every epoch, exiled virtue finds an asylum in certain souls. Charles IX. says, in speaking of Elisabeth of Austria: "I can felicitate myself on having the wisest and most virtuous wife, not only in France or Europe, but in the whole world." The wife of Henry III., Louise de Vaudemont, is also a model of conjugal piety. The eye rests with pleasure on these tranquil countenances which have never been disturbed by evil passion. Such types but throw into greater prominence the violent wickedness of other women. And thus we find every shade of the feminine character, the noblest and purest, as well as that which is vilest and most depraved.

Many recent works have shed new light upon this

epoch. The old memoirs have been rejuvenated by substantial and interesting commentaries. Criticism has redoubled its zeal and skilful investigators have discovered riches hitherto unknown. We desire to profit by their researches, and give an account of their labors, by outlining the women of the sixteenth century according to the publications which have appeared in these latter times. We are persuaded that the more this difficult and dramatic period is studied, the more numerous will be found its fertile sources and inexhaustible mines, whether from the picturesque or the psychological point of view. Writers like M. Vitet and M. Mérimée, musicians like the immortal author of the *Huguenots*, painters like Paul Delaroche, have proved that no period is better calculated to impress the imagination of an artist than this century whose tragic events would have been worthy to inspire a Shakespeare. The romancers have been less fortunate. Instead of imitating Walter Scott, who, in general, takes nothing from history but the framework and spirit of the period where his action passes, they have seized upon historical personages themselves, and have been unable to reproduce their actual physiognomy.

Thus, to cite but one example, Catherine de' Medici has been so greatly disfigured as to make her, so to say, unrecognizable. The real Catherine does not resemble the ogress under whose lineaments she has been represented by certain modern

romancers. She has not that sinister glance, that
deadly mien, that mysterious and savage aspect
which one ascribes but too willingly to her who
instigated the Saint Bartholomew massacre. By
emphasizing the features, and overloading the tints,
they have made a spectre, not a woman. Instead of
a real type, they have painfully succeeded in creating
a phantasmagoric personage. Catherine de' Medici
such as she was, with her self-possession, her frigid
cunning, her supreme elegance, her imperturbable
tranquillity, has something striking in far other wise.
It is its calmness, its moderation, which give this
physiognomy an originality so great. This gentleness in crime, this absence of anger in the most
bloody tragedies, this politeness like that of an
executioner for his victims, this Machiavellianism
equal to every trial, which nothing alarms, nothing
surprises, and which, with tranquil dexterity makes
sport of every law of morality and humanity, this
is the real character of Catherine. Nothing needs
to be added to, or subtracted from, such types. The
exaggerations are not merely detrimental to historical studies, but are equally regrettable from the
picturesque point of view,— art itself suffers from
them as well as truth. "If you desire romance,"
M. Guizot has said, "why do you not turn to
history?"

II

THE HISTORIANS OF CATHERINE DE' MEDICI

CATHERINE DE' MEDICI is the figure that dominates all others at the court of the Valois. We shall group the heroines of this epoch around her, and she will be the connecting link which binds them together in the rapid sketches we are about to attempt. We shall confront her with the Duchess d'Étampes, Diane de Poitiers, Mary Stuart, Elisabeth of Austria, Jeanne d'Albret, Louise de Vaudemont; and in every crisis, every drama of her time we shall encounter her action and her influence. The most contradictory judgments have been passed upon her. According to some, she was merely an intriguer without talent, ability, or breadth of view, living from hand to mouth, caught in her own snares, and with difficulty working out the schemes of a changeable and untoward policy. According to others, she brought to the service of a cause truly national, that of French unity, an intelligence, ability, and strength of character worthy of the greatest praise. Thus she is sometimes represented as the ruin, and again as the salvation of France; sometimes as a mischief-making demon, and sometimes as the precursory genius of Richelieu, and of Louis Quatorze.

In the front rank of the authors disposed to belittle her, we must cite M. de Chateaubriand,[1] who says in speaking of her: "If one follows all her proceedings, one perceives that in the whole vast realm of which she was the sovereign, she beheld only a larger Florence, the broils of her petty republic, the risings of one quarter of her native city against another, the quarrel between the Pazzi and the Medici in the struggle of the Guises and Châtillons." M. Michelet, who is fond of a sharply defined thesis, has gone much farther:[2] he has even been unwilling to admit the importance of the famous Queen-Mother. "Our historians," says he, "have been so honest, or, to speak plainly, so innocent, that they have all taken Catherine de' Medici seriously. Not one of them has fathomed this nonentity." For him, the illustrious mother of three kings is but a stage queen, having merely the externals, the attire of royalty, and patiently accepting "that rôle of peace-making Queen who, in ceremonious interviews, thrones it with her lively court amid the loves and graces." M. Michelet admits that she had a taste for the arts, but in little things. "She remained," he says, "exactly on the level of the small Italian principalities." He denies

---

[1] *Analyse raisonnée de l'Histoire de France.*
[2] M. Michelet, *Guerres de religion.*

her everything, even audacity in crime. He makes of her a more than prudent woman, very fearful for her children, who contrives everything, and is afraid of everything. She does not even succeed in arousing his anger. He judges her with cold disdain. Unwilling to find anything great in her, not even wickedness, he denies her "that profound dissimulation which could have been making ready for Saint Bartholomew's for so many years." "Never, he adds, "had she either the idea or the courage required for a revolt against facts. . . . Her admirer Tavannes overrates her, I think, and exaggerates in attributing to her the idea of Coligny's death. She consented to it, she granted it; but never without external pressure, or a great alarm, would she have dared such an action. She had no more heart than she had sense or temperament." It is as much as he can do to grant that "as a mother she pertained, however, to nature." But he takes pains to compare this maternal tenderness to that of an animal. "She was a female," he says, "and loved her young."

M. Armand Baschet has protested vigorously against this verdict of the celebrated historian. "Desiring to be more than true," he has said to him, "you are worse than false. The infinitely little things you search for, in order to confirm your judgments, plunge you into an infinity of contradictions. To listen to you, one would think Catherine de' Medici knew not even the first word about politics. The one concession you make to her is that she loved the arts, and even then you add: 'in little things; she remained exactly on the level of the small Italian principalities.' You forget that this level is that of Raphael, Urbino, Donatello, Michael Angelo, Cellini of Florence, Titian, and Paul Veronese of the state of Venice." M. Armand Baschet continues his refutation with real ardor: "Where do your contradictions lead you?" he exclaims. "You are even unwilling to admit that Catherine was capable of daring to commit that great political crime of the attack on the Admiral. But in that case, without meaning or intending to do so, you acquit her of the crime that has made her odious to the consciences of so many. Then why, in other pages, such animosity on your part against her power? If she was a nonentity, why discuss her, why even refuse to acknowledge her? One day you attack her as one attacks a great being; on another you completely forget that she directed all public affairs. Her who was a working politician, you refuse to consider under any other aspect than that of a fine woman, a fine figure of a queen-mother. She must be considered otherwise."[1]

M. Armand Baschet, notwithstanding this brilliant reply to M. Michelet's ideas, none the less recognizes all the evil sides of her character. Other

---

[1] M. Armand Baschet, *La Diplomatie vénitienne.*

writers, less restrained in their admiration, and perhaps led astray by their fondness for paradox, have celebrated Catherine with a sort of enthusiasm. Honoré de Balzac, notably, has composed a work in her honor, which he describes as *Études philosophiques*. In the eyes of the illustrious romancer, "the figure of Catherine de' Medici appears like that of a great king. The calumnies once dispelled by facts, recovered with difficulty from the falsities and contradictions of pamphlets and anecdotes, everything can be explained to the honor of this extraordinary woman, who had none of the weaknesses of her sex, who lived chastely in the midst of the amours of the most licentious court of Europe, and who, in spite of her meagre purse, was able to build admirable monuments, as if to repair the losses occasioned by the demolitions of the Calvinists, who inflicted as many wounds on art as on the body politic."

Nothing gives pause to Honoré de Balzac in his admiration for his heroine, nothing, not even the massacre of Saint Bartholomew's. "Could one succeed otherwise than by cunning?" he exclaims. "Any power, legitimate or illegitimate, must defend itself when it is attacked; but, singular thing, while the people are heroic in their victory over the nobility, power passes for an assassin in its duel with the people. Why, in our days, should we deny to the majestic adversary of the most barren of heresies, the grandeur she derives from this very struggle? The Calvinists have written much against the stratagem of Charles IX. But go through France: when you behold the ruins of so many beautiful churches that were destroyed, when you estimate the enormous wounds inflicted on the social body by the Protestant reformers, when you learn what retaliations they made, when you deplore the evils of individualism, you will ask yourself on which side the scoundrels were."

As indulgent to legitimate as to morganatic queens, M. Capefigue also undertakes the defence of Catherine, and the volume he devotes to her is a mere apology from beginning to end. Fascinated by the artistic tastes and the elegance of the Queen-Mother, he flatters her as assiduously as Brantôme does. He finds "that no one has ever raised to their true level the Valois, that choice family to which France owes its finest palaces, its masterpieces of art, chasing, painting, sculpture, printing, book-making, binding." He will not forgive either novelists or historians for representing Catherine "as a sort of Medea of the Renaissance, never appearing but with poniard in hand, and hiding poison in the flowers of her bouquet, the perfume of her gloves, or the folds of her Florentine robe."

For his part, he makes of her a type of gentleness, conciliation, wisdom, and it is apropos of her that he says: "Those who have studied history in its larger aspects know what martyrdom is endured by governments inclined to temperance and moderation; nearly always they succumb under the labor, and once down, they are torn to pieces by all the petty-minded." We think the truth lies between the two extremes of these contradictory theses. Doubtless it is necessary to be on one's guard against the apologies which tend to disguise vice and change the meaning of words. It is Machiavelli himself who says: "One must not pretend that there is any merit in massacring one's fellow-citizens, in betraying one's friends, in being devoid of faith, piety, and religion; by such means one may acquire power, but not glory."[1] Let us be as severe on the Saint Bartholomew as on the September massacres, and be no more indulgent to the crimes of kings than to the excesses of peoples. There is no theory more false and dangerous than the mania for rehabilitations, the predetermination to find attenuating circumstances, the love of paradox, the claim to say to history: "Adore what thou hast burned, and burn what thou hast adored!" Nothing is further from our intention than a eulogy of Catherine de' Medici. But while affirming her faults, her vices, and even her crimes, we do not wish to exaggerate them. We desire above all to display the society in the midst of which they were produced. Individuals cannot be understood but by getting at the foundations of societies, and the first requisite for justly estimating

---

[1] Machiavelli, *The Prince*, ch. viii.

a historic figure is to have conscientiously studied its epoch both in the mass and in detail. Isolated from her contemporaries, Catherine de' Medici is a monster. Brought back within the circle of their passions and their morals, their prejudices and their theories, she becomes once more a woman.

Rarely does one find a character which is all of one piece. Very few persons are absolutely good or absolutely bad. In general, the human creature is, as Montaigne has said so well, essentially versatile and various. In nearly all hearts there are bizarre contrasts, strange contradictions, which at first glance seem enigmas, and which cannot be understood unless one bears in mind the extreme variability of the soul. The same sky is by turns tranquil and tempestuous, radiant and gloomy. The same person will be successively good and wicked, gentle and ferocious, generous and stingy, believing and incredulous. Catherine de' Medici is a complex character such as occurs in civilizations that are at once elegant and brutal. She is not, at all moments of her life, a woman without heart and pity. No matter what is said about her, she is susceptible of maternal tenderness. She loves her children, and is devoted to their interests. She has a certain religion, but it is badly understood, ill-regulated. The sixteenth century, which understands the beautiful, understands neither the good nor the true. Catherine de' Medici is like her century.

Do not demand from her, then, either greatness

of soul. true moral force, or the virtues which are
the poetry and the honor of woman. But recognize
in her, will, intelligence, inflexible perseverance.
Recollect the almost insurmountable difficulties of
her task. Admit that it would have required an
almost superhuman genius to stay, at such an epoch,
the torrent of evil in its course, and to make an
upright and honest policy successful at a time when
the doctrines of *The Prince* were the model and
ideal of statesmen. Catherine felt the influence of
the corruption of her times. Its vices are reflected
in her. She was still more its victim than its
inspiration. Place her in other surroundings, in
our century, for example, and perhaps she might
always have been a good mother of a family, a calm
and gentle woman, as she was in the earliest period
of her life, before her lips had touched the bitter
fruit of power.

It must be admitted, Catherine did not inspire
her contemporaries with that reprobation and horror
which is the usual impression of the historians who
have written her life. On the contrary, she usually
awakened sympathy in those around her. A child,
she excited pity by her misfortunes, and the most
frenzied demagogues of Florence were unwilling to
destroy this feeble scion of the Medicean family.
A young girl, she made her appearance in France
as a symbol of pacification. She brought to her
new country the alliance and the apostolic benediction of her uncle, Clement VII. Never was any

festivity more magnificent, more imposing, more agreeable to all France than that of her union, at Marseilles, with the future Henry II. The woman whose hands were afterwards to weave the Saint Bartholomew plot, had adopted a rainbow as her emblem, with the motto: "I bring light and serenity." On arriving at court, she at once pleased everybody by her grace, affability, her modest air, and, above all, by her extreme gentleness. She was the assiduous companion of her father-in-law, Francis I., the amiable and intelligent alleviator of the fatigues of the blasé and prematurely aged King.

During the reign of Henry II. she wisely avoided every danger. Faithful to her wifely duties, she gave no cause for scandal, and, recognizing that she was not strong enough to overcome her all-powerful rival, she waited. At this time, the Venetian ambassador, Giovanni Capello, wrote of her: "The Queen is loved and respected, and deserves to be so by every one, for her personal qualities and her benevolence. The whole kingdom is of this opinion." When she became regent, she began by moderation. Taking the virtuous L'Hôpital as her adviser, she tried, as she wrote to the Bishop of Limoges, her ambassador in Spain, "to rehabilitate gently whatever the malice of the times might have deteriorated in the kingdom."

Gentleness having failed, she tried to succeed by violence; but if she committed cruelties it was not for the pleasure of being cruel. Machiavelli enjoins the prince, who wishes to rid himself of his enemies, to strike without threatening, to exterminate without a lingering persecution. Catherine struck so quickly that she exterminated a party, as one kills a man, at one blow. Such were the maxims of the epoch. The sixteenth century had lost the notion of justice and injustice. Its moral sense was at fault. The principles of government, given vigor by Catherine, then passed for wisdom itself. No greater ability than that of cunning was known: divide to reign was the adage in vogue. Catherine did not create the vices of her time; but, if she is not their author, she is, we must admit, their complete personification. Why did she not inspire in her contemporaries the same repulsion as in posterity?

'Tis because she was identified with their ideas and their errors. Whatever their opinions or their party, they recognize themselves in her.

Assuredly, when Brantôme sounds the lyric trumpet to celebrate the graces and virtues of the Queen-Mother, when he speaks of her with an enthusiasm that amounts to tenderness, Brantôme is in perfectly good faith. How he admires not only the Queen-Mother but her squadron of maids-of-honor, "creatures more divine than human," who have "their free will to be religious of Venus as well as of Diana!" How he is enraptured by their charms when, in the solemn processions of Corpus Christi, Palm Sunday, and Candlemas, he points them out to us, carrying their palms or torches with such grace! How he loves this court, "true paradise of the world, school of all honesty and virtue, ornament of France!"

How he venerates her, that sovereign "made by the hand of the great King Francis, who had introduced this fine and splendid revelry!" He represents her under the aspect of a good, amiable, attractive woman, with a ready laugh, a jovial disposition, and not afraid of a jest. He credits her with solid qualities, as well as agreeable ones.

For him she is an intrepid female warrior, a "Queen Marphise," whose courage drives the foreigners from Rouen. She is "a Semiramis, another Athalie," who "secures to her children in their reigns, several enterprises prepared for them in their minority with such prudence and industry that every one thinks her admirable." Over the accusation of cruelty, Brantôme passes lightly. "She has been strongly accused," he says, "of the Paris Massacre. . . . There were three or four others who were more ardent than she, and who urged her greatly; making her believe that the threats people were uttering on account of the wounding of M. the Admiral would cause the killing of the King, and her children, and all the court." Far from seeing in her an evil genius, he always describes her as constantly laboring to extinguish the flames of civil war which she had not enkindled, "having a wholly noble heart, exactly like that of her great-uncle, Pope Leo, and the magnificent Seigneur Lorenzo de' Medici"; a good Christian, who never missed Mass or Vespers, "which she rendered as agreeable as they were devout, by means of the singers of her chapel." He extols her conciliatory sentiments, her grief "at seeing so many nobles and wealthy people perish," her wisdom, "her goodness," and it is with the accent of sincerity that he exclaims on two different occasions: "How unfortunate was the day on which this Queen died!"

History has not yet said its last word about Catherine de' Medici. A writer, distinguished for his charming style, and the laborious patience of his investigations, Count Hector de La Ferrière, has for several years had in course of preparation the hitherto unpublished letters of Catherine. This voluminous correspondence, borrowed in great part from the archives of Saint Petersburg, should throw complete light on all the phases of one of the most troublous careers of which history makes mention. A collection of immense interest, *la Diplomatie vénitienne*, by M. Armand Baschet, has already opened previous sources of information on the same subject. The ambassadors of the Republic of Venice, those great masters of the art of observation and description, have made portraits of Catherine which are masterpieces of resemblance. They have judged her calmly, without anger, and without enthusiasm, with no bias toward either indulgence or severity. They, who saw her daily, who talked with her continually, who were present at all her entertainments, and were charged to give an account of all her doings to their government, were able to know her better than others could. Their despatches go into the most circumstantial and precise details. These singular relations will aid us, better than any other documents, to explain the character of Catherine de' Medici, and to attempt to bring out its qualities and its defects.

III

THE CHILDHOOD OF CATHERINE DE' MEDICI

LITTLE was known of the childhood of Catherine de' Medici. A learned diplomatist, M. Alfred de Reumont, formerly Prussian Minister plenipotentiary to Florence, has composed a work in German on this subject which has been translated into French [1] by M. Armand Baschet, and which throws fresh light on the earliest years of the famous Florentine. As M. de Reumont has very justly remarked in the preface to his book, Catherine de' Medici is a historical personage of too much importance not to awaken a thirst for information concerning the circumstances amidst which she grew up, and the persons who directed her education. "She was in the flower of her youth when she left Italy, but the family misfortunes which had saddened her cradle, the tempests unchained around the walls of the cloister where she found asylum, the character of her protectors, all exerted an influence greater than might be believed over her moral

---

[1] *La Jeunesse de Catherine de Médicis*, by A. de Reumont, translated, annotated, and enlarged by Armand Baschet. 1 vol. : Plon.

and intellectual faculties." Surrounded from infancy by snares and dangers, the heiress of the Medici escaped as by a miracle. She early learned the art of temporizing, of reckoning with her enemies, of avoiding dangers by calmness and prudence. Her earliest memories brought back to her the clash of arms, the furious and revengeful shouts of popular insurrections. It was her destiny to live in the midst of tempests. The thunder rumbled over her cradle as it did above her tomb.

Catherine de' Medici was born at Florence, April 13, 1519, in that magnificent abode enriched by so many marvels of art. "The Medici," says M. Charles de Moüy, "present themselves to history amidst the sacred group of the Renaissance. We see them erect and smiling among the architects, painters, and sculptors; their fine profile defines itself clearly amongst these august faces; they have their place in this choir of demigods. Michelozzi and Brunelleschi dispute the honor of building them a palace; in the courts and apartments of that dwelling, the most beautiful contemporary works charm the eyes of those great politicians, enamoured of pictures and vases, statues and manuscripts, of all modern elegances and all ancient souvenirs. The *David* and the *Judith* of Donatello, the *Orpheus* of Bandinelli, surmount fine columns; Greek marbles, which have escaped the vicissitudes of events, display to dazzled eyes forms of incomparable beauty."

Catherine was the great-granddaughter of the illustrious Lorenzo the Magnificent, the peacemaker, orator, artist, statesman, the *Pensieroso* of Michael Angelo. She was the great-niece of Pope Leo X., who, like Pericles and Augustus, was to give his name to his century. At once citizens and princes, the Medici, true kings in all but name, governed the Florentine Republic. Catherine's father, Lorenzo II., exercised almost absolute power. He had married a Frenchwoman of great family, Madeline de La Tour d'Auvergne, born of Jean, Count of Bologne, and Catherine of Bourbon, daughter of the Count of Vendôme. The marriage of Lorenzo, who bore the title of Duke of Urbino, was celebrated at Amboise, in 1518, amidst extraordinary pomp, Francis I., who presided at the festivities on this occasion, making it a point of honor to dazzle his guest.

Ten days were entirely given up to banquets, balls, and tournaments. The wedding-feast was spread in the court of the castle, which had been transformed into a tent, its walls hung with splendid stuffs. After having received from the Most Christian King the ribbon of Saint Michael, a company of a hundred lancers, and the promises of unalterable friendship for his person and country, Lorenzo de' Medici returned to Florence with his young wife. The married pair received a triumphal welcome. So much silk was employed for the entertainments given in their honor that the city exhausted all its supplies and had to send for more to Venice and Lucca. This union, concluded under such brilliant auspices, was doomed to speedy interruption by death. On April 13, 1519, the Duchess brought Catherine de' Medici into the world, and on the 28th of the same month she breathed her last sigh. Six days later, her husband, who had been attacked, some time before, by an incurable malady, followed her to the tomb.

Catherine, at the age of twenty-two days, was orphaned of both father and mother. All the enemies of her family, whose sole legitimate representative was Pope Leo X., raged about her cradle like prophets of misfortune. Ariosto, affected by the destiny of this child, a little flower passed over by the tempest, composed at this time those touching verses which, by a graceful allegory, he places in the mouth of a woman personifying Florence, and looking at the frail scion of the house of Cosmo: —

> Verdeggia un ramo sol, con poca foglia,
> E fra tema o speranza sto surpresa,
> Le lo mi lasci il verno o lo mi taglia.

"A single branch grows green again with a little foliage; between fear and hope I remain uncertain whether winter will spare it or tear it from me." Leo X. extended his protection to Florence, which he considered as one of his dominions. He sent thither Cardinal Julius de' Medici (the future Pope Clement VII.), the natural son of a brother of

Lorenzo the Magnificent. When Cardinal Julius, who had governed Florence wisely, assumed the pontifical tiara, he entrusted the care of the Republic to a legate, Silvio Passerini, Cardinal of Cortona, who supervised Catherine's education.

She lived in Florence until the revolution of 1527 broke out. Rome was taken by assault, and delivered up to pillage, by the troops of Constable Bourbon, on the 6th of May. This news, as soon as it was known, acted on men's minds with the speed of lightning. On learning that Pope Clement VII. was a prisoner in the castle of Saint Angelo, Florence seized the occasion to fling off the pontifical yoke. May 11, the whole city was in open revolt. Philip Strozzi placed himself at the head of the insurrection. The Cardinal of Cortona, and the two young bastards of the elder branch of the Medici, Hippolyte and Alexander, were driven from the territory of the Republic.

The popular party triumphed. In one of the sessions of the great council, Nicholas Capponi caused Christ to be proclaimed "perpetual King of Florence," and an inscription placed over the principal door of the public palace confirmed this nomination. Dante de Castiglioni tore down the blazon of the Medici from the churches of Saint Laurence, Saint Mark, and Saint Gallo. The only legitimate representative of the elder branch of this illustrious family was little Catherine, who was barely eight years old. The younger branch, descended from a brother of Cosmo the Elder, and later the ancestors of the Grand-Dukes of Tuscany, had neither political position nor authority with the parties. The people were unwilling to transfer either to bastards or a woman the power of Cosmo or Lorenzo the Magnificent. Fearing the claims which might be put forward on behalf of Catherine, the democrats, instead of exiling her, kept her as a hostage and shut her up in cloisters which served the purpose of prisons.

Here, then, we have Catherine in her ninth year, surrounded by snares and perils, amidst the relentless enemies of her family. She is at first sent to the Dominican nuns of Saint Lucia, in the via San-Gallo. Then, on December 7, 1527, she is closely veiled and taken to the convent of the *Santissima Annunziata delle Murate*. Affable and gracious, the *duchessina*, as she is called by the Florentines, is beloved by the nuns. In this cloister, where all parties are represented, and each nun prays for her own, she is skilful enough to wound no one, and soon acquires the difficult art of living amidst discords. But now a terrible storm mutters over Florence. The Pope and the Emperor have come to terms; the pledge of their alliance is to be the ruin of the unhappy Republic. The treaty of Cambrai is signed. The King of France abandons his Italian allies. Charles V. withdraws his troops from various provinces of the peninsula in order to concentrate them on the

Florentine territory. He confides the task of reducing Florence, and accomplishing the vengeance of Pope Clement VII., to one of his best generals, the Prince of Orange. The sombre presentiments of Michael Angelo are about to be realized. To look at the statue of the *Pensieroso*, one would say that Lorenzo the Magnificent was beholding in the distant future the calamities of his country. The fatal hour has struck. Clement VII. turns against his native city the same army which three years before had besieged him in the Castle Saint Angelo, and which had sacked Rome with such pitiless barbarity. The new Vandals hurl themselves upon their prey. Spite of its slender resources, Florence determines to struggle courageously. What is to become of Catherine during this terrible siege which was to last ten months? Exasperated by famine, epidemics, and sufferings of every kind, there are demagogues who would like to avenge upon the innocent child the severities of her great-uncle, the Pope. "Put her in a brothel instead of a convent!" cries Leonard Bertolini. "That will spoil the Pope's fancy for marrying her to some prince or noble."

Others of the *arrabiati*, as the enthusiastic democrats were called, proposed binding Catherine fast to the most exposed place on the ramparts, to find out what direction the balls of the troops of the Prince of Orange would take when faced by this scion of the house of Medici. It is learned, one day, that the *duchessina*, precocious heiress of the craftiness of her progenitors, has already a talent for making friends; that imprisoned partisans of her family have received in their dungeons mysterious baskets from this child, whose fruits and flowers conceal escutcheons embroidered with the arms of the proscribed race. At once it is resolved that Catherine shall remain no longer in the cloister of the Murate. Salvestro Aldobrandini is sent, with three commissioners, to withdraw her from this convent, and take her back to the Dominicanesses of Saint Lucia, who are supposed to be more favorable to the people's party, and who will guard the daughter of the Medici with greater rigor. Aldobrandini presents himself before the grating of the Murate cloister and makes a demand for Catherine. The nuns experience an indescribable emotion, for they believe that the poor child will leave her asylum only to go to her death. The abbess is refusing to surrender her, when the child, dressed like a nun, appears before the commissioners of the Republic, and says sweetly: "Go, and tell my masters that I will become a nun and spend my whole life with these venerable mothers." Aldobrandini, affected by Catherine's grace, speaks to her respectfully. He tells her that it is only a question of putting her in a more secure place, the cloister of the Murate, situated but a few steps from the ramparts, being too much exposed to the attacks of the imperial troops. On their knees the nuns implore Heaven for the safety of the child, whom they are unwilling to abandon. Aldobrandini dares not insist any further. He describes to the government the tears and supplications of the nuns. But the government is inflexible. It formally commands the abbess to submit, and, July 20, 1530, Catherine, after much weeping, bids adieu to her companions, and goes on mule-back to her former convent of Saint Lucia.

She remained there until the end of the siege. The capitulation took place August 12. After ten months, the city, reduced to the last extremities, opened its gates. More than eight thousand citizens and fourteen thousand soldiers had perished. The Archbishop of Capua, Nicholas de Schonberg, was given the direction of affairs by the Pope until July 3, 1531, when Alexander de' Medici, Catherine's natural brother, became the head of the Republic.

Liberated on the day when the blockade ended, Catherine had returned to her dear convent of the Murate, where the nuns welcomed her with transports of joy. She was afterwards summoned to Rome, by Clement VII., and the sight of the Eternal City impressed the young imagination of the child, and aided to strengthen that taste for the arts which had already been awakened in her by the contemplation of the marvels of Florence. She was eleven years old when Antonio Suriano, Venetian ambassador to the court of Rome, foreseeing that this cherished niece of Clement VII. might yet have a great part to play, wrote concerning her: "This child has a very lively disposition and displays a charming wit. She owes her education to the care of the nuns of the Murate convent at Florence, women of great renown and of saintly life." Catherine never forgot the nuns who had surrounded her childhood with such affection, and at various times she gave them tokens of her gratitude. She was pleased also with Salvestro Aldobrandini, on account of the respect he had shown her at the time of his unpleasant mission, and this man, whose son was one day to wear the pontifical tiara as Clement VIII., owed his escape from the death to which he had at first been doomed to the intercession of the grateful child.

The Pope thought at once of marrying his great-niece, and several offers were made him for the *fanciulla*, as the Venetian ambassador, Antonio Suriano, styles her. Among other aspirants may be named the Duke of Milan, the Duke of Mantua, the King of Scotland, the Duke of Urbino. Clement VII., whose interest it then was to be on good terms with France, in order to protect himself against the exorbitant power of Charles V., rejected all these proposals and eagerly accepted the overtures of Francis I., who asked Catherine's hand for his second son, Henry, Duke of Orleans. Very proud to see a Medici enter the royal family of France, Clement VII., disregarding the Emperor's attempts to prevent this alliance, wished it to be concluded without delay. The Duke of Orleans was only fourteen years of age, and Catherine but thirteen. But the Sovereign Pontiff was unwilling to wait any longer, and resolved to marry the couple himself at Marseilles. The idea that the descendant of Florentine bankers was about to approach the throne of Charlemagne overwhelmed the soul of Clement VII. with joy.

Before leaving Italy, Catherine bade farewell to Florence by a splendid banquet to which all the illustrious ladies of the Republic were invited. She departed September 1, 1533. No doubt, on quitting her native city, which she was never more to see, she cast a lingering glance on that beautiful Medici palace where she was born, that brilliant abode which reminded her of so many glories and so many sufferings.

First impressions are the most enduring. The little Florentine was never to forget Italy. A bitter feeling against popular seditions abode with her. Convinced from earliest childhood of all the dreariness and danger attaching to high positions, she already understood that the art of governing is not easy. She had reflected, both in the Murate convent and beside the pontifical throne of Clement VII., on human vicissitudes and the irreparable griefs of power. It was to her father that Machiavelli had dedicated his famous work, *The Prince*. She inherited as a patrimony the political wisdom and astuteness of her ancestors.

Fate reserved for her the spectacle of other struggles more bloody than those of the Medici and the Pazzi. The scene widened before her, but the policy of the Valois resembled that of the petty Italian principalities, and, on a larger stage, she found anew the same intrigues, the same passions, and the same crimes. An immense horizon unrolled before the *duchessina*. The Florentines, as they regretfully watched the departure of this young girl who had shared their misfortunes and whom all parties respected, had no inkling of the turns of fortune which awaited the heiress of Cosmo on French soil. They cordially wished her a happy destiny, and were not without anxiety concerning the part she was to play in that famous court on which the eyes of all Europe were then fixed. Who could have foreseen that she would behold three of her sons ascend successively the throne of France, and that she would display all the resources of her Tuscan genius in conjunctures so terrible? The childhood of Catherine de' Medici had prepared her for the crises and storms of her career. The prologue was worthy of the drama.

IV

CATHERINE DE' MEDICI AT THE COURT OF FRANCIS I.

THE city of Marseilles was in great joy on October 12, 1533. The signals of the tower of If and of Notre Dame de la Garde had just announced that the pontifical fleet was approaching, with Pope Clement VII. and his niece, the betrothed of the King's son, the young Catherine de' Medici, on board. The steeples of the Major responded to the municipal belfry on the Place de Linche in ringing welcome to the august voyagers. Numerous boats, containing a crowd of gentlemen and musicians, left the shore to go and meet them. Three hundred pieces of artillery rent the air with their joyous salvos. The populace were on their knees. At the head of the fleet came the principal galley, which carried the Blessed Sacrament, according to the custom of the Popes when travelling by sea. Carpeted with crimson satin and covered with a tent of cloth-of-gold, the vessel of Clement VII. was richly sculptured in the Venetian fashion. Ten cardinals and a great number of bishops and prelates accompanied the successor of Saint Peter.

The solemn entry into the town was surrounded with extraordinary pomp. Throned on the *sedia gestatoria*, the Vicar of Jesus Christ was borne on the shoulders of robust men. Preceding him, on a white horse led by two equerries in sumptuous costumes, was the Blessed Sacrament, in a magnificent ostensory. The crowd, receiving the Apostolic benediction piously, rained flowers along the path of the procession; priests chanted canticles, and there rose a cloud of incense in the air. Vested in their purple, the cardinals, on horseback, followed the Pope by twos. Then, giving her hand to her uncle, John Stuart, Duke of Albany, and wearing a robe of gold brocade, came the fourteen-year-old Florentine, with her black eyes, her dull complexion, her gentle and intelligent expression. Curiosity, so great already, would have been far more excited, could the part this young girl was called to play in the destinies of France have been foreseen. The next day, Francis I. attended by his court and all the foreign ambassadors, went as the Most Christian King, to pay homage to the Holy Father. For the Pope and the King, two palaces had been made ready, separated from each other only by a street, and united by a great wooden bridge, forming a vast hall hung with rich tapestries, and intended for the consistories as well as for the interviews between the two sovereigns.

The Pope's attendants, bragging much about the advantages of the pontifical alliance, claimed that

Catherine would give to the house of France "three rings of inestimable price: Genoa, Milan, and Naples." Francis I. had never displayed more courtesy, or made a greater show of luxury. The young Duke of Orleans testified a lively sympathy for his young betrothed, and all France participated in his joy. The marriage was celebrated October 23, in the cathedral church, the Major, by the Pope, who said the Mass, and gave the nuptial ring to the spouses. Catherine wore a robe of white silk enriched with precious stones and ornaments of Florentine wrought gold. Her head was covered by a veil of Brussels point. She looked like the Italian Madonnas in their glittering frames. The Pope and the King did not separate until November 27, when His Holiness went on board of the pontifical galley, and Francis I. took the road to Avignon, whence he was to return to Fontainebleau.

This residence, which Catherine occupied, had never been more gorgeous. At the age of thirty-nine, Francis I. retained all the tastes of his early youth, and his court was not a school of morality. Brantôme describes him as inciting "his worthy gentlemen to have mistresses under penalty of being regarded by him as dolts or blockheads, and promising them his good offices with such as were inhuman; he was not contented with merely seeing them follow his example; he wanted to be their confidant. Often, too, when he saw them in great discussions with their mistresses, he would accost them, asking what good things they had said, and, if he did not think them good, would correct them and teach them others." It was not merely in matters of gallantry that Francis I. might be esteemed a master. A Venetian ambassador, Marino Cavalli, wrote concerning him: "This Prince has very good judgment and great knowledge: listening to him, one recognizes that there is neither study nor art which he cannot discuss with much pertinence, and criticise in a manner as positive as those who have specially devoted themselves to it. His acquirements are not limited to war, the manner of provisioning and commanding an army, arranging a plan of battle, preparing quarters, assaulting or defending a town, directing artillery; he not only understands all that appertains to maritime warfare, but he has great experience in hunting, painting, literature, the languages, and the different exercises befitting a handsome and brilliant chevalier." Catherine understood at once how much was to be gained in the society of this learned, amiable, and powerful King. She wished to become his pupil, and seeking every occasion to follow and ply him with homage, she set to work to become an assiduous companion, a sort of maid-of-honor to him.

Francis I. had a passion for the chase. Catherine became a great huntress. "She prayed the King," says Brantôme, "to permit her to be always at his side. They say that, being subtle and crafty, she did this as much or more for the sake of watching the King's actions, extracting his secrets, and listening to and knowing everything, as for the sake of hunting." After this reflection, Brantôme adds: "King Francis was so pleased with such a prayer, and her ready fondness for his company, that he granted it very cordially, and besides his natural affection for her, his liking continually grew, and he delighted in giving her pleasure at the hunt, where she never quitted the King, but always followed him at full speed; she rode well and was daring, and had a very graceful seat, being the first one who threw her leg over the saddle bow, insomuch that her grace was even more striking and apparent there than on a floor." Catherine followed from city to city, from castle to castle, this monarch whose custom it was to change his abode incessantly. Marin Giustinian, Venetian ambassador to France from 1532 to 1535, says concerning this: "Never, during my embassy, did the court remain in the same place for more than fifteen consecutive days." Agreeable by the quickness of her intellect, as well as her evenness of temper, the young Florentine sought to make friends, not merely of the King and the Princes, but of all who approached her She lived on good terms with "the little band of court ladies," as Brantôme says, "ladies of family, damsels of reputation," whom Francis I. assiduously sought for among "the most beautiful and most noble," and who appeared "in the court like goddesses from heaven."

Catherine needed all her address and prudence to avoid the snares already laid for her. Aristocratic prejudices were enlisted against her. The French nobles did not think the escutcheon of the Medici sufficiently gilded by the pontifical tiara of Leo X. and Clement VII. They said it was, after all, but a family of merchants, and that even with the best will in the world the marriage of the Duke of Orleans could not be considered other than a *mésalliance*. It was claimed, also, that the Pope had not kept his promises very well, and had in fact been of no advantage. Two years after the marriage, the Venetian ambassador, Giustinian, wrote: "M. d'Orléans is married to Madame Catherine de' Medici, which dissatisfies the entire nation. It is thought that Pope Clement deceived the King in this alliance. However, his niece is very submissive. The King, the Dauphin, her husband, and also the King's youngest son, seem to love her much." Besides, Catherine, who had only married the King's second son, did not at this time seem destined to play an important political rôle. The sole ambition which she and her husband could hope to realize was that, when the war between Charles V. and France was over, they might receive the investiture of the Duchy of Milan or that of Urbino.

An unexpected event abruptly changed this situation. The Dauphin, who had followed the King to the war of Provence, died suddenly at Tournon,

July 15, 1536. The Duke of Orleans became the heir to the throne, and assumed the title of Dauphin. He was eighteen years old, and Catherine seventeen. The position of the new Dauphiness was becoming very difficult. Though she had been married for three years, she had no children, and people said she never could have any. A beautiful and imperious woman, accustomed to power, Diana of Poitiers, had subjugated the heart of Catherine's husband, and Catherine, with rare penetration, saw at once that it would be impossible to contend with her. And yet Diana of Poitiers, born in 1499, was twenty-three years older than the Dauphiness. But she was an enchantress, an Armida, a woman full of seduction and prestige, whose charm was like a talisman to bewitch the feeble Henry. A great fund of timidity underlay the character of this young Prince. His childhood had passed very sadly. Sent to Spain with his brother, in 1526, as a hostage for the fulfilment of the treaty of Madrid, he had spent four years there at Valladolid, in a convent of monks, where he endured a real captivity. When he returned to his father's court, he had been obliged to relearn his own language. Lacking confidence in himself, humble and silent in the presence of the King, he thought he needed a protectress, an Egeria. He had caught a glimpse of the beautiful widow of the Seneschal of Normandy, Diana of Poitiers, Countess of Brézé, who "dressed prettily and pompously," says Brantôme, "but all in black and white." Diana was a real marvel at this period. She was Henry's first, or rather, his only, real passion. A child, he dared not imagine that a day would come when he might lift his eyes to this idol. The woman who feigned hypocritical tears for her deceased husband seemed to him a model of goodness and virtue. Diana, like a knowing coquette, saw at once what she could make of the naïve and tender soul of the ecstatic youth. She inspired him with one of those passions, platonic to begin with, sensual later on, which seizing hold on all the faculties of a man, dominate alike his mind, his imagination, and his heart. Beginning by giving her young admirer only a faint glimmer of hope, she pretended to permit herself to be loved, but only, as is commonly said, in all honor and virtue. Even the court was for some time deceived by this comedy. The Venetian ambassador, Marino Cavalli, wrote concerning the Dauphin: "He is not much addicted to women. His own suffices him. For conversation, he confines himself to that of Madame, the Seneschale of Normandy. He has a real tenderness for her, but people believe there is nothing lascivious in it, and that it is an affection like that between mother and son. They say that this lady has undertaken to instruct, correct, and counsel M. the Dauphin, and to urge him on to all worthy actions." People very soon found out what to think of this so-called maternal affection. Although nineteen years younger than his idol, the young Prince had a love for her which was anything rather than filial. She was not long in becoming his recognized mistress. In 1541, at a fête given in the wood of Berlaudière, near Châtellerault, under the designation of a tournament of knights errant, he publicly wore the Seneschale's colors, and thereafter never quitted her.

During the last years of the reign of Francis I., a feminine duel raged between the two favorites, the Duchess d'Étampes, mistress of the King, and Diana of Poitiers, mistress of the Dauphin. The court was divided into two camps, and the King, instead of putting a stop to the quarrels, disputes, and intrigues, took a certain pleasure in them. It was a war of slanders, calumnies, and epigrams. Very proud of being ten years younger than her rival, the Duchess who, according to her flatterers, was the most learned of beauties and the most beautiful of learned women, triumphed insolently, and wanted to see the whole court at her feet. Queen Eleanor, the sister of Charles V., a gentle, modest woman, kept herself apart, and sought consolation in piety and in reading, of which she was passionately fond. The Duchess d'Étampes had all power in her hands. The Emperor was well aware of this. When he was in France, the King had said to him, pointing to his favorite: "Brother, there is a beautiful lady who thinks I ought not to let you depart until you revoke the treaty of Madrid," and he contented himself with answering coldly: "If the advice is good, you must follow it." But the same day at dinner he let a diamond of great value drop before the Duchess, who was giving him his napkin, and refused to take it back, saying: "Madame, it is in too fair hands."

The wily monarch knew how to make an ally of his rival's mistress. She became the head of the party which desired to base French policy on an agreement with the Emperor. Diana supported the contrary opinion, and the struggle between the two women attained the proportions of a great affair of state. Poets and artists took part in this rivalry of women which occupied the court more than that between Francis I. and Charles V. While Primaticio endlessly reproduced the features of the Duchess d'Étampes in the decorations of the royal galleries, Benvenuto Cellini chose as his model Diana of Poitiers, the beautiful huntress, and in his Memoirs the famous engraver has detailed in the most picturesque fashion his quarrels with the King's mistress and Primaticio. The poets enlisted on the side of the Duchess d'Étampes celebrate her as a resplendent, unparalleled beauty, and were one to judge by their French and Latin epigrams, the Seneschale was nothing but a toothless, hairless, old woman, who owed her remnant of deceptive brilliancy to paint.

A less intelligent woman than Catherine would have ranged herself openly on the side of the Duchess, and tried to form a league, a coalition, with the powerful favorite, for an attack on the Seneschale. But this bold stroke would not have been in keeping with the temporizing genius of the Florentine. She understood that in declaring against Diana she would run a risk of being repudiated, and instead of clashing with a force which was now irresistible, she employed all her skill in remaining on equally good terms with both the favorites, irreconcilable enemies though they were. Thus the woman, who was thereafter to occupy so great a place, now sought only to efface herself; she seemed a real model of simplicity and reserve. Francis I., to whom she had never occasioned any vexation, was astonished and enraptured. He attributed her precocious wisdom to his instructions, and was both pleased and flattered by it. As to the Dauphin, in spite of the lack of warmth in his affection for his wife, he could not avoid doing justice to her physical and moral qualities.

"She was," says Brantôme, "of a fine and ample figure, very majestic, always very gentle when necessary, beautiful and gracious in appearance, her face fair and agreeable, her throat very beautiful, white, and full, very white in body likewise. . . . Moreover, she dressed well and superbly, always having some new and pretty invention. In brief, she had beauties fitted to inspire love. She laughed readily, her disposition was jovial, and she liked to jest." The artistic elegance that surrounded her whole person, the tranquil and benevolent expression of her countenance, the good taste of her dress, the exquisite distinction of her manners, all contributed to her charm. And then she was so humble in presence of her husband! She so carefully avoided whatever might have the semblance of a reproach! She closed her eyes with such complaisance! Henry told himself that it would be very difficult to find another woman so well disposed, another wife so faithful to her duties, another princess so accomplished in point of instruction and intelligence. The *ménage à trois* continued therefore, and if the Dauphin loved his mistress he certainly had a friendship for his wife. And, on her part, whenever she felt an inclination to complain of her lot, Catherine bethought herself that if she quitted her position she would probably find no refuge but the cloister, and that, taking it all round, the court of France, in spite of the humiliations and vexations one might experience there, was an abode less disagreeable than a convent.

At the end of nine years of marriage, she had still no children, and was constantly troubled by fear of a divorce. "It is unknown," says Varillas,[1] "whether Francis I. had been deterred from such a step by its visible injustice, the oaths by which Clement VII. had bound him never to send away this Princess who was his niece, or the pity inspired by Catherine, whose condition was then so deplorable that no place

---

[1] Varillas, *Histoire de Henry Second.*

of refuge would have been open to her, the new Duke of Florence being too politic to receive her in his dominions where her rights exceeded his; or, finally, by the address of Catherine herself, who spared no pains to preserve the rank her uncle had acquired for her." The account given by the Venetian ambassador, Lorenzo Contarini, explains how prudently Catherine averted the dangers impending over her: "She went to the King and told him she had heard it was His Majesty's intention to give his son another wife, and as it had not yet pleased God to bestow on her the grace of having children, it was proper that, as soon as His Majesty found it disagreeable to wait longer, he should provide for the succession to so great a throne; that, for her part, considering the great obligations she was under to His Majesty, who had deigned to accept her as a daughter-in-law, she was much more disposed to endure this affliction than to oppose his will, and was determined either to enter a convent or remain in his service and his favor. This communication she made to King Francis I., with many tears and much emotion. The noble and indulgent heart of the King was so greatly moved by it that he replied: 'Daughter, do not fear that, since God has willed you to be my daughter-in-law, I would have it otherwise; perhaps it will yet please Him to grant to you and to me, the grace we desire more than anything else in the world.' Not long afterwards she became pregnant, and in the year 1543 she brought a male infant into the world to the great satisfaction of everybody."

Not long before, a Venetian ambassador, Matteo Dandolo, had written concerning Catherine: "Her Majesty is so much liked by both the court and the people, that I think there is no one who would not shed some of his blood to procure her a son." She was as fruitful in the later years of her marriage as she had at first been sterile. Between 1543 and 1555 she had ten children. As soon as she became a mother she felt reassured. Her fear of divorce departed, and the wily Princess inwardly congratulated herself on the prudence which had extricated her from a difficult situation. Much younger than Diana of Poitiers, she waited for time to put her in the right and brilliantly avenge her. The astrologers, who were her counsellors, had promised her domination. Relying on their words, she waited. An interior voice said to her: "Thou shalt govern!" She did not doubt it for an instant, and each day brought her nearer to her goal. To her might be applied the famous saying: Genius is a long patience.

DIANE DE POITIERS

V

DIANA OF POITIERS

WITH Henry II.'s accession to the throne begins the definitive triumph of Diana of Poitiers. At the age of forty-eight, the all-powerful mistress enslaves a King who is twenty years her junior. The huntress utters a cry of joy; this is the time for spoils. The King loads Diana's tools with wealth and favors, and, on the recommendation of the favorite, who seizes all the avenues of power, he aggrandizes the house of Guise beyond measure. This numerous family, established in France but a few years only, acts as one man, and conceives the project of setting aside all the princes of the blood. Posing as the heir of Charlemagne, it reclaims, in an underhanded way, its more or less chimerical rights over Anjou, Provence, the Two Sicilies, and Jerusalem. The six sons of Duke Claude de Guise aspire to all the great offices of the kingdom. The third son, Claude, Marquis of Mayence, is Diana's son-in-law. He claims for himself and his mother-in-law all vacant estates in France.

The Archbishop of Rheims, Charles de Guise, brother to Diana's son-in-law, is the assiduous courtier of the favorite. In his diocese, this Archbishop of twenty-three plays the saintly bishop and father of the Church; at court he is the flatterer of the King's mistress, and his intrigues promptly gain him a cardinal's hat. Created Duchess of Valentinois, Diana disposes of ecclesiastical benefices, makes one of her trusty adherents keeper of the royal treasury, in order to have "the key of the coffer," and monopolizes wealth, lands, and precious stones with insatiable avidity. Henry II. bestows on her all the taxes levied at the accession of a new king on the holders of purchasable offices, corporation immunities, and other privileges. At the coronation she has a place of honor, and in the account of the ceremony she is treated as a real sovereign of the left hand.

> Et celle-là qui, en la cour royale
> Est en faveur, la grande sénéschale,
> Doit-elle pas ici le rang tenir
> Où par vertu on la voit parvenir ?[1]

The Duchess d'Étampes, vanquished and humiliated, vanishes from the scene. She is obliged to restore the jewels she received from the deceased King, and relegated to her estates, she drags out a monotonous existence. Her husband, Jean de

---

[1] And she who, in the royal court — Is in favor, the great seneschale — Should she not hold the place here — Which by virtue she is seen to have attained ? — *Le Sacre et Couronnement du très-puissant et très-chrétien Roy Henry, deuxième du nom.* Paris, André Ruffet, 1549.

Brosse, the complaisant spouse who had so greatly
profited by his wife's adultery, brings a shameful
action against her. He sues her for the salary of
the government of Brittany, to which he had held
the title for some years while she had drawn the
revenues. Henry II. was not ashamed to meddle in
such an affair in order to serve Diana's vengeance.
He appeared at the inquiry and made his deposition.

Her contemporaries, astonished at the victorious
prestige of the aged mistress, credited her with some
magic power, some enchanted ring. "We are not
in a natural world. This is an enchantment, and
it can only be carried out by violent spells and
dramatic strokes. The Armida of fifty years who
holds a king of thirty in lease, must daily use her
magic wand. Inebriated with fanfares, prophetic
emblems, and the dream of conquering the world,
he makes with closed eyes the decisive actions
whereby the idol signifies his divinity."[1] In
thickets of myrtle and roses, amidst statues, fountains, and gushing springs, in the depths of dark
and game-abounding forests, the King leads an
enchanted existence. Fondly persuaded that he is a
hero, a model, because he is the most humble servant
of the woman of his thoughts, he treats adultery as a
sacred thing, a duty. Fidelity to his aged mistress
is the ideal of this brain, crazed by the romances of
chivalry and the ritual of amorous mysticism which

---

[1] Michelet, *Guerres de religion*.

is the fashion of the day. Henry would consider it a crime to return to the right path. Having reached the culminating point of a false conscience, he has succeeded in deluding himself if not others. "I supplicate you," he writes to Diana, "to remember him who has never known but one God and one love, and be certain that you will never have cause to be ashamed of having given me the name of servitor, which I entreat you to preserve for me forever." The *Amadis Espagnol* is the chivalric Bible of the new reign. As M. Michelet says again: "To the sun of Francis I. succeeds another star, the moon, romantic, equivocal, of doubtful lustre."

Burning scaffolds shed their horrible glow over all this phantasmagoria. June 10, 1549, Henry II. causes Catherine de' Medici to be crowned at Saint Denis. A few days later, his ceremonious entry into Paris takes place. June 23 begins a series of tournaments which last fifteen days. A naval combat on the Seine follows the tilting; thirty-two galleys amuse the court with these new games. The festivities end with a religious procession from the church of Saint Paul to that of Notre-Dame, where the voluptuous monarch, honestly imagining that cruelty will atone for adultery, renews his vow to pursue and extirpate heresy. After Mass he dines in public at the bishopric, and after dinner places himself at one of the windows of the Tournelles Palace to see the execution of four wretches con-

victed of Lutheranism. Among them is a man
whom the King knew, his tailor, his "seamster,"
as was said in those days. Accompanied by Diana
of Poitiers and the Bishop of Macon, Henry II. had
chosen to interrogate the man of the people for the
sake of enjoying his timidity and embarrassment.
Hubert Burré was not dismayed. He refuted the
sovereign's arguments, then the bishop's, and when
the favorite ventured to speak, "Madame," exclaimed
the poor artisan, "content yourself with having
infected France, and do not mingle your filth with
anything so sacred as the truth of God!" On the
scaffold the seamster recognizes the King, and while
the executioners are putting him to the horrible
torture of slow fire, he casts on the monarch a look
of so much suffering and so much courage that
Henry II. is troubled, and turns pale.

Pleasure dispels remorse. To the image of the
tailor in the flames, an avenging image which long
haunts the King, succeeds that of Diana the huntress,
the crescent on her forehead, the golden quiver on
her shoulder, the silver bow in her hands. The
marvellous Castle of Anet is the temple of his idol.
A veritable veil of stone lace envelops this fairy-like
abode. On the azure and gold of the pillars amorous
devices are engraved. Strange spectacle! Diana
will not grow old, and she does not. What is her
secret? M. Michelet reveals it. "To be affected
by nothing, to love nothing, to sympathize with
nothing. Of the passions to keep only what will

give a little rapidity to the blood, of the pleasures, those that are mild and without violence, the love of gain and the pursuit of money. Hence, absence of soul. On the other hand, the cultivation of the body. The body and its beauty uniquely cared for, not weakly adored as by the majority of women, who kill themselves by their excessive self-love, but by a virile treatment, a frigid régime which is the guardian of life."

At all seasons of the year Diana plunges into a cold bath on rising. As soon as day breaks, she mounts a horse, and, followed by swift hounds, she rides through dewy verdure to her royal lover, to whom, fascinated by her mythologic pomp, she seems no more a woman, but a goddess. Thus he styles her in verses of burning tenderness: —

> "Helas! mon Dieu! combien je regrette
> Le temps que j'ai perdu en ma jeunesse!
> Combien de fois je me suis souhaité
> Avoir Diane pour ma seule maîtresse.
> Mais je craignais qu'elle, qui est déesse,
> Ne se voulût abaisser jusque-là." [1]

Diana, at the height of favor, tolerated Catherine de' Medici, and Catherine took good care not to contend with her. "When Henry came to the crown, the Seneschale, informed by the King himself

---

[1] Alas! my God! how much I regret — The time I lost in my youth! — How many times have I desired — To have Diana for my only mistress. — But I feared that she, who is a goddess, — Would not stoop so low as that.

that the Queen had never sought to lower her in his esteem, preferred to have her in the place she occupied rather than another who would not be so patient, and, consequently, she never took any pains to thwart her. Catherine, on her part, contented with being Queen, and with the fecundity which Fernel, the chief physician, had, under God, procured for her, confined herself to the care of bringing up her children, and, abandoning all else, she left almost entire possession of the new King to the Seneschale."[1] This *ménage à trois* has been described in the most painstaking way by a writer whose patient researches have cast full light on the figure of Diana, M. Georges Guiffret.[2] He shows us the mistress constituting herself the protectress of the legitimate wife, monopolizing the cradles, settling all questions concerning the health of the newly born, insisting on receiving letters like this from the physician of the royal family: "Without your diligence and goodness of heart, the Queen would be already almost hopeless; but God has so prospered your efforts and listened to your prayers that she will finally recover her health." Diana made herself the sick-nurse, but she took good care to receive a salary therefor which would repay her trouble. By a letter signed at Blois, January 17, 1550, Henry II. gave her 5500 livres of Tours (about

---

[1] Varillas, *Histoire de Henry second.*

[2] *Lettres inédites de Diane de Poitiers,* published by M. Georges Guiffret, 1 vol., 8 mo: Renouard.

66,000 francs of our money), "on account," said he, "of the good, praiseworthy, and agreeable services she has heretofore rendered to our dear and much-loved companion, the Queen." Two years later, the Venetian ambassador, Lorenzo Contarini, wrote these characteristic lines: "The Queen continually visits the Duchess, who, on her part, renders her the kindest offices in the mind of the King, and it is often she who exhorts him to go and stay with the Queen." At ceremonies, audiences, and receptions, Catherine preserved her rank, but it was very necessary for her to be contented with the exterior signs of royalty; always cool and prudent, she knew that her hour had not yet come. She was waiting.

Everybody, at this time, considered her to be merely a good mother of a family, who was superintending the education of her children in the most assiduous and intelligent way. In 1550, she lost Louis of France, Duke of Orleans, and in 1556, Victoire and Jeanne of France, twin sisters. There remained to her four sons (Francis II., Charles IX., Henry III., the Duke of Alençon) and three daughters, whose grace and precocious beauty were much admired: Madame Elisabeth, born in 1545, promised at first to Edward of England, but afterwards given to Philip II.; Madame Claude, born in 1547, who became Duchess of Lorraine; Madame Marguerite, born in 1553, who was the celebrated Queen Margot. Along with her three little daughters, Catherine de' Medici brought up the Queen of Scotland, Mary Stuart, who had been taken to France at the age of five, in 1548, and who was destined to marry the Dauphin. The list of themes and translations given as exercises to these princes and princesses has been preserved. The Marquis du Prat, in his *Histoire d'Elisabeth de Valois*, has quoted this note, dictated by Catherine to the little Queen of Scotland for her to translate into Latin: —.

"The true grandeur and excellence of the prince, my very dear sister, does not consist in dignity, in gold, in purple, and other luxuries of fortune, but in prudence, wisdom, and knowledge. And by so much as the prince wishes to differ from his people in his mode and fashion of living, by so much should he be removed from the foolish opinions of the vulgar. Adieu, and love me as much as you can."

Under her apparent reserve Catherine already cloaked profound meditations. She reflected on all the court intrigues without meddling in them, learning in silence the difficult and complex art of manœuvring between parties. The ambassadors were already impressed by the exquisite tact she displayed in conversation, and her talent in questioning her interlocutors. She showed, for the first time, what she was capable of, on August 14, 1557. Foreigners were then threatening to invade the kingdom, and in order to arrest their successes on the northern frontier, it was necessary to obtain considerable subsidies from Parliament. Catherine, who was directing public affairs in her husband's absence, repaired herself to Parliament, and the Venetian ambassador, Giacomo Soranzo, thus describes the proceeding: "The Queen expressed herself with so much eloquence and feeling that she touched all hearts. . . . The session terminated amid such applause for Her Majesty, and such lively marks of satisfaction with her conduct, as words can give no notion of. Nothing is talked about all over the city but the Queen's prudence, and the happy way in which she proceeded in this undertaking."

The time was approaching when Catherine could gratify that passion for governing which was the basis of her character. Diana of Poitiers was not to triumph much longer. The reign of Henry II. ended, as it had begun, with fêtes, prodigalities, and persecutions. At a time when the country was groaning under the burden of interminable wars, and strict economy was indispensable to the healing of its wounds, the feeble and ostentatious monarch plunged into the most exaggerated outlays. The marriage of the Dauphin to Mary Stuart was celebrated April 24, 1558, with ceremonies marked by a truly prodigious luxury. The youthful Queen-Dauphiness wore a golden crown ornamented with pearls, diamonds, rubies, sapphires, emeralds, and other jewels of inestimable value. A gallery twelve feet high, and hung with vine branches laden with grapes in the antique manner, led from the court of the bishop's palace to the open space in front of Notre-Dame. The royal dais, sown with lilies, was placed before the door. Preceded by the beadles in grand costumes, halberd in hand, and by drummers and fifers, the Duke of Guise, who acted as master of ceremonies, appeared first on the platform, where the Bishop of Paris was awaiting the royal family. When the cortège arrived before the church door, the King drew a ring from his finger, which he handed to Cardinal de Bourbon, Archbishop of Rouen, and there, under the portico, this prelate united the Dauphin and the Queen of Scotland "in presence of the Reverend Father in God, Mgr. the Bishop of Paris, who made a learned and elegant speech to the spectators."[1] Then the Duke of Guise, accompanied by two heralds-at-arms in coats of mail, came on the platform, and called the people nearer. "Largess! largess!" cried the heralds-at-arms, flinging gold and silver pieces among the crowd. "Then might have been seen such a tumult and shouting among the people that one could not have heard it thunder, so great was the clamor of the spectators as they threw themselves on each other in their inordinate desire to have some." There was a magnificent fête that evening at the Tournelles Palace. "I leave you to imagine the pleasure and

---

[1] *Archives de l'Histoire de France*, by Cimber and Danjou. This passage is cited in the interesting volume published by M. Armand Eudel, of Gard, under the title, *Recueil de fragments historiques sur les derniers Valois*.

delectation that the princes and lords, the princesses, ladies, and demoiselles then took in the rejoicings of such an assembly. And at the dress ball, there were masques, mummeries, ballads, and other pastimes in such great triumph that it is next to impossible to write of them." Twelve artificial horses, with trappings of gold and silver cloth, on which rode Monsieur d'Orléans, Monsieur d'Angoulême, the children of the Dukes of Guise and Aumale, and other young princes, drew the coaches of numerous pilgrims dressed in cloth of gold and silver, sparkling with jewels, and chanting epithalamiums. Then six vessels, covered with crimson velvet, advanced by irregularly undulating movements which imitated the progress of vessels through the waves. Each vessel carried a prince who, in thus making the round of the hall, took on board the lady whom he desired to embark with him on his vessel. King Henry II. chose the Queen-Dauphiness; the Dauphin, the Queen his mother; the Duke of Lorraine, Madame Claude ; the King of Navarre, the Queen his wife; the Duke of Nemours, Madame Marguerite; the Prince of Condé, the Duchess of Guise. "I omit several other delectations, mummeries, melodies, and divers recreations; I will briefly say that the major part of those who were in the aforesaid hall hardly knew whether the torches and cressets illuminated it better than so many sorts of rings, brilliants, gold, and silver."

Does one get a just idea of the iniquities, violences, vexations, that were required to nourish this fatal luxury? What sufferings, what tears, to realize these great victories of opulence and sensuality! It is not only wild beasts that are stricken by the darts of the beautiful huntresses, — their arrows pierce the hearts of the poor. It is by means of rapine and destruction that they build these elegant dwellings where the refinements of art heap marvels upon marvels. To the festivities succeed the persecutions. Voluptuousness and cruelty might be the motto of this century. Provided a few heretics are burned from time to time, the King is at peace with himself. Never was any man more the sport of a false conscience. His persistence in adultery is his chief pride. He is bent on acting as a lover to his sexagenarian mistress, although in reality his affection is now only that of a friend. He does not even see the hatreds heaped up against him by the shameless favoritism, the mad follies which are the scandal of his reign. He takes seriously the strange parody of knightly manners which in his day is already anachronistic rubbish. Born with good dispositions, and a gentle, indulgent character, flattery has made him ridiculous and hateful. The fault brings its chastisement. The house of Guise, so imprudently aggrandized to please the favorite, will ruin that of Valois. The Protestants, exasperated by indescribable cruelties, will plunge into terrible rebellions. The blood of the victims cries for vengeance. June 10, 1559, the King repairs to

Parliament to strike the heretics with terror; he finds intrepid men there. "It is not a thing of slight importance," exclaims Councillor Anne Du Bourg, "to condemn those who, in the midst of the flames, invoke the name of Jesus Christ. . . . What! shall crimes worthy of death, shall blasphemies, adulteries, horrible debaucheries, perjuries, be committed every day with impunity in the sight of Heaven, and every day new tortures be invented for men whose only crime is to have discovered the Roman turpitude by the light of Holy Scripture, and to demand a salutary reformation!" Councillor Du Faur expresses himself with still greater violence: "We must understand," says he, "who they are who trouble the Church, lest that should happen which Elijah said to King Ahab: It is thou that troublest Israel." Exasperated, Henry II. causes the two bold orators to be arrested, and sends them to the Bastille. Condemning them in advance to the scaffold, he intends to see them burned with his own eyes. But he is reckoning without Montgomery's lance.

The fêtes had just begun anew. On June 20, the famous Duke of Alva had espoused, by proxy, in the name of Philip II., the young Elisabeth of France, and on the 27th, the contract of marriage between the Duke of Savoy and Madame Marguerite had been signed. The 29th, a tournament took place before the Tournelles Palace, almost at the foot of the Bastille, where Councillors

Anne Du Bourg and Du Faur were imprisoned. At this period there were in circulation two unpleasant predictions, one old and the other new, which pointed out with sufficient precision the kind of death by which the King was menaced. The old one had been made by Luke Gaurico, a celebrated Italian astrologer, in whom the Queen had great confidence. She had entreated him to draw the horoscope of Henry II., and he had predicted that the Prince would be fatally wounded in a duel at the age of forty. Gaurico had been derided, people declaring that their royalty exempted sovereigns from that kind of danger. But, within a week, a new prediction, entirely conformable to the old one, had disquieted people's minds. The King, without being disturbed, remarked to the Constable that prophecies were sometimes fulfilled, and he would like as well, or better, to die in a duel than otherwise, providing it were by the hand of a brave man. Henry did not imagine he was speaking so truly. Still wearing the colors of his aged mistress, he was tilting brilliantly in the lists, when Montgomery's lance struck him in the face and pierced through the right eye to the brain. A few days later he breathed his last. The superstitious Catherine believed more firmly than ever in the supernatural power of astrologers.

VI

MARY STUART

TO the influence of Diana of Poitiers and of Montmorency succeeded that of Mary Stuart and the Guises. Frail, scrofulous, undecided in character, and slothful in mind, married before the age of puberty, and submissive as a slave to his wife, Francis II. might be said to be crushed under the weight of his crown. Diana of Poitiers disappeared from the scene. The young King sent her word that her evil influence over the deceased monarch deserved a great punishment, but that in his royal clemency he would not trouble her any further; nevertheless, she must restore all the jewels she had received from Henry II. It was thus that the gems which had passed successively with the favor of sovereigns, from the Countess of Chateaubriand to the Duchess d'Étampes, and from the Duchess d'Étampes to the great Seneschale, returned to the crown. Catherine de' Medici, who never cared to avenge herself for the mere pleasure of vengeance, was satisfied with requiring Diana to surrender to her the magnificent castle of Chenonceaux in exchange for the gloomy domain of Chaumontsur-Loire, and took no further pains to annoy her former rival.

The rivals now are Catherine de' Medici and Mary Stuart, one forty years of age, and the other seventeen; one who had never been really beautiful, the other dazzling and admirable; the one a cool schemer, mistress of herself, hiding her emotions under an impenetrable mask, and possessing the temperament of a statesman; the other inexperienced, ardent, impetuous, carried away by the vehemence of her character, and making an open display of her sensations and caprices. The one has already been subjected to many trials; a child, she had been entangled in great catastrophes; a young woman, she had seen her pride humbled both as wife and queen. The other knows yet neither the dangers nor the sorrows of life; flattered from her cradle, suffering no contradiction, proud of her double crown, prouder still of her beauty, she is intoxicated by the incense which an idolizing court burns in her honor.

The grave L'Hôpital himself addresses her Latin verses wherein he declares her the most beautiful and accomplished person of her times in all respects. The borders of flattery are enlarged for her sake. Mythology is brought into requisition for its most charming images, and lyrism for its most hyperbolical expressions whereby to celebrate this wonder of wonders. She is regarded as an exceptional, a divine being. Brantôme but echoes all the courtiers when he goes into ecstasies over the precocious learning, the incomparable brilliancy, of the young Queen, when he describes her in her national Highland costume, "in the barbarous fashion of the savages of her country, appearing like a true goddess in a mortal body and a coarse dress," singing very well, and accompanying her voice with a lute, "which she touches firmly with that beautiful white hand and those fair and well-formed fingers," which would inspire envy "in those of dawn." When she marries, "both court and city resound with cries that a hundredfold blessed is the Prince about to be united with this Princess, and that although the kingdom of Scotland was a thing of price, yet the Queen is worth still more, because though she had neither sceptre nor crown, yet her person alone, and her divine beauty, were worth a kingdom; but, since she is a queen, she brings a double fortune to France and to her husband."

How resist this enchantress who still impassions posterity, and after the lapse of centuries finds fanatical admirers? Between his mother and his wife the young King does not hesitate. Absorbed even to ecstasy by a passion which was to be his first and last, the royal stripling lives solely for his fascinating companion. Catherine knows the human heart too well to enter into a strife which would have been still more hopeless against the youthful Mary Stuart than the aged Diana of Poitiers. And besides, what would be the use? Catherine does not desire her son's death, but she knows he will not live. The astrologers have told her so. What matter is it if Mary Stuart, full of family prejudices, considers her mother-in-law a woman of low birth, and even treats her sometimes as "the daughter of Italian merchants"? Believing herself far superior in wisdom and experience to the young Queen, whom she regards as a madcap, Catherine, who for more than twenty years has put up with the Seneschale, can easily put up with her for a few months. Since the days of Francis II. are numbered, she mounts her batteries in advance, and making ready in silence for the great struggles about to begin, she studies, analyzes, compares, and waits. The conspiracy of Amboise does not disturb her. An impassible spectator of the executions, she is present at them, as the Roman matrons were at the gladiatorial combats.

Regnier de La Plance has related these horrible events with much detail. The streets of Amboise, strewn with dead bodies, streamed with blood. The Loire was covered with corpses fastened to long poles. During a whole month nothing was done but "decapitate, hang, and drown people." "But what was strange to behold, and unusual in all forms of government, they were led to execution without any sentence having been pronounced on them in public, nor any cause assigned for their death, nor even their names mentioned. . . . One thing observed with regard to some of the principals

was that they were reserved until after dinner,
contrary to custom; but the Guise party did it
expressly for the sake of giving some pastime to
the ladies, who, as they saw, were growing tired of
being in the place so long." Catherine de' Medici,
Mary Stuart, and all the court ladies looked on at
these atrocious scenes from the upper part of the
terrace, "and the sufferers were pointed out to them
by Cardinal Lorraine, who showed signs of rejoicing,
and when any of the victims died more steadfastly,
he said: 'Look, Sire, at these shameless madmen!
Even the fear of death cannot humble their pride
and treason. What would they have done if they
had got hold of you?'" The Duchess of Guise,
daughter of the Duke of Ferrara and Renée of
France, having been taken almost by force to this
spectacle, came back from it in such grief that she
dissolved in tears on entering the room of the Queen-
mother. Catherine, on beholding her so afflicted,
asked what was the matter, what had happened to
make her "so sad, and complain so strangely." —
"I have every reason in the world," she replied,
"for I have just seen the most piteous tragedy. . . .
In short, I do not doubt that a great calamity will
fall on our house, and that God will exterminate
us for the cruelties and inhumanities which we
commit."

The triumphant house of Guise wished to kill
the King of Navarre and the Prince of Condé. The

MARIE STUART

When Dauphiness of France

Prince, having been condemned, was about to be executed, when Francis II. fell ill. Catherine, alarmed at the omnipotence of the Guises, thought it wise to oppose them by means of the Bourbons. She caused the execution of Condé to be delayed, and the King's death, which occurred December 5, 1560, saved him. Francis II., who was only sixteen years old, had reigned for seventeen months. "It was remarked," says Varillas, "that he was born during an eclipse, that he had been married amid the fires of warfare, and that the hall which had been arranged for the trial of the Prince of Condé and several other guilty persons was used for his lying-in-state."

Catherine's hour had come. At last she was about to govern. Mary Stuart, who at first withdrew to the convent of Saint Peter, at Rheims, where her aunt was abbess, breathed out her grief in poetic lines, which Brantôme has preserved for us:—

> "Si en quelque séjour,
> Soit en bois ou en prée,
> Soit pour l'aube du jour
> Ou pour la vesprée,
> Sans cesse mon cœur sent
> Le regret d'un absent;
> Si je suis en repos,
> Sommeillant sur ma couche,
> J'ay qu'il me tient propos,
> Je le sens qui me touche.

En labeur, en recoy,
Toujours est près de moi."[1]

Mary, who loved France passionately, would have liked to stay in her own domain of Touraine and Poitou; but Catherine, who was jealous of the intelligence and beauty of her daughter-in-law, desired nothing more ardently than her return to Scotland. Henry II. had been governed throughout his reign by a woman older than himself. Would it be surprising if Mary Stuart, who was but eight years older than Charles IX., should some day exert influence over him? "As to which it is in nowise doubtful," says Brantôme, "that if, at the time of his Parliament, King Charles, her brother-in-law, had been of full age instead of very young and small, and had also been in such a mood of love for her as I have seen him in, he would never have allowed her to depart, but would resolutely have espoused her. For I have seen him so much in love that he could never look at her portrait without his

---

[1] If in some place I stay,
In forest or in fell,
Whether at break of day
Or at the vesper bell,
Still, still my heart is sore
For one who comes no more;
If I am in repose,
Sleeping upon my bed,
There is who cometh close,
Whose hand on me is laid.
In toil or thought I see
Him who is near to me.

eyes becoming so fixed and enraptured that he could scarcely remove or satisfy them, and have often heard him say that she was the most beautiful princess ever born into the world, and that he considered his brother only too happy, and thought he ought not to regret lying in the grave, since in this world he had possessed this beauty even for so short a time, and that such enjoyment outweighed that of his kingdom."

Philip II. had a momentary inclination to play the same part in Scotland that France had, and to marry his son Carlos to Mary Stuart. At the beginning of the year 1561, Cardinal Lorraine had talked of this project with the Spanish ambassador, Chantonnay. Catherine de' Medici opposed it with all her might, such an alliance seeming to her a serious danger for the house of Valois. The Bishop of Limoges, French ambassador at Philip's court, was ordered to do all that was possible to prevent such a marriage, and the prospect which Catherine dreaded so greatly was never realized.

The Queen-mother, not contented with this first success, redoubled her efforts to induce her daughter-in-law to leave France. Certain emissaries urged Mary to return to her own dominions in order to re-establish the Catholic religion there, and extinguish, if possible, the flame of civil dissensions. Her uncles of Aumale and Elbeuf persuaded her instinctively, and without premonition of the woes from which it would have saved her, to remain in the land of her affections; but Cardinal Lorraine, whether in the interests of Catholicism, or fearing lest his niece might lose the Scottish crown, or desiring to avert the enmity of Catherine de' Medici, strongly advised Mary Stuart to return to her kingdom, and his advice finally prevailed. The Cardinal tried to persuade his niece to leave in his care the jewels and precious objects she had received in France, lest they might be lost through some accident of the voyage. Mary declined this proposition, saying that since she was going to risk her life on the sea, she surely might risk her jewels also.

The voyage was not altogether safe, by reason of the hostile dispositions of Queen Elizabeth. The English cruisers were to be dreaded, and Mary Stuart asked her rival for a safe-conduct which would enable her to pass within view of the English shores without danger; but this safe-conduct was refused her. She did not hide from Throckmorton, the English ambassador, the painful surprise she experienced at this refusal. "Sir," she said to him, "nothing afflicts me more than to have so far forgotten myself as to beg of the Queen, your mistress, a favor of which I had no need." In July, 1561, she went to Saint-Germain to bid adieu to the young King and the court before quitting that land of France to which, eight years later, she was vainly to solicit Elizabeth's permission to return at the price of a ransom, "as was the custom among all princes, even enemies." "I hope," she said at that time to

Throckmorton, "that the wind will be favorable to me, and that I shall not have to land on the English coast. If I do land there, Mr. Ambassador, your Queen will keep me in her hands, and can do with me what she pleases. If she is so cruel as to desire my death, let her have it, let her sacrifice me. Perhaps that fate would be better for me than life. May the will of God be done!"

Mary Stuart set sail from Calais, August 14, 1561. Brantôme, who accompanied her on the voyage, relates in touching words, the beautiful Queen's farewells to France. Just as she was embarking, she beheld on the horizon a vessel which foundered instead of entering the port. Most of its passengers were drowned. "Ah! my God! what an omen!" exclaimed the royal exile.

The mournful voyage had begun. Mary, "without dreaming of another action, leaned her two arms on the poop of the galley, on the side of the helm, and melted into great tears, constantly turning her beautiful eyes toward the port she had sailed from, and always saying these words: Adieu, France! adieu, France! and continued this doleful exercise nearly five hours, until, as night began to fall, some one asked if she would not remove from there, and take a little supper. Then redoubling her tears more than ever, she said these words: 'Truly it is at this hour, dear France, that I wholly lose sight of you, since night, obscure and jealous of my satisfaction in seeing you as long as I can, drops a heavy veil before my eyes to deprive me of such a happiness.'" The famous piece of verse —

> "Adieu, plaisant pays de France,
> O ma patrie,
> La plus chérie
> Qui as nourri ma jeune enfance,"[1]

is apocryphal,[2] they say; but the sentiments it expresses are doubtless Mary Stuart's. When night was come, "she commanded the helmsman, as soon as day should break, if he could still see and discover the land of France, to awaken her and not be afraid to call her. As to which fortune favored her; for the wind having ceased, and oars resorted to, very little progress was made that night, so little that when day appeared, the land of France appeared also, and the helmsman, not failing to obey the command he had received, she rose up in her bed and began to contemplate France again as long as she could; but the vessel moving further away, her contentment departed also, and she saw her beautiful land no more. Then were again renewed these words: 'Adieu, France! it is over! Adieu, France! I think I shall never see you again.'" The voyage

---

[1] Adieu, pleasant land of France —
O my country —
The most cherished —
Which nourished my young childhood.

[2] M. Feullet de Conches, in Vol. IV. of his *Causeries d'un Curieux*, attributes this piece of verse to Meusnier de Querlon, which appeared for the first time in the *Anthologie française*.

lasted five days, and the arrival was as sad as the departure. "One Sunday morning that we arrived in Scotland," says Brantôme again, "such a great fog arose that we could not see from the poop to the prow, so thick that we were obliged to cast anchor in open sea, and take soundings to find out where we were. This fog lasted all day and all night until eight o'clock the next morning, when we found ourselves surrounded by so many reefs, that if we had gone forward, or to either side, we should have foundered on the rocks and all perished. Concerning which the Queen said that as far as she was concerned, she would not have cared much, as she desired nothing so greatly as death." It was not Mary Stuart alone who was struck by such omens. "Having seen and recognized the land of Scotland on the morning the fog lifted, there were those who predicted that this fog signified they were about to land in a disorderly kingdom, troubled and unpleasant."

Poor Queen! what humiliations, what griefs, will be yours during the twenty-seven years you have still to live, or, rather, to suffer! How bitterly you will expiate the brilliancy of your youth and your double crown! Yet a little while, and instead of enthusiastic admirers you will have nothing but rebellious and insolent subjects. They will force you to drink to the dregs the chalice of bitterness. The diadem will scorch your forehead like a ring of fire. Humiliated and vanquished, betrayed as queen, betrayed as woman, accused of odious crimes, steeped in calumnies and insults, you will be obliged to seek a refuge near your enemy, and this refuge will be a captivity of twenty years, and, after the prison, death. The headsman will seize hold of your beautiful tresses, whitened by grief; your eyes, those eyes which cast so soft and radiant a light, will be bandaged; they will place your august and charming head upon the fatal block. Then you will repeat the psalm: "*In te, Domine, speravi, non confundar in æternum*"; and at the moment when you utter the words: "My God, into thy hands I commit my spirit," "*In manus tuas, Domine, commendo spiritum meum*," a blow from the axe will put an end to all your sufferings. Then they will fling a scrap of frieze, torn from a billiard table, over your body, once so admired, so flattered, and not one of those sworn to defend you will rise up to avenge you.

"Well, they may say what they like, but many a noble heart will take sides for Mary Stuart, even though all that is said about her should be true." In recalling this speech, which Walter Scott places in the mouth of one of the characters in his romance, *The Abbot*, M. Sainte-Beuve adds that this will be the last word of posterity as well as of her contemporaries, the verdict of history as well as of poetry.

"Vanquished in the order of realities, the beautiful Queen has regained everything in the realm of imagination. There, from century to century, she has found knights and lovers. Some years since a distinguished Russian, Prince Alexander Labanoff, undertook, with incomparable zeal, a search among the archives, collections, and libraries of Europe, for all the pieces emanating from Mary Stuart, in order to bring them together, and make of them a body of history, and, at the same time, an authentic reliquary, not doubting that interest, — a serious and tender interest, — would spring more powerfully from the bosom of truth itself." Dead, as it were, during her lifetime, Mary Stuart has had the privilege of exciting at once enthusiasm and anger.

As M. Feuillet de Conches has said so well in his remarkable *Causeries d'un Curieux*, she belongs to "the number of those political personages concerning whom polemists of all parties continue to fling burning coals at each other. Look at the passionate books that are written about her. Would not one call them great combats fought over the tombs of the heroes of antiquity?" The innocence of Mary Stuart in Darnley's murder has been impeached by M. Mignet, who, on this point, is an able and vigorous prosecutor. But the memory of the Queen has none the less found ardent and convinced defenders. A learned professor, M. Wiesener,[1] has revised the indictment and made an emphatic protest against M. Mignet's thesis. He maintains that the pretended letters of Mary to

---

[1] See also the admirable *Histoire de Marie Stuart* by M. Dargaud.

Bothwell, and the coarse verses attributed to the
Queen, are apocryphal. He recalls that Bothwell,
then taking shelter in Denmark, when believing
himself on the point of death, avowed himself the
author of the murder, and, at the same time, declared
that the Queen had taken no part in plotting or
executing the crime. Finally, let us cite a letter
written to Mary, November 8, 1575, by her mother-
in-law, the Countess of Lennox, a letter intercepted
by Cecil's spies, and found by Miss Agnes Strick-
land in the State Papers Office. It shows that even
Darnley's mother, after having pursued Mary with
violence, had in the end fully recognized her
innocence.

Innocent or guilty, Mary Stuart will always excite
profound sympathy. M. Sainte-Beuve has said as
much in eloquent terms: "That gentle charm with
which she was endowed, and which acted on all who
approached her, resumes the ascendancy and works
upon us from a distance. It is neither with a regis-
trar's text, nor even with the reason of a statesman, that one judges her, but with the heart of a
chevalier, or, say rather, of a man. Humanity,
pity, religion, poetic and supreme grace, all these
invincible immortal powers, have an interest in
her person, and cry aloud in her behalf across the
ages." Even if we admit that Mary Stuart had
been guilty, which for our own point we strongly
doubt, are we not still more affected by the sanctity of her repentance? In the night preceding

her execution she searched the Old and New Testaments for an example of some great sinner whom God had pardoned, and chose the history of the good thief to be read to her. "He was a great sinner," said she, "but not so great as I; I entreat our Saviour, by the memory of His passion, to remember and have mercy on me as He did on him."

VII

CATHERINE DE' MEDICI REGENT

TO Francis II. had succeeded Charles IX.; to an imaginary majority, a real minority. The little King was only ten years old. At last Catherine de' Medici reigned. Never had a more overwhelming burden rested on a woman's shoulders. A Blanche of Castile's force of soul would not have been great enough to struggle against the formidable tempests about to be let loose on France. Catherine foreboded them. "My own," she wrote to her daughter, Elisabeth, Queen of Spain, "recommend yourself well to God, for you have seen me as contented as you are, never expecting to have any other tribulation than that of not being loved according to my liking by the King, your father. And God has taken him from me, and not content with that, He has taken your brother also, whom I loved as you know, and has left me with three little children, and a kingdom so divided that there is not a single one in whom I can wholly trust who has not some private prejudice." True, history has a right to be severe towards this woman. Yet, for all that, it must recognize the terrible obstacles she had to surmount, and give her credit for the courage with which she accepted the struggle. The Venetian ambassadors who witnessed her indefatigable efforts, have spoken of them with a sympathy approaching tenderness. "I do not know," says one of them, Giovanni Correr, "what prince would not have made mistakes in such a great confusion; how much more, a woman, a foreigner, without trusty friends, frightened, and never hearing the truth from those about her. For my part, I have often been surprised that she did not become thoroughly confused, and give way to one of the two parties, which would have been a final calamity to the kingdom. It is she who has preserved the remnant of royal majesty still to be found there. This is why I have always pitied rather than blamed her, and she has often reminded me of it when speaking of her distresses and the woes of France." It is a mistake to fancy Catherine as always impassible. No doubt, like the majority of great politicians, she had learned how to mask her feelings. But there were moments when nature resumed her rights, and the mask itself was inundated with tears. "I know," says Giovanni Correr again, "that she has more than once been found weeping in her chamber; but she at once dried her eyes and dissembled her sadness; and in order to mislead those who estimated the state of affairs by the expression of her countenance, she wore a calm and joyous aspect when abroad."

It must not be believed that the Queen-mother

had always had settled projects, fixed plans. There is no science more contingent than that of politics. Assuredly, Catherine knew what she wanted; her aim was to save the house of Valois, and solidify the royal authority. But the means to do this varied with events. Justice demands us to recognize that she began by trying the paths of gentleness, moderation, and impartiality. In a time when there were as yet no constitutions, she acted, at the beginning of her regency, like a true constitutional sovereign. She sought to balance powers, she tried conciliation, she induced mortal enemies like the Duke of Guise and the Prince of Condé to embrace each other. A prophetic inkling of the ideas of 1789 animated the States-General of Orléans. A profound thinker who had divined the future, Chancellor L'Hôpital, spoke as a great orator of our days might do. He announced principles which in his time seemed paradoxes, but which in ours are axioms. We believe that at this time Catherine was sincere, that she seriously desired the good of the kingdom, that her intentions were upright; but, and it is a sad confession to make, had she continued in this path, her century would probably have neither understood nor followed her.

In troublous and violent epochs, the masses listen to nothing but exaggerations. Moderate people are considered lukewarm. There is no longer either impartiality or justice. The moral sense and the reason disappear together. Doubtless, truly noble souls are not immoderately affected by these aberrations of public opinion. Persevering without uneasiness in the path of right and duty, they remember the old adage which is the device of virtue, Do what you ought, come what may. But Catherine was not one of those grand characters which events do not affect. From the day on which she became convinced that mildness would not succeed, she never recoiled from crime.

It is incontestable that the Queen-mother hesitated momentarily between the rival cults. She had been greatly impressed by the progress of Protestantism. In 1555, there was but a single reformed church in all France; in 1559, there were two thousand. The Spanish ambassador, Chantonnay, wrote, September 6, 1561: "Take into consideration that whatever is lawful at Geneva, as to sermons, administration of the sacraments, and similar things, may be done with impunity throughout the kingdom, beginning in the King's own house, and he is thought stupid who does not do the worst he can." The Prince de la Roche-sur-Yon, who superintended the education of Charles IX., showed himself favorable to the new religion. Surrounded as she was by a great number of Protestant ladies, Catherine questioned whether it were the interest of the dynasty to remain loyal to the Catholic faith.

She liked much the notion of replenishing the funds by seizing ecclesiastical property. Her Huguenot courtiers said that nothing could be easier than to make France Protestant, and that where Henry VIII. and Gustavus Wasa had succeeded so easily she could not fail. Would not a word from Catherine suffice to change the religion of the kingdom, as had happened in England and in Sweden? Nothing was more dangerous than such counsels, and the Queen-mother soon repented of having, for several months, entertained an inclination to follow them. It is evident, none the less, that at the beginning of her regency she inclined toward the new ideas. Either through fear of the Guises, or in hopes of turning the reform movement in favor of the royal authority, she gave the Protestants great hopes, and had a disguised Calvinist, the Bishop of Valence, preach before the young King. He spoke, says a Venetian ambassador, "on all the points as clearly as if he had been in the middle of Geneva." Cardinal de Chavillon performed the ceremony of feet-washing in the Cathedral of Beauvais, with his wife at his side.

The development of Protestantism in France is at once a curious and painful spectacle. Certain it is that in both cults there were some honest, convinced souls, led by conscience and the passion for truth; Protestants who wished that manners and morals might be quickened with the primitive purity of the best days of Christianity, and Catholics who, while sincerely loyal to the faith of their fathers, beheld with sacred and profound sorrow the attacks made on unity of dogma. But, close beside these choice souls, what light, superficial, inconsistent spirits! What mean and miserable considerations blended with religious questions! For some, Protestantism was an affair of interest, ambition, or rancor; for others it was a caprice, an infatuation, a whim. There was a moment when well-bred men of the Catholic party chose to display a more or less decided predilection for the doctrines of Geneva. Marot's French Psalms were fashionable literature. The labor of searching the Bible was left to a few grave doctors. Were scholasticism and theology harmonious with the gay and careless humor of the young nobles of the court of Charles IX.? And yet the religious passions reappeared at intervals in these frivolous natures. How many times the same man who would have staked his religion at night on a throw of the dice, had veritable attacks of fanaticism on the morrow! The Germans, who served in the Calvinistic troops, never lost their wonder at this versatility. "These French weathercocks," said they, "for whom people are killed to-day, are ready to embrace each other to-morrow."

The fluctuations of public opinion, not yet decided, exercised some influence over the mind of Catherine, "a wise woman," says the Venetian ambassador, Michel Suriano, "but timid, irresolute, and always a woman." It has been said, wrongly as I believe, that she was completely incredulous. It is probable that, like many other souls, she had her moments of faith and her moments of scepticism.

Brought up in the Catholic religion, she retained up to a certain point the impressions of her childhood. She certainly believed in hell and in paradise, in the devil and in God. But she varied as to other doctrines. There were hours when, like Montaigne, she would have been tempted to say: What do I know? There were others when the religious sentiment regained entire possession of her soul. Nothing absolute can be found in her. Her character is full of contradictions, and the historians who will conscientiously analyze her life, will waver, like her contemporaries, between sympathy and dislike for this mobile nature.

From the day when she gained the twofold conviction that Protestantism was sapping the foundations of royal authority, and that Catholicism was assured of success, Catherine no longer hesitated. The first wars of religion opened her eyes to the tendencies, by turns republican and feudal, of the Calvinist leaders, to the ambition of the Prince of Condé and Admiral Coligny, to the danger to the great cause of French unity arising from the new ideas, and to the anti-national character of the Huguenot alliance with England.

Brantôme describes the exasperation she displayed when the English made their appearance in Normandy. "When Rouen was besieged," he tells us, "I saw her in all the rages in the world, when she saw the English success enter there; . . . hence she turned every stone to take the place, and never

failed to come every day to Fort Saint Catherine."
She was not less vigorous in driving the foreigners
from Havre in 1563, and assuredly one of the finest
epochs of her life was that in which she induced
Catholics and Protestants to unite in this enterprise
and to set patriotism above party disputes.

"To return to our Queen," says Brantôme again,
"her enemies have charged that she was not a good
Frenchwoman. God knows it, and with what zeal
I saw her urged to drive the English out of Havre-
de-Grâce, and what she said about it to Monsieur
the Prince, and how she made him go there with the
gentlemen of his party and Monsieur Andelot's first
companies, and other Huguenots, and how she led
the army in person, being usually on horseback like
a second fair Queen Marphisa, exposing herself to
musket-shots and cannonades, like one of her captains, always watching the battery fire and saying
she would never be easy until she had driven the
English from France, hating worse than poison those
who had sold it to them. Thus she did so much
that it made her French."

It is impossible to deny that, with all her faults,
Catherine had the national sentiment. When she
saw that the heart of the nation beat for the Catholic
cause, she would have no more of the Reformation.
Moreover, she had too much intelligence not to
comprehend that to abandon the honor of protecting
the faith to the Guises, was to destroy, for their
behoof, all the prestige of the crown. "The

churches were the theatre of all the fêtes and all the joys of the people; their palaces were more splendid than those of the kings, where, kings in their turn, they forgot all their hard labors and their miserable dwellings in dreams of heaven. What was offered them in place of all this magnificent Catholic symbolism, this immense poem in action which incessantly unrolled with the rolling year? Abstract worship of the spirit, in temples void and empty to eyes of flesh, enthusiasm for moral reform, praise of the Christian's dignity sounding in the chants of a new harmony, the sole act of an iconoclastic worship."

There was, in the first place, in religion as well as in the French character, a strife between the northern and the southern spirit. But the southern influence was not slow to conquer. The people were attached with all their soul to the pomp and poetry of the religion of their fathers. It was perceived that in France Catholicism was the soul of the family, the city, and the nation. Catherine, who had written to the Pope to ask for the suppression of images, communion under both species, and prayers in the vulgar tongue, "because it is impossible to reduce either by arms or by laws those who have separated from the Roman Church, their numbers being so great," — Catherine changed her mind. She watched with attentive eyes the spectacle that was unrolling before her eyes. When she beheld the Huguenots, like true Vandals, destroying the masterpieces of the Middle Ages, dragging crucifixes and relics through the mud, raging at everything which to the people meant civilization, happiness, and glory; when these modern Saracens respected not even the dead; when they profaned, at Angoulême, the sepulchres of the ancestors of the reigning family; when they burned, at Cléri, the bones of Louis XI., and at Sainte-Croix the heart of Francis II.; Catherine, as she listened to the cry of wrath and vengeance which rose from the Catholic masses told herself that the Valois must range themselves on the side of the people, if they would not perish in the tempest. Moreover, the Catholic triumvirate, which had so alarmed Catherine, no longer existed. The Marshal of Saint-André had been killed at the battle of Dreux, and the Duke of Guise assassinated before Orleans. Protestantism was now the danger for authority. Ideas of moderation had no longer any influence. The civil war assumed a savage character on both sides; whole garrisons had their throats cut. The wells were choked with human bodies; the soldiers became headsmen. Roadside trees turned into gibbets. "The civil war," says Castelnau in his Memoirs, "were an inexhaustible source of all villainies, thefts, robberies, murders, incests, adulteries, parricides."

And yet Catherine did not despair of appeasing all hatreds, ending all discords, and bringing out the royal authority victorious from all its trials.

"She thought she could dispel the turbulent humor, which she attributed rather to an ambitious movement, and the love of vengeance than to religious sentiments. She hoped, also, that the obedience of the people would increase as the King grew older, so that the seditious could not thenceforward lift their heads with so much assurance. She told me one day that if she alone among all the queens of France had encountered such evils, she would believe herself the most unfortunate woman in the world; but she was consoled when she remembered that always, during the minority of kings, the great had endeavored to seize hold of affairs."[1]

Nothing discouraged her. The more difficult the situation, the more astuteness, patience, and activity she displayed. Her life was an incessant labor. M. Michelet himself, the pitiless detractor of Catherine, does justice to "her facile pen, always ready and always trimmed. At the head of the Laubespins, the Pinarts, the Villeroys, and other French secretaries, at the head of the Gondis, the Biragues, and other Italian secretaries, must be placed that untiring female scribe, Catherine de' Medici. If there is no despatch to draw up, she makes up for it by writing letters of politeness, compliment, or condolence, even to private persons. . . . The great ladies of the period, Catherine, Mary Stuart, Marguerite of Valois, write fluently a language

---

[1] Despatch of the Venetian ambassador, Giovanni Correr.

already modern, agreeable, and easy, wherein the few obsolete expressions seem but an amiable Gallic naïveté, and impart a deceptive air of antique candor." M. Armand Baschet has remarked very truly: "A just, veracious, and great history of Catherine de' Medici would be impossible, except after studying her private letters. Her ability, her penetration, her astonishing facility in obviating all difficulties come out in all her expressions. . . . Subtle and eager, such is Catherine, and in her (how rare a quality!) subtlety restrains eagerness. Her style has the most unexpected and extraordinary turns; and however diffuse may be the arrangement of her sentences, they always have an underlying fund of wit and judgment." Count Hector de La Ferrière, who is now preparing the collection in which Catherine's unpublished correspondence is to appear, may be sure in advance of the interest with which so curious a publication will be received. All the intellectual vigor of this "stateswoman" will be made evident by it.

I think I see her in her Louvre, living by her intelligence, her head, far more than by her heart, never losing sight of her plans and ideas, pursuing her ends by the most crooked paths, displaying in all circumstances the resources of an adroit and pliant character. "At table, and while walking, she is constantly conversing with some one on affairs. Her mind is bent, not merely on political matters, but on so many others that I do not know how she can endure and go through so much."[1] Notwithstanding all her preoccupations, she still finds time to think of letters and the arts. She makes Amyot preceptor to Charles IX., takes pleasure in Montaigne's conversation, and, in 1564, begins the erection of the Tuileries after the plans of Jean Bullant and Philibert Delorme.

Calm, smiling, happy, apparently at least, amidst the gravest perils and most horrible tragedies, I behold her feared by her children, held in great consideration even by her enemies, pleasing even the most rebellious by the courtesy of her manners and the sweetness of her words, overwhelming with attentions every one likely to be of use to her, writing to the Calvinist leader, the Prince of Condé himself, when she needed his influence to counterbalance that of the Guises:

"Cousin, remember to guard the children, the mother, and the realm; I thank you for what you are doing for me; if I die, I will instruct my son to requite you for it." Experience has ended by giving her an imperturbable calmness. Having come to despise humanity, she has arrived at indifference in her judgments on her contemporaries. To her, more than to any other personage, may be applied that line of a great poet: —

"Sans haine, sans amour, tu vivais pour penser."[2]

---

[1] Despatch of the Venetian ambassador, Sigismond Cavalli.
[2] Without hate, without love, thou livest to think.

To reign, is what one should say. To rule is Catherine's joy. "All her actions," says the Venetian ambassador, Sigismund Cavalli, "are founded on that invincible passion which, even during her husband's lifetime, was recognized in her, — the passion for domineering; *un affetto di signoreggiare.*" She yields to this lust for power, but without conceit, without arrogance, and with a sort of good-nature. Amiable, attractive, and exquisitely polite, she takes pains to make herself agreeable to all who approach her. She never likes to displease the person whom she speaks with. "But it imports those who treat with her to proceed with extreme circumspection, for she has a singular mastery over her speech. If she chooses, she will give a response which, though apparently determinate and definitive, is, nevertheless, inconclusive."[1] Her tact and her memory, qualities so useful to sovereigns, being extremely good, she always appears keenly interested in the persons surrounding her. They know her to be false, wily, capable of great treachery, and yet those who talk with her are nearly always enchanted. Her conversation is by turns jovial and instructive. She is conversant, not merely with French affairs, but with those of all other kingdoms and European states.

Mistress of herself, she has the great art of self-control. If she is dissatisfied with one of her officials

---

[1] Despatch of Sigismund Cavalli.

or attendants, she expresses her displeasure in affectionate terms. "When she calls any one 'my friend,'" says Brantôme, "it is either because she thinks him a fool, or is angry; so true is this, that she had a noble servant named M. de Bois-Février, who said as much when she called him 'my friend': 'Ah! Madame, I would like it better if you called me your enemy, for it amounts to saying that I am a fool, or that you are angry with me, for I have known your disposition this long while.'"

Nothing affects Catherine less than the pamphlets written against her. When there is any wit in the satire she says: "Oh! oh! here are people very well up in our affairs." If the libel is badly done: "These are gossips and dunces!" she exclaims. Doubtless, she remembers her illustrious ancestor, Lorenzo the Magnificent, who was accustomed to repeat concerning the pamphleteers: "We do what we like, let them say what they please."

One day, while talking with the King of Navarre in a lower room, she hears two soldiers, who do not suppose her so near, singing insulting songs about her, while roasting a goose beneath the window. The King of Navarre wished to go down and punish them. "Let them alone," says Catherine; "there is no cause for anger, and that is not our game." Then, showing herself to the soldiers: "What has your Queen done to you?" says she. "She is the cause why you are roasting the goose."

Up to the fatal moment when the Saint Bartholomew Massacre spotted her black robe with an ineffaceable stain of blood, she was much oftener accused of moderation and mildness than of violence and cruelty. The parties reproached her with being too conciliating, and with wishing to pacify everybody. It was by means of the beautiful girls in her train, her flying squadron as they were called, that she attacked and vanquished her harshest enemies. She wanted to blunt hatreds by pleasures, to change shouts of rage into voluptuous chants; and this woman, destined a few years later to wear a sinister aspect, never appeared, during the childhood of Charles IX., but with a smile on her lips and the olive-branch in her hand.

VIII

ELISABETH OF FRANCE, WIFE OF PHILIP II.

CHARLES IX. entered his fourteenth year June 27, 1563. August 17, Catherine and Chancellor L'Hôpital conducted him to the parliament of Rouen to hold a bed of justice. The young King, in a childish voice, pronounced a little discourse in which he was made to declare that having attained the age of majority, he would not permit any one to disobey him.

Soon afterwards, accompanied by all his court, he passed through all the southern provinces of the kingdom. It was Catherine's notion that this journey, which occupied two years, would increase the prestige of royal authority, and contribute to the prevalence of conciliatory ideas. In June, 1565, Charles IX. halted at Bayonne, whither his sister Elisabeth, wife of Philip II., went to join him under the care of the Duke of Alva. Nearly three weeks were spent in balls, jousts, and banquetings. The court of France made a parade of unbridled luxury in order to disguise from the Spaniards the sorry condition of the national finances. The novelties of the day, Spanish pastorals, the idyls of Boscan

ELISABETH OF FRANCE

and Montemayor, imitated by Ronsard, charmed these august personages. There was nothing but interludes, ballets, and allegories. Thus, as M. Michelet has said, the chants of nymphs and shepherdesses covered the whispered conversations between Catherine and the famous minister of the vengeance of Philip II. If Protestant writers may be believed, he counselled at this period the massacre accomplished seven years later on. Davila relates what the Duke might have said then to Catherine de' Medici: "Nothing is more pernicious than to permit peoples to live according to their consciences, and thus allow as many varieties of religion to be introduced into a state as there are caprices in the heads of men. Controversies on the faith have always served as pretexts for the discontented. We must deprive them of this pretext, and without sparing either sword or fire, extirpate the evil to its very roots."

People long remained convinced that a strict alliance was at this time concluded between France and Spain, and that the Duke of Alva found means to persuade Catherine that a Sicilian Vespers had become indispensable in dealing with the Huguenots. But things did not take place in this way, and it is now averred that the Queen-mother, far from accepting the counsels of the celebrated Spanish minister, was not yet inclined to give up the see-saw policy which was her preference. The despatches addressed to Philip II. by the Duke of Alva are known at present, and it is plain from them that the Duke failed in all his attempts, whether to obtain the dismissal of the Chancellor de L'Hôpital, or to have the preachers suppressed who were authorized by the Edict of Amboise in the provinces bordering on Spain. Nothing but vague protestations of friendship could be obtained in either case. The Duke of Alva found Catherine "more than cold for the holy religion," in spite of the "lofty energy and consummate prudence" employed by Queen Elisabeth to induce her mother to associate herself more intimately with the Spanish policy. No definite resolution was taken. "The Catholic Queen, my daughter," wrote Catherine to Constable de Montmorency, "left us July 3; the King, my son, took her back to the same place where he had received her, which is on the bank of the river. We have talked of nothing during our meeting but caresses, entertainments of good cheer, and, in general terms, of the desire felt by each for the continuance of the good friendship between their Majesties and the preservation of peace between their subjects, the principal cause and occasion of the said meeting being simply to have the consolation of seeing the said Queen, my daughter."

During the whole time of her stay at Bayonne, the Queen of Spain, who was young and charming, had testified a lively pleasure at finding herself once more among her compatriots. "She showed herself neither more nor less familiar with the ladies and young girls of the court than when she was a girl, and inquired very particularly about those who were either absent, or married, or newly arrived since her departure. She did the same with the gentlemen, asking those who had been there who the others were, and often saying: 'He or she were at court in my time, I knew them well; these others were not, and I desire to know them.' In a word, she contented everybody."[1]

Born in 1545, Elisabeth of France, Queen of Spain, had just turned twenty. She had been married for five years and a half to Philip II., whose gloomy and taciturn disposition was in contrast with the grace and amiability of his young companion. It is related that at the close of the year 1559, when she first set foot on Spanish soil, Elisabeth was received by Cardinal Mendoza who, in a harsh voice, addressed her in these words from Psalm xliv.: "*Audi, filia, et vide, et inclina aurem tuam obliviscere populum et domum patris tui.*" "Listen, my daughter, and incline thine ear: forget thy people and thy father's house."

The Bishop of Burgos went on with the succeeding verse: "And the King shall desire thy beauty, because he is thy lord and master." "*Et concupiscet rex decorem tuam, quoniam ipse est dominus tuus.*" Elisabeth had at first been intended for Don Carlos, the son of Philip II. But, as Brantôme puts it, the King " who had just become a widower by the decease

---

[1] Brantôme, *Dames illustres*.

of the Queen of England, his wife, having seen the portrait of Madame Elisabeth and finding her very beautiful and much to his taste, cut the grass under his son's feet and took her for himself, beginning all charity at home. Afterwards, according to what I have heard from a reliable quarter, the said Carlos, having seen her, became so much in love with her, and so full of jealousy toward his father, that it lasted all his life, and was so vexed with him for having despoiled him of his beautiful prey that he never loved him."

The marriage of Philip II. and Elisabeth had been celebrated January 31, 1560, in the palace of the Duke de l'Infantado, and Don Carlos, though suffering from an attack of fever, had been one of his father's witnesses at the ceremony. In the excellent work [1] he has devoted to the hero of Schiller's drama, M. de Moüy has treated as fabulous the mutual inclination attributed by many historians to the Queen and her step-son. He says on this subject: "As to writers who amuse themselves by describing the emotions of Don Carlos and the Queen on this solemn day, and the sudden passion they experienced for each other, they have forgotten, doubtless, to adduce any proofs for such a story, and also the age of the prince, who was hardly more than fourteen, and who, sick, unsightly by nature, and still a child physically and morally, could evidently neither feel love nor inspire it."

---

[1] *Don Carlos et Philippe II.*, by Charles de Moüy.

Contrary to the opinion of Brantôme, M. de Moüy does not believe that Don Carlos ever had what is called a passion for his step-mother, and he explains in this way the very special character of the Infant's sentiment: "Don Carlos beheld in Elisabeth a compassionate friend, who was attached to him precisely on account of his infirmities and weakness, and whose feminine susceptibility, moved at sight of him by affectionate pity, had a more penetrating accent than that of the gentlest man, and found within itself the secret of an exquisite delicacy. He who had never known a mother's love, was allured by the goodness of a woman who united in herself the majesty and rank of a mother with the youth and grace of a sister. He consecrated to her one of those strange sentiments which exceptional situations give birth to in the heart of man, a sentiment at once filial and fraternal, austere and tender, to which was added that infinite gratitude of weaklings for those who take an interest in their sufferings." Whatever may have been the character of the affection of Don Carlos for Elisabeth, it is incontestable that the conduct of the Queen was above all suspicion.

Few sovereigns have left in Spain so touching a renown. "When she went to churches, monasteries, and gardens, there was such a great press to see her, and such a great crowd and throng of people that one could not turn round amongst the rabble, and very happy was he or she who could say in the evening: 'I saw the Queen.'" They called her the Queen of

Bounty, *Isabel de paz y bondad.* Whenever she fell ill all her subjects were in prayers and tears. She was sincerely attached to her new country. "Her Spanish," says Brantôme, "was as attractive as it could possibly be, and she learned it in three or four months that she was there." People were pleased with the rapidity with which she adapted herself to the manners and customs of her realm. "Subjected to an often painful obedience, she performed her duties without a murmur; accustomed to the brilliant festivities of the court of the Valois, to the cheerful aspect of that '*pleasant* life,' so dear to Mary Stuart's memory, she knew, and that without showing regret, how to inure herself to the severe discipline of the palace of Philip II."[1]

Her mother, Catherine de' Medici, would like to have learned from her the secrets of Spanish policy; but the young Queen refused such a rôle and answered her in respectful but evasive terms. Every one rendered homage to her physical and moral qualities. "The nobles could not look at her," says Brantôme once more, "lest they should be smitten, and so awaken the King's jealousy and consequently risk their lives. It was the same with churchmen, through fear of temptation." Although sincerely devoted to Spain, she remembered France with affection. "The French were received by her, on their arrival in Spain, with a countenance so benign, that from the greatest

---

[1] M. de Moüy, *Don Carlos et Philippe II.*

to the least none ever left her without feeling himself much honored and well contented." She had never been willing to discontinue French, "but always read it in the best books that could be had from France." She opened her mother's letters with emotion and even a sort of fear, for "she so honored and respected her, that never did she receive letters from her without trembling and alarm." Brantôme adds with feeling: "Behold the goodness of this princess and her virtue of honoring and fearing (being so great) the Queen, her mother. Alas! the Christian proverb was not well kept in her regard, that he who would live many years must honor his father and mother, since, doing all this, she died in the most fair and pleasant springtime of her youth."

A tragic legend has been connected with Elisabeth's memory. Her contemporaries suspected Philip II. of having poisoned her, and posterity has been affected by this mysterious and terrible accusation. Brantôme timidly re-echoes it. It is related, he says, that a "Jesuit, a very worthy man, speaking in his sermon one day of Queen Elisabeth, let slip a remark that it had been very wickedly done to cause her death and so innocently, for which he was banished to the farthest Spanish Indies. This is very true, so people say. There are still other conjectures about which one must be silent. But, at all events, she was the best princess of her time." The latest investigations of historical criticism exonerate Philip II. from the crime imputed to him, and everything leads to the belief that Elisabeth died a natural death. M. Gachard and M. de Moüy, in their works on Don Carlos, have arrived at the same conclusions. Everything goes to prove that the pretended passion of the Infant for his step-mother had no influence whatever on the tragic end of that prince. The Spaniards saw nothing but what was natural and legitimate in the respectful sympathy testified by Don Carlos for his step-mother. No one sought to incriminate this affection. The French ambassador at Philip's court expressed himself concerning it with perfect confidence in his letters to Catherine de' Medici. The Infant was not afraid of giving little presents to the Queen with which she liked to adorn herself, and in the Spanish court, severe and rigid though it was, not one voice was raised to accuse Elisabeth.

We do not believe, then, that the daughter of Catherine de' Medici should be involved in the terrible scenes which filled the imprisonment and death-agony of Don Carlos with horror. Sick in soul and body, the heir of so many crowns spent a few years in the greatest evils that can be inflicted on a man. He was, as has been said so well, a poor, pale prince, weakly, trembling, one of those historic figures before which thoughtful posterity hesitates between disdain and pity.

Although mad, he was interesting, because he had suffered so much. He died, at the age of twenty-three, July 24, 1568. He had been a prisoner since

January 18, and death was his deliverance. Elisabeth, while having no love for the Infant, did not behold this gloomy catastrophe unmoved. When he was dead, Don Carlos, in accordance with a desire he had expressed, was dressed in a Franciscan habit, and the cowl of a Dominican. At the door of the palace his body was received by Spanish grandees, and by them carried to the church. The King who, according to etiquette, could not be present at the funeral service, watched from his window the departure of the lugubrious procession.

The year 1568, which began so inauspiciously for the family of Philip II., was to end in a manner not less lamentable. Queen Elisabeth descended into the tomb two months and a half later than Don Carlos. She died in childbed, October 3. The French ambassador, Fourquevaulx, has described her last moments in a letter expressive of real sorrow: "The King her husband," he wrote to Charles IX. and Catherine de' Medici, "had visited her this morning before daybreak, to whom the said lady, speaking like a very wise and Christian princess, and bidding him farewell forever in this life, in language which no queen ever spoke with better sense or more sanely, mentioned to him his daughters, the friendship of your Majesties, the peace of her realms and her ladies, with other words worthy of admiration, and fitting to pierce the heart of a good husband, such as was the said lord King, who replied with the like constancy, being unable to believe she was so near her end, and granted all her requests and demands. Then he withdrew to his chamber, very much afflicted and sorrowful." Elisabeth wished to see for the last time the old servitor of her grandfather, Francis I., her father, Henry II., and her brothers, Francis II. and Charles IX.

"Monsieur Fourquevaulx," she said to him lying on her deathbed, "you see me in the way to depart presently from this miserable world to go to another Kingdom more agreeable, and I hope to possess near my God the glory that shall have no end. . . . I beg you to say to the Queen, my mother, and the King, my brother, that I supplicate them to take my death patiently. I will pray for them and for my brothers that God will guard and long maintain them in His most holy protection." And, as Fourquevaulx tried to reassure her by saying that she exaggerated the gravity of her illness, and that she was not going to die: "No, no, Monsieur the Ambassador," she replied in a voice enfeebled by the last sufferings, "I would much rather go to see what I hope and believe I presently shall see." An hour afterward she expired, "so easily," adds Fourquevaulx, "that we should not have known the moment when she yielded up her spirit, but that she opened her two clear and lustrous eyes, and it seemed to me as if they were still commanding somewhat from me, for they were turned straight upon me. We presently withdrew, leaving the whole palace in tears."

Thus died, at the age of twenty-four, this beautiful

Queen, in whose destiny there is something so melancholy and so sweet. She had shed a soft lustre over the gloomy palaces of her pitiless and fanatical husband. When this lustre was extinguished, night fell again on all surrounding Philip II. The angel of mercy was no longer there to pacify the savage charracter of the sovereign who has been called the Demon of the South. Spanish poets consecrated to the memory of the beautiful sovereign, who had passed from morning to evening, plaintive elegies, bearing the imprint of sorrow and tears. "O Death inexorable," cries one of them, Pedro Lainez, "thou smitest the feeble and the strong, the ignorant and the wise, the haughty king and the obscure pauper, and thy hand makes them equal in that hour supreme. . . . Charming Queen, most perfect creature that has ever been encountered in these regions which the sun illumines and the ocean laves, before death came to strike thee, thy tender youth seemed to assure thee long years of happy life, and we have all admired thy beauty like that of the lily and the rose."

Above the tombs of Don Carlos and of Elisabeth, opened so soon after one another, to engulf such youth, such grandeur and such hope, a sombre romance has been reared. Men have sought to make it believed that the two victims of a destiny so fatal had been united by love before becoming so by death, and that Philip II., inflexible in his vengeance, was the executioner of his wife after having been that of his son. There are already gloomy sides enough in the life of the King, dear to inquisitors, to dispense one from blackening still further his appalling figure. We believe, with M. de Moüy, that Queen Elisabeth has her sympathetic poetry, and needs not the fictitious prestige that belongs to ardent and persecuted passions. "She has the charm of women who die young after a gloomy life, of mothers whom their children have not known, of queens who have welcomed human grandeurs and death with the same resigned and melancholy smile. She was, during her short life, the object of that respectful admiration which the heart of peoples does not squander, and which flattery does not imitate." The destiny of these young women, so promptly harvested by death, vividly impresses the soul and recalls the lessons of Bossuet in presence of the catafalque of the Duchess of Orleans. Whoever gives ear to the past hears always a plaintive voice issuing from the depths of history. Nothing is more striking than the contrast between a palace and a sepulchre. The dead who wore a crown come from their tombs to say to us: "*Memento, homo, quia pulvis es.*"

IX

THE CHILDHOOD OF MARGUERITE DE VALOIS

CATHERINE DE' MEDICI was afflicted by the death of her daughter, the Queen of Spain. But nothing dries tears so quickly as political anxieties. Carried away by the whirlpool of affairs, by the ardor of the strife, Catherine had no time to give to sorrow. The successes she obtained at this period diverted her from her grief. Death was disembarrassing her by degrees of the principal rivals she had met with in her path: Constable Montmorency was slain at the battle of Saint-Denis, and the Prince of Condé at the battle of Jarnac. Always on the go, always at the breach, this untiring woman discouraged nobody, and made no definite break with any party. She had not abandoned her idea of pacifying all, and although Philip II. advised her to prosecute to the utmost the war against the Protestants, she treated with the vanquished of Jarnac and Montcontour, and had Charles IX. sign the edict of Saint-Germain, which was more favorable to their cause than if they had been the victors (August 8, 1572). They were granted admission to all employments, the exercise of Calvinistic worship in two cities of every province, and in all those where it was already established, besides four places of safety during two years, Rochelle, Montauban, Cognac, and Chartres.

It has been often said that this arrangement was only a snare laid for the Huguenots by the Queen-mother. We do not believe it. We think, with M. Lavallée, that "it was another effort to make the two religions live together, to give some repose to exhausted France, possibly to attempt to subdue or render more pliable during the peace the Calvinists, who were indomitable in spite of their defeats." Thereupon all seemed to quiet down. There were no more riots, no more combats. People attended either Mass or preaching without fear. Catherine triumphed. "A reign of twelve years since her husband's death had inspired her with great confidence in herself; she was no longer watched by those favorites, ministers, and generals whom it had been necessary for her to treat with circumspection; she was reigning, feared and obeyed by her sons whom she continued, however, to oppose to each other; for the spirit of intrigue had not abandoned her on her rise to power; on the contrary, the dissimulation to which she had accustomed herself when she had everything to fear had become to her the science of the throne and of supreme ability."[1]

It is curious to study the interior of the royal family at this epoch. Charles IX. is twenty years

---

[1] Sismondi, *Histoire des Français.*

old, the Duke of Anjou eighteen, the Duke of Alençon sixteen. Their sister Marguerite (Queen Margot) is seventeen. Violent jealousies disturb them. Charles IX. begrudges the Duke of Anjou, the future Henry III., the affection shown him by their mother, and the easy triumphs she has let him score. The Duke of Alençon, already treacherous and uneasy, has the ambition which so often torments the younger sons of illustrious families. Catherine applies in her family the same principles as in government: she spies, she intrigues, she rules by petty means. She mistrusts Charles IX., who is violent and irascible even to frenzy, and reflects with terror that he may turn against her the lessons she has given him. An instant would suffice to break the chains so skilfully forged. There are hours when the mother and son, who watch each other, remind one of Agrippina and Nero.

It is at this moment that Brantôme's ideal, Marguerite of Valois, begins to play a part. She was born May 14, 1553. Her education, like that of her sisters, was conducted by a woman eulogized by the writings of the time, Madame de Curton. "To speak of the beauty of this rare princess, I think that all that are, or will be, or ever have been, near hers, are ugly, or are not beauties, for the brightness of hers so burns the wings of all others in the world, that they neither dare nor can fly or appear around it."[1] To vivid coloring, hair of the most beautiful

---

[1] Brantôme, *Dames illustres.*

black, a soft and tender glance, the figure of a nymph, and the gait of a queen, she unites the graces of the mind, gaiety of character, and the charms of imagination. The bad examples she has before her eyes give an evil turn to her finest qualities.

The memoirs she has left give us the most curious details concerning the court of the Valois. Marguerite relates that in her childhood she suffered a real persecution at the hands of her brother the Duke of Anjou, because she was too good a Catholic. The prince who, some years later, was to be the chief instigator of the Saint Bartholomew massacre, had then an evident inclination for the reformed religion. "My brother of Anjou," says Marguerite, "had been unable to escape the impression of that wretched *Huguenoterie*. He was incessantly calling on me to change my religion, often throwing my Hours into the fire, and giving me Huguenot psalms and prayers instead, forcing me to take them, the which, as soon as I had, I gave to Madame de Curton, my governess, whom God gave me the grace to keep Catholic, and who often conducted me to the house of that good man, Cardinal de Tournon, who advised and strengthened me to suffer all things to maintain my religion, and gave me more Hours and rosaries to replace those which my brother of Anjou had burned." But the young prince returned to the charge, "and his other particular friends who had undertaken to ruin me," adds Marguerite, "finding the rosaries again, insulted me, saying this was childishness and folly; that it was plain I had no understanding, because all who had any intelligence, no matter what their age or sex, had withdrawn from the abuses of this bigotry." But the little prince threatened his sister in vain, and she thus ends her story: "I answered such threats, bursting into tears, the age of seven or eight years which I had then reached being tender enough, that he might beat me or kill me if he liked, but that I would suffer everything rather than damn myself."

A few years later, the Duke of Anjou, then one of the props of the Catholic cause, wished to make a confidant and an ally of Marguerite. He was eighteen years old and had just gained the battle of Jarnac. His mother had gone to the castle of Plessis-lez-Tours to congratulate him, and he was on the point of returning to the army when he drew his sister aside into one of the alleys of the park, and said to her: "Sister, the nurture we have had in common does not oblige us to love each other more than does our new relationship. So you may have understood, that, among all your brothers, I have always been more inclined to wish you well than any other, and I have recognized, also, that your nature disposes you to return the same friendship. Until now we have been naturally led to this without any design of ours, and without this union being of any use to us except the mere pleasure of conversing together. That was well enough in our childhood, but now it is no longer the time to live like children. You see the great and lofty positions to which God has called me, and to which I have been raised by the Queen, our good mother. You ought to know, that as you are the one thing in the world which I most love and cherish, I shall never have any grandeurs or goods in which you do not participate."

After this insinuating preamble, the Duke of Anjou frankly requested his sister's aid. "I know you have enough intelligence and judgment," said he, "to be of use to me with the Queen, our mother, in maintaining my present fortune. Now, the chief means for this is to remain in her good graces. I am afraid absence may injure me, and yet the war and my appointments constrain to be almost always at a distance. Meanwhile, the King, my brother, is always near her, and flatters and humors her in everything. . . . I find it is necessary for me to have some very faithful persons near the Queen, my mother, who will be on my side. I know none so suitable as you, whom I consider as my second self." The young prince concluded by advising his sister to be as much as possible with Catherine, who would initiate her into affairs, and no longer treat her as a child. "It will be a great happiness to you," said he, "to be loved by her. You will do much for yourself and for me, and I shall esteem you as, after God, the preserver of my good fortune."

Marguerite describes very well the astonishment and joy caused her by such overtures. The sixteen-year-old girl then was about to become a political woman. "This language was very new to me," she says, "who had thus far lived without purpose, thinking of nothing but dancing and going to the chase, not having even the curiosity to dress myself, or to appear beautiful, since I was not yet old enough for that ambition, and having been brought up with such constraint toward the Queen, my mother, that I not merely did not dare to speak to her, but when she looked at me I was paralyzed with fear lest I had done something to displease her."

At the first moment, the young princess was frightened by the part her brother proposed to her. "I was very near replying," she says, "like Moses to God, in the vision of the burning bush, 'Who am I? Send whom Thou oughtest to send.' However, finding in myself what I had not supposed to be there, powers hitherto unknown to me, excited by the meaning of these words, although I had been born with plenty of courage, on inwardly recovering from this first astonishment these words pleased me, and, in an instant, I seemed to be transformed, and to become something more than I had ever been before."

Marguerite promised her brother her assistance, and that very evening, with a sort of rapture, she heard her mother saying to her in an affectionate tone: "Your brother has reported to me the discourse you have had together, and he does not consider you a child. Hence I will not do so either. It will be a great pleasure to me to talk with you as I do with your brother." "These words," adds Marguerite, "made my soul feel what it had never felt before, — a satisfaction so unmeasured that all the satisfactions I had had until then seemed to me nothing but symbols of this boon; I looked back scornfully at the exercises of my childhood, dancing, the chase, and companies of my own age, and despised them as things too vain and foolish. I obeyed this agreeable command, and never missed a single day to be among the first at her levee and the last at her couchee. She did me the honor to talk with me sometimes for two or three hours, and God gave me the grace to make her so satisfied with me that she could not sufficiently congratulate herself on it with her women."

Marguerite's story is characteristic. She makes evident the sentiment of respectful fear awakened by Catherine de' Medici, as well as the charm she exercised on all around her. Doubtless Marguerite loved her mother, "that good mother," she says, "who lived only for her children, ready to abandon her life at any hour to preserve theirs and their estate." She loved her, but yet she feared her more.

The pact concluded between the brother and sister was not of long duration. Influenced by his favorite, Du Guast, the Duke of Anjou became at the end of some months Marguerite's irreconcilable enemy. The cause of this great hatred was the inclination his sister suddenly experienced for the Duke of

Guise. Born in 1540, Henry de Guise was then twenty years old. He dazzled the court by his grand appearance, his luxury, and his chivalrous manners. "These Lorraine princes," said the Maréchale de Retz, "have such a gentlemanly air that beside them other princes seem like common people." Ambitious and eager for all kinds of success, the young duke aspired to the princess, and on May 3, 1570, the Spanish ambassador wrote: "There is no public matter at present in France but the marriage of Madame Marguerite with the Duke of Guise."

In a remarkable work, full of curious information drawn from the best sources,[1] M. Réné de Bouillé has related how everything at first concurred to favor this bold and ambitious wooing. "The Duke of Anjou, under a perfidious show of friendship, was constantly bringing Guise into his sister's apartments; he expressed to him, even in her presence, solely for the sake of compromising both of them, and in terms as positive as they were familiar and hypocritical, his desire to have him very soon for a brother-in-law. One of the Queen's ladies, the Countess of Mirandole, who was much attached to the Guises, kept up, as it seems, a correspondence with the young duke in which the princess occasionally wrote some even affectionate lines with her own hand. One of these letters, intercepted in June, 1570, sud-

---

[1] *Histoire des ducs de Guise*, by Réné de Bouillé, former minister plenipotentiary. 2 vols. Amyot.

denly exploded the Duke of Anjou's artfully contrived mine. Charles IX. fell into a violent fury. He forbade Henry of Guise to see Marguerite again, and strongly denied that any such marriage had been intended. The King's anger, excited by his mother, was so great that to avoid a vengeance which seemed imminent, the Duke of Guise found it expedient to hurry on a marriage with the widow of the Prince of Porcian."

Several historians have intimated that Marguerite had been the prince's mistress. There is no doubt that, in the second period of her life, she was very dissolute; but nothing authorizes the belief that she fell before her marriage. There is absolutely no plausibility in the pretended evidence adduced. For our own part, we wholly disbelieve in these insinuations. The laws of etiquette were too severe at the time to render it possible for a Daughter of France, especially one watched by a prudent and suspicious mother, to commit such a fault. Is it probable that Henry of Guise, who aspired to marry Marguerite, could have entertained the thought of dishonoring her beforehand?

We must not too lightly credit the inventions of pamphleteers. There are enough real crimes to make the invention of fictitious ones needless. The Duke of Anjou's wrath against his sister is very easily explained. When he saw the woman in whom he had expected to find a trusty confidant and ally permitting herself to be dazzled by a man for whom he had already a profound aversion, his vexation knew no bounds. In the eyes of this irritated brother, Marguerite's sentiment was an unpardonable crime, a defection from the Valois cause. From his earliest childhood the Duke of Anjou had cherished against the rival policy, whose ambition and audacity he had instinctively divined, those sentiments of hatred and jealousy which afterwards opened under the feet of the Duke of Guise, and his own as well, the abyss in which both were swallowed up.

Reassured by the marriage of the Duke of Guise with the Princess of Porcian, Charles IX. began to think of marrying himself. He asked the hand of Elisabeth of Austria, second daughter of Maximilian II., Emperor of Germany, a mild and tolerant prince who carried out a conciliatory policy in his dominions. This offer was accepted, and the nuptials were celebrated November 26, 1570, at Mézières, whither the Archduchess had been conducted by the Archbishop Elector of Trèves, Chancellor of the empire. The principal leaders of the Huguenots were invited to the marriage festivities, but they excused themselves, and remained in their asylum at La Rochelle, although Admiral Coligny had written in respectful terms to Catherine de' Medici to protest his devotion to the King, and his forgetfulness of the past. At the same time, Charles IX. sent an ambassador to the Elector of Saxony, in order to renew, through the intermediation of that Prince, a defensive alliance with the Protestants of Germany.

Elisabeth of Austria was crowned Queen of France, March 25, 1571, in the Basilica of Saint Denis, by the hands of Cardinal Lorraine, abbé of that church, who was fated to place the diadem on the heads of successive queens, and to cast the last handful of earth on the mortal remains of kings. The ceremony was delayed by quarrels on points of precedence and etiquette. Instead of being celebrated in the morning it did not begin until three o'clock in the afternoon. The grand almoner came to Cardinal Lorraine, who was officiating at the altar, to say that the Queen had not taken an early breakfast as usual, because she was to receive Holy Communion, and that she had just told him she was afraid of fainting if she did not eat something to keep up her strength. The Cardinal began by replying that "it was not a thing permitted by the Church; that the Queen should consider whether she could not endure the fatigue until the end." Then, changing his mind, he added, "that, in fine, since this was impossible, she might take something very light, more as a stay to the stomach than to please her taste." The courtiers who were near Elisabeth advised her to profit by this authorization. She firmly refused to break her fast, and amidst a concert of laudations, she "received the Holy Communion towards six o'clock in the evening, as upright and gay as though it were six in the morning."

This pious Queen excited neither suspicion nor jealousy in Catherine, distrustful though she was. She was a true Christian, a saint, wholly occupied in good works, and understanding none of the intrigues of the Machiavelian and corrupt court which she had entered. An angel astray in hell, she did not even suspect the brutal passions, the ferocious hatreds at work on this terrible and brilliant stage. The naïve and candid German was bewildered in her strange surroundings. Charles IX., who had poetical and even kindly moments, did not contemplate unmoved the calm and gentle countenance of his young companion. People remarked the same contrast between them as between a clear blue sky and one furrowed by the lightnings of a great tempest. She was mildness at the side of violence.

X

JEANNE D'ALBRET

AFTER the peace of Saint-Germain Charles IX. sincerely desired the reconciliation of parties. Schemes of conquest allured his inflammable soul. He dreamed of military glory, and wished to lead both Catholics and Protestants, once more united under the same banner, against the foreigner. To give an evident pledge of this policy, he resolved on a marriage between his sister Marguerite and Henry of Navarre, the son of Jeanne d'Albret, the future Henry IV. Very serious obstacles impeded this union. The Pope was unwilling to give the necessary dispensations, and the Queen of Navarre, who had always been an inveterate defender of the Protestant cause, was slow to confide in the brilliant promises that were made to her.

This woman of virile character holds a great place among the heroines of the sixteenth century. Her severe, almost savage, countenance is in strong contrast with those of the elegant and sensual beauties of her epoch. She is the ardent Calvinist, the warlike and despotic Queen, who loves combats and Protestant sermons, who draws an immense strength from her enthusiasm, and who frustrates, with the aid

JEANNE D'ALBRET

of a handful of poor, ignorant, but intrepid mountaineers, the best-laid plots of her powerful neighbors. It is not easy to imagine what activity, perseverance, and audacity she needed to hold her own against the perils of a most threatening situation, to resist the rebellion of her own subjects, the encroachments of France, and the attacks and conspiracies of Spain. Taken, so to say, between two fires, on the north and on the south, she escaped only as by miracle from the flames which incessantly threatened to spread over her dominions, and destroy all within them.

She had exhibited her rare qualities from childhood. Charles V. recommended his son, Philip II. in his will to marry this "Princess of robust health, admirable character, virtuous, and with a heart worthy of her birth." Happily for France, which had so great an interest in preventing the Spaniards from getting a foothold in the strategetic positions of Béarn, Charles V.'s intentions were not realized, and Jeanne d'Albret espoused Antoine de Bourbon, Duke of Vendôme, who descended in the direct male line from Robert, Count of Clermont, the fifth son of Saint Louis. Antoine of Bourbon, who had well merited his sobriquet of the Barterer, having been by turns Catholic, Calvinist, Lutheran, and then Catholic again, died at the siege of Rouen, November 17, 1562. Jeanne, his widow, then definitively declared for the reformed religion, and in a public ceremony received communion, along with her children, according to the Genevan rite. Divided by religious animosities and local jealousies, her subjects gave themselves up to the most bloody dissensions. Before making herself beloved, Jeanne determined to be feared. As absolute as Calvin himself, she did not recoil from pitiless measures. Béarnais were forbidden under penalty of death to be present at Mass, or in religious processions. Ecclesiastical property was confiscated, altars demolished, pictures defaced, statues broken to pieces, and the ashes of saints scattered to the winds. The two parties rivalled each other in cruelty. At Montluc, the terribly Catholic people opposed Montgomery, the man whose lance had killed Henry II., and who had plunged eagerly into Protestantism. The enemies of the Queen of Navarre, exasperated by the audacity of this Princess, "who had nothing of the woman about her but her sex," as d'Aubigné says, plotted repeatedly against her liberty and her life. To-day, they wanted to abduct her, and hand her over to the inquisitors of Philip II. To-morrow, she was threatened with a French invasion, which would have wrested her sceptre from her. Whether in the defiles of the Béarn Mountains or in the intrenched Huguenot camp at La Rochelle, her presence revived a failing courage. Her natural eloquence, the lightning flashes from her eyes, her reputation as a Spartan matron and an intractable Calvinist, all contributed to give her a great influence with her own party. The military leaders, Coligny, La Rochefoucauld, Rohan, La Noüe, submitted their plans of campaign to her.

A strong and violent nature, a woman of the mountains, with a haughty heart, an active mind, a heated imagination, Protestant in her soul, convinced even to fanaticism, full of hatred for the Pope and Philip II., at least as intolerant as her adversaries, and like them committing inhuman actions in the name of the Gospel, Jeanne d'Albret is a type of exceptional energy. Surrounded by snares and enemies, she sought an asylum amid rocks and inaccessible peaks. Shielding herself behind the devotion of her loyal Béarnais, she bravely accepted the challenge of Rome and Spain. Proud of the national device: "I am what I am, *Sum id quod sum*," she had been tempered in the vivifying air of mountain summits. In her eyes, the court of France was a receptacle of debaucheries and infamies. Chaste, she admitted of no excuses for voluptuousness. A woman of duty, she despised pleasure. Impassioned even to fury for her religious ideas, she wrote to Catherine with a sort of rage: "If I held my states and my son in my hand, I would rather throw both into the sea than take them to Mass." The Protestants, all whose prejudices, rancors, and passions she espoused, regarded her as a heroine, a saint. A Biblical poetry encircled her as with a halo.

To her son, the future Henry IV., born December 13, 1553, she had given an education which was to make a hero of him. On the day when he was born, his grandfather, Henry d'Albret, exclaimed in a transport of haughty joy: "My sheep has brought forth a lion!" Then, rubbing the lips of the newly born with garlic, "Child," said he, "drink from this cup of old wine, and thou wilt be a brave Gascon and true Béarnais." Henry d'Albret, who knew "how greatly the severe nurture and discipline of a country serves to render the mind and courage more firm and generous and capable of great and praiseworthy undertakings," wished his grandson to be "brought up without delicacy, and with no superfluities." He was put out to nurse, like a little peasant, in the village of Bilhères, near Pau, and later, when he had ascended the throne of Saint Louis, the woman who had suckled him asked as her recompense an authorization to have the arms of France graven on her cabin, with the Béarnais inscription: "*Saube-garde dou rey.* Safe-guard of the King." Henry's earliest education was that of the poor. Bareheaded, barefooted, fighting with ragged children, braving the heats of summer and the frosts of winter, eating brown bread and cheese, more agile than the chamois, and sporting on the brink of precipices, he was early accustomed to fatigue and dangers. Mingling with shepherds and laborers, "he did not acquire those brilliant and premature attainments with which the memory of infant princes is overburdened; but he learned to be sincere, judicious, and compassionate for the woes of others."[1] He bathed in the water of springs. He

---

[1] *Histoire de Jeanne d'Albret*, by Mademoiselle Vauvilliers.

drank from the torrent. Gay, nimble, bold, fearing neither frost nor storm, the hardy young *compagnon* was full of confidence in his lucky star. "Thus the destinies of France were mysteriously unveiled in a remote Béarnais valley, and the future was to justify the Spanish proverb which one may still see graven above a door in the old dungeon of Coaraze, and which is believed to have been inspired by Moslem fanaticism: '*Lo que a de ser no puede faltar.* That which must be cannot fail to happen.'"[1]

It is said that from the infancy of Henry of Navarre and Marguerite of Valois, the court of France had dreamed of their future union. According to Favyn's account, the little Prince, when five years old, was presented by his father to King Henry II. "The King, charmed with his pretty face, asked him if he would be his son. But the child replied at once, in his Béarnais dialect, and turning toward Antoine of Bourbon: '*Quet es lo seigne pay.* This is Monsieur, my father.' The King, pleased with this jargon, asked him: 'Since you will not be my son, will you be my son-in-law?' The little Prince replied promptly and without taking thought: ' *O be!* Yes, willingly!'"

When Charles IX. sent to propose a marriage between Henry of Navarre and Marguerite of Valois, Jeanne d'Albret, who had the pride of her race, was

---

[1] *Histoire des peuples et des États pyrénéens*, by M. Cénac-Moncaut.

certainly much flattered by the idea that her son might become the brother-in-law of the King of France, and that the union would be considered by all Europe as a victory for the Protestant cause. On the other hand she had a vague presentiment that this matrimonial project concealed some ambush. Accustomed to rely on herself in the first place, she undertook the preliminary negotiations and leaving Henry of Navarre in his dominions, started for the court of France, to which she would not summon her son until all disputed points were settled.

Before repairing to Blois to regulate the conditions of the marriage, Jeanne d'Albret published in Béarn the national code, known as the *Stile de la reine Jehanne*, the provisions of which are of Draconic severity. Accompanied by her daughter, Catherine of Bourbon, whose history has been so well related by Madame the Countess of Armaillé, she departed from the castle of Pau early in 1572, never to return. She received a very cordial welcome at the court of France. Little Catherine of Bourbon, who was barely thirteen, was charmed with her future sister-in-law, Marguerite, and in the evening after their first meeting she wrote to her brother, who had remained in Béarn: "Monsieur, I have seen Madame Marguerite, whom I think very beautiful; I have asked her to keep you in her good graces, which she promised me; she was pleasant to me and gave me a pretty little dog which I love." It has been pretended that Charles IX., who was very respectful to

Jeanne d'Albret, had the following dialogue with
Catherine de' Medici afterward: "Well, Madame,
do you think I played my part well?" — "Yes, very
well indeed, my son; but that is nothing unless you
keep on." — "By God's death! mother, let me do it
alone, and you will see I will get them all in the
net!" This conversation, which no one overheard,
is not in the least probable, and we believe that
Charles IX. has been represented as more perverse
and hypocritical than he was.

Jeanne d'Albret's arrival in Paris made a great
sensation. Protestants venerated the Queen of
Navarre as the strong woman of Scripture; Catholics
regarded her with mingled admiration and anger,
hatred and esteem. She was a heretic, a damned
soul, but she had made herself feared, she had forced
the great powers of the earth to reckon with her, and
in this century where force was everything, such a
woman must necessarily have prestige and reputation. The sentiment she inspired in the people was
complex. They respected the daughter of the Marguerite of Marguerites, the niece of the great Francis I.; but they were irritated against the ally of the
German Protestants and Elizabeth of England.

At Paris, the Queen of Navarre thought herself
transported to another Babylon. Everything she
saw and heard scandalized her. The elegant debauchery, boldly displayed before her eyes, made her
indignant. The Calvinist of austere tastes could
not accustom herself to this luxury which exhaled

corruption as well as perfumes. She discovered snares hidden in the thickets of rose and myrtle. Sombre forebodings disturbed her. Anxious for both herself and her children, she was full of self-reproach for having allowed herself to be entangled in the webs of silk and gold which entwined her. Charles IX. overwhelmed her with compliments and caresses. He called her "his dear aunt, his all, his best beloved," and his courtiers treated her with profound deference. But Jeanne, who had an observing disposition, found some falsity in these smiling faces. There was venom underneath the honeyed speech.

Nothing better describes the preoccupations and the anguish of the Queen of Navarre than her letter to the son whom she still hesitated to summon and whom she was never more to see. " Your betrothed," she wrote him, "is beautiful, very circumspect, and graceful, but brought up in the worst company that ever was, for I do not see a single one who is not infected by it. . . . I would not for anything in the world have you come here to live. This is why I desire you to marry, and withdraw yourself and your wife from this corruption; for bad as I supposed it to be, I find it still worse than I thought. It is not the men here who invite the women, but the women who invite the men. If you were here, you could not escape from it without a great grace from God."

At certain moments, Jeanne d'Albret, believing Catherine capable of every perfidy, thought herself on the brink of ruin. At others, resuming confidence, she reflected that her suspicions might be exaggerated and unjust, and she experienced those alternations of hope and despair which occur in the crises of private as in those of public life. As to Catherine, pleased to find her enemies under her hand, and still asking herself whether she was going to spare them or to strike, she redoubled her amiability, courtesy, and affectionate protestations.

Assuredly it must have been a curious spectacle to see these two illustrious women face to face with each other, both queens, both mothers, both eager for power, accustomed to domination, inspiring profound fear in all around them, both of them witty and intelligent, observing each other with uneasiness, suspicion, jealousy, representing adverse mysteries and causes. These reunited rivals were themselves astonished at their seeming intimacy, and public common-sense reflected that such a friendship could not be sincere. Jeanne made the same reflection. She saw the storm approaching and yet she did not go away. Something more powerful than her will detained her. She had for some years been enfeebled by great sufferings, and was a prey to a sort of prostrating sadness; at such times her friends could only revive her by speaking of her children. Exhausted by emotion, sickness, and a presentiment of the great catastrophe impending over her co-religionists, the courageous Queen of Navarre was at the end of her physical resources. The preparations for her son's marriage revived her for an instant.

Sustained by a feverish energy, she visited the ateliers of renowned artists, selected toilettes, jewels, ornaments, and carried her shopping expeditions as far as the Pont Saint-Michel, where Catherine's perfumer, René the Florentine, was established. On the morrow she was taken with frightful pains, and breathed her last five days afterward, June 9, 1572.

Libels printed in Geneva pretended that she had been poisoned by the scented gloves she purchased in the shop of the perfumer, whom the Protestants represented as an assassin in the pay of the Queen-mother. It must be remembered that no proof exists in favor of this suspicion. Madame the Countess of Armaillé, says concerning this in her excellent work on Catherine of Bourbon: "The accusation has been frequently reproduced, and ought always to be rejected, as one of the fatal results of the credulous passions of France in the sixteenth century. If L'Estoile, Olhagaray, De Thou, and Mézeray have not feared to add their testimony to the common prejudice, it must be remembered that the first of these historians drew his article from the filthy libel entitled: *Le Discours merveilleux*, and that the others have been impelled by partisanship rather than by an intelligent conviction based upon ascertained facts. Against them, and speaking with the accent of truth, are ranged Cayet, in his *Chronologie novennaire;* Favyn, in his *Histoire de Navarre;* the physician, Caillard, and the surgeon, Desnœuds, in their reports. The latter, who were zealous Protestants and authors of various writings against the court of Charles IX., would not have failed to denounce the crime if they had discovered or suspected the least trace of poison."[1]

Jeanne d'Albret died with great courage, as she had lived. Not a complaint, not a murmur escaped her in the midst of cruel sufferings. Catherine de' Medici, who came to see her on her death-bed, was struck by this noble patience. A few hours before her agony, Jeanne dictated the provisions of her will. In it she recommended her son to remain faithful to the religion in which she had reared him, never to let himself be carried away by "the lures of voluptuousness and corruption," and to banish "atheists, flatterers, and libertines." She begged him to take his sister Catherine under his protection and to be "after God, her father." "I forbid my son," she added, "ever to use severity towards his sister. I wish, on the contrary, that he should treat her with gentleness and kindness; that, above all, he should have her brought up in Béarn, and that she shall never leave there until she is old enough to be married to a prince of her own rank and religion, and whose morals shall be such that the spouses may live holily together in a good and holy marriage."

The Protestants were in despair. Admiral Coligny wept for the valiant friend who had so often revived

---

[1] *Catherine de Bourbon, sœur de Henri IV.*, by Mademoiselle the Countess of Armaillée. 1 vol. Didier.

Huguenot courage. Clothed in a robe of white satin, embroidered with silver, and a royal mantle of violet velvet, Jeanne d'Albret's dead body was exposed on a funeral couch in a chamber hung with black. No candle was burned beside this couch. No voice intoned the prayers which the Catholic liturgy consecrates to the memory of the departed. The funeral obsequies were conducted with austere simplicity. The corpse was laid in a coffin without a blazon, without ornament, like the coffin of a pauper. Then it was taken to Vendôme to be laid beside that of Antony of Bourbon. Navarre lost even the ashes of its queen.

Thus died, at the age of forty-three, the intrepid woman who had mingled in the most terrible events, and had struggled against ill-fortune, with a sort of asperity, an indomitable vigor. Catherine de' Medici made a show of weeping for her.

XI

THE MARRIAGE OF MARGUERITE DE VALOIS

HENRY of Navarre had decided to leave Béarn, and, turning toward Paris, he had just arrived at Chaunay in Poitou when he received news of his mother's death. It was like a thunderbolt to him. Seized by a violent fever, he thought at first of retracing his steps; but Coligny, who had been deceived by the false promises of the court, and thought that the marriage of the young prince would be the dawn of a new era, wrote letter after letter to induce him to continue his route. In spite of his sad misgivings, the new King of Navarre yielded to the admiral's persuasions, and made his entry into Paris escorted by five hundred gentlemen who, like himself, wore mourning.

At the Louvre nothing was heard of but balls and masquerades. The young nobles, both Huguenot and Catholic, rivalling each other in courtesy, elegance, and gaiety, were enacting ballets together. Catherine de' Medici spent whole nights in organizing festivities. The entire court was in a fever of luxury and pleasure.

Coligny was delighted. The respect and affection

of Charles IX. moved him even to tears. He seemed to behold himself already at the head of a magnificent army, powerful and victorious. The regions of Flanders, the only Burgundian fiefs which had not as yet returned to the French crown, were at last to be subdued; the courage of Protestants would give the King these fine provinces whose restoration had been the traditional ambition of his ancestors. The admiral felt his very heart pierced by keen enthusiasm at the idea that his military talents would henceforth be employed not in civil war but on a theatre worthy of him. As he looked at the standards of Jarnac and Montcontour hanging from the arches of Notre-Dame, he exclaimed: "Those are mournful trophies; but they will soon give place to others more agreeable for us to contemplate." The King had declared that the happiest day of his life was that in which he had seen the tranquillity of his realm assured by the admiral's arrival.

As for Henry of Navarre, he was still hesitating on what was as yet new ground to him; profoundly afflicted by his mother's recent death, he thought incessantly, and with painful regret, of that elect woman in whom he had found a counsellor, protector, and friend from his tenderest infancy. He had but meagre sympathy for his betrothed. The young girl, brought up like a coquette, amidst all the refinements of a subtle elegance, was unsuitable for the mountain prince who was a child of nature. Gay, witty, jovial, skilled in bodily exercises, but little versed in the fine language of the brilliant court cavaliers, the Béarnais found it troublesome to put off his simple costume, and put on a doublet of cloth-of-silver and a silken mantle. He retained the large felt hat of the Calvinists.

Meanwhile Charles IX. was hastening his sister's marriage with feverish impatience. It is pretended that, exasperated because the dispensations of Rome were delayed, he cried: "I am not a Huguenot, but neither am I a dunce, and if the Pope acts too much like a fool, I shall take Margot by the hand and have her married in open sermon!"[1]

On Sunday, August 17, 1572, Cardinal Bourbon affianced Henry of Navarre to Marguerite of France. After a grand supper, followed by dancing, the princess was led in great triumph to the episcopal palace, where she slept. The marriage took place next day at Notre-Dame. A magnificent amphitheatre, with side galleries, one of which, passing through the nave, led to the choir, and the other to the bishop's palace, had been erected in front of the church. The King of Navarre, escorted by the Dukes of Anjou and Alençon, the King's brothers, the Prince of Condé, and the Marquis of Conti, the Dukes of Montpensier, Guise, Aumale, and Nevers, the marshals, Admiral Coligny, and many nobles belonging to both religions, repaired to the bishop's palace. A splendid August sun made the gildings and the

---

[1] *En plein prêche.* The *prêche* signified a Protestant sermon.

weapons glitter. The princes "wore uniform coats of pale yellow satin, covered with raised embroideries, and enriched with pearls and precious stones. It was observed that, with the exception of the bridegroom, all the Protestants affected very simple dress, while the Catholic nobles displayed the greatest ostentation."[1] The Venetian ambassador, Giovanni Michieli, was dazzled by the quantity of precious stones exhibited. He says, "the cap, the poniard, and the raiment of the King represented five or six hundred thousand écus. Monsieur d'Anjou, among other jewels on his cap, had thirty-two pearls of twelve carats, famous pearls bought for the occasion at Gonella at a cost of twenty-three thousand golden écus. More than a hundred and twenty ladies were brilliant in the most splendid stuffs, brocade, cloth-of-gold, velvet brocaded in gold and laced with silver."

The bride appeared conducted by the King, her brother. She has herself described her splendid costume. She was "dressed royally, with the crown and *couët* of speckled ermine" (the *couët* was a piece of fur which, beginning below the breast, wound around the figure to the waist). She wore on her shoulders a large blue mantle, with a train four ells long, which was carried by three princesses. On arriving in front of the church the youthful spouses were married by Cardinal Bourbon according to a

---

[1] *Histoire de Marguerite de Valois*, par A. Mongey.

particular formula agreed upon by the two parties. "Marguerite, on being asked whether she accepted the King of Navarre as her husband, replied not a single word; this disquieting the Cardinal, he gave her a little push at the back of the head to make her give that sign of consent in lieu of speech. . . . It was at this moment that the Duke of Guise, who had stretched up above the other nobles to watch Marguerite's face and eyes, received such a keen and threatening glance from Charles IX. that he nearly lost consciousness."[1] The surrounding crowd was hostile, but made no murmur. Only, when the Mass began, and the Protestant gentlemen went to promenade in the cloister of Notre-Dame while it was being said, the Catholics looked angry. At the end of the ceremony, Henry of Navarre embraced his wife. They returned afterwards to the bishop's house, where a superb repast had been prepared, during which heralds-at-arms flung gold medals to the crowd, engraven with the initials of the married pair, interlaced and surrounded with the motto: " *Constricta hoc discordia vinclo.* This tie fetters discord." On other medals there was a lamb and a cross with the device: " *Vobis annuntio pacem.* I announce peace to you."

There was a ball at the Louvre in the evening. On silver rocks and gilded shells women appeared disguised as nymphs, naiads, and goddesses. The celebrated Etienne Leroy sang in his melodious voice.

---

[1] A. Mongey.

All the pomps of mythology were brought into requisition, and the court poets had rivalled each other in their nuptial odes.

The festivities were still more brilliant two days later. The Duke of Anjou, who directed it, had devised an allegorical entertainment whose truly infernal significance was not fully understood until several days afterward. In a hall of the Bourbon palace, neighboring the Louvre, a paradise had been constructed whose entrance was defended by the King and his two brothers, fully armed. On the opposite side was hell, "in which there were many devils and little imps making a racket and playing monkey tricks, and a great wheel, entirely surrounded by little bells, revolving in the said hell. Paradise and hell were divided by a river in which there was a bark conducted by Charon. At one end of the hall were the Elysian fields, that is to say, a garden adorned with foliage and all sorts of flowers, and the empyrean heaven, which was a great wheel with the twelve signs of the zodiac, the seven planets, and numberless little stars. . . . This wheel was in continual motion, and caused also the revolution of this garden in which were twelve richly accoutred nymphs."[1] Several knights-errant led by the King of Navarre, presented themselves at the gate of Paradise. But the three paladins, who guarded its entrance (Charles IX. and his two brothers), repulsed

---

[1] *Mémoires d'État de France sous Charles IX.*

them, sword in hand, and pushed them into Tartarus, where they were dragged away by devils and furies. Meanwhile the nymphs began to dance a ballet which lasted over an hour. The Protestant knights still remained in hell, and those of their coreligionists, who witnessed this strange spectacle, found the allegory by no means agreeable. At last a Mercury and a Cupid, borne by a fantastic animal, descended from heaven. The singer, Etienne Leroy, played the part of Mercury. He intoned a hymn in honor of the conciliation, and Charles IX. went to deliver the captives imprisoned in Tartarus. Afterwards there were fireworks, and the whole palace seemed to be in flames.

Never had the King and the Queen-mother displayed more gaiety. Admiral Coligny was wholly joyful, and ridiculed the alarms of the Huguenots who had seen an omen and a menace in this mythological allegory. One of them, Lagoiran, thought it prudent to depart, and taking leave of the admiral, he said to him: "I am going away because of the good reception they are giving you, preferring to save myself with the fools rather than to perish with those who esteem themselves wise."

The festivities ended on Thursday by a tourney in front of the Louvre, which was a real masquerade. On one side appeared Charles IX., his two brothers, and the Dukes of Guise and Aumale, disguised as amazons; on the other, the King of Navarre and several nobles of his suite, wearing turbans and Turkish costumes of rich brocade.

The next day (Friday, August 22, 1572), the festivities were at last over, and the courtiers were resting after so many pleasures, when a terrible piece of news began to circulate all of a sudden, and rekindled in an instant the flames that smouldered beneath the ashes. Admiral Coligny, just as he was quitting the Louvre on foot, walking slowly and reading a petition, had been struck by a musket-shot which took off the forefinger of his right hand.

The Protestants accused the Duke of Guise, who had always professed his conviction that Coligny was his father's murderer. Suspicion also hovered about Catherine de' Medici, jealous of the influence exercised over her son by the Huguenots and their chief. When the crime was announced, Charles IX. was playing tennis with Téligny, the admiral's son-in-law, and the Duke of Guise. He furiously broke his racket, exclaiming: "Am I never to have any repose?" Then, after a hasty dinner, he went to the admiral's house, accompanied by the Duke of Anjou and the Queen-mother. "My father," said he, "the pain and the wound are yours; the insult and the outrage mine." He promised a striking vengeance, and showed the most affectionate interest toward the admiral.

He offered the Calvinist nobles lodgings around their chief, invited the King of Navarre and the Prince of Condé to bring their friends to the Louvre to sleep, proposed to the wounded man to come and install himself close to the royal chamber, in the apartments of his sister, the Duchess of Lorraine. Looking at the Guises with a "bad expression and worse words": "It is I who am attacked," said he. "It is all France," added Catherine de' Medici.

In spite of the King's promises the Huguenots were not reassured. They organized a resistance in case the instigators of the murder were not punished. The admiral sent in all haste for six thousand troopers and ten thousand Swiss. Threatening shouts were uttered before the Guise mansion. The Catholics also repaired to arms. The markets, the trades, the confraternities, the monks, were all in agitation.

As for Charles IX., he wavered between the most contradictory ideas, and as yet knew not what direction his anger would take. Catherine was sometimes an object of respect, sometimes of aversion to him, and he thought himself by turns protected and betrayed by her. His jealousy and suspicion included not only his mother, but his brothers, his ministers, and all the great nobles. There were still moments when Coligny seemed to him a loyal subject, a great captain about to open to him magnificent horizons of glory and conquest. At others he remembered the civil wars that had been directed by this famous rebel.

During this time Catherine was trembling. There was a war to the death between her and the admiral, cloaked under the appearances of reciprocal courtesy. She told herself that if Coligny got the upper hand, he would throw on her the responsibility for his attempted assassination; that she would be in disgrace, and, perhaps, even exiled in company with her favorite son, the Duke of Anjou. The King was escaping from her. She wanted to regain him. She sent to him Count de Retz, Chancellor Birague, Marshal de Tavannes, and the Duke of Nevers, who took every means to irritate the irascible monarch against Coligny and his adherents. They reminded him of that day at Meaux when he had nearly been abducted by the rebels, — a memory which made on his pride "the impression of a red-hot iron on a wound." They told him that if he, the King, were unwilling to put himself at the head of the Catholics, the Duke of Guise would become their supporter, their idol, possibly their chief; that, outflanked simultaneously by the two opposing factions, the royal authority would be crushed and ruined; that the hour had come to end the plots and conspiracies once for all; that it was needful to make himself dreaded before making himself beloved. The young monarch hesitated still.

XII

CATHERINE DE' MEDICI AND THE SAINT BARTHOLOMEW

THE freshness of a beautiful August night enticed people to defer the hour of slumber. Some Protestants, who were late in returning home, had remarked a certain number of armed men, but had been told by them that they had been ordered for some new tournaments to be given the next day. All alarm had been dispelled. The Huguenots reposed in peace.

Apparently, the Louvre had never been more tranquil. Catherine de' Medici, with her daughters, Madame Claude, Duchess of Lorraine, and Marguerite, Queen of Navarre, beside her, seemed entirely at ease and held her usual drawing-room. The Duchess had been forewarned of what was going to happen. Marguerite knew absolutely nothing about it. She gives a curious account of this scene in her Memoirs: "The Huguenots suspected me because I was Catholic, and the Catholics because I had married the King of Navarre, who was a Huguenot. So much so that no one said anything about it to me until in the evening, when I was at the couchee of the Queen, my mother, sitting on a box near my sister of Lorraine, whom I observed to be very sad, the Queen, my mother, who was speaking to several persons, noticed me and told me to go to bed. As I was making my courtesy, my sister took me by the arm and stopped me, and beginning to cry very hard said to me: 'My God! sister, do not go there!' which frightened me extremely. The Queen, my mother, saw this, and calling my sister scolded her very much, and forbade her to say anything to me."

The Duchess of Lorraine, who knew that in a few moments the Calvinist nobles were to have their throats cut close to the chamber of the Queen of Navarre, entreated Catherine to keep her daughter with her. "My sister said to my mother," adds Marguerite, "that there was no advantage in sending me to be sacrificed like that, and that without doubt, if they discovered anything, they would revenge themselves on me. The Queen, my mother, replied that if it pleased God no harm would come to me, but however that might be, I must go lest they should suspect something. . . . I plainly saw they were contesting some point, but I did not hear their words. She roughly ordered me again to go to bed. My sister, bursting into tears, bade me good-night without daring to say anything else; and I went off quite dismayed and bewildered, without being able to imagine what I had to fear. As soon as I was in my chamber, I began to pray God to be pleased to take me under His protection, and keep me safe without knowing why or wherefore."

When she entered her apartments, Marguerite found her husband there surrounded by thirty or forty Huguenots. All night long they talked of nothing but the admiral's wound, and determined to demand justice from the King as soon as day broke. "For me," says the Queen, "my sister's tears were constantly in my mind, and I could not sleep for the apprehension they had put me in. Thus the night went by without my closing my eyes." But already the dawn of Saint Bartholomew's day had begun to whiten the horizon. It would soon be four o'clock in the morning. The King of Navarre said he would go and play tennis until King Charles should awaken. He went out with his nobles, and began a game of tennis in the lower halls of the Louvre. "For me, seeing that it was day, concluding that the danger my sister had spoken of was over, heavy with sleep, I told my nurse to fasten the door so that I might sleep at my ease. As I was sleeping, a man came rapping at the door with feet and hands and crying: 'Navarre! Navarre!' My nurse, thinking it was the King, my husband, ran quickly to the door. It was a gentleman named M. de Tejean, who had a sword thrust in the elbow, and a halberd thrust in the arm, and who was still pursued by four archers who followed close after him into the chamber. He, desiring to save himself, threw himself on my bed. Feeling these men who were holding me, I threw myself between the bed and the wall, and he after me, keeping me all the time across his body."

M. de Tejean was saved from death by Marguerite. As to the other Calvinists, lodged like him in the Louvre, "the archers pricked them from chamber to chamber, so that they should throw themselves down the stairs, or through the windows of the court, where slaughterers drawn up in ranks, with serried pikes, would receive and finish them." Throwing a night mantle over her shoulders, the Queen of Navarre started for the chamber of her sister, Madame de Lorraine, which she reached more dead than alive. At the moment she entered it, a gentleman named Bourse, trying to escape from the archers who pursued him, was pierced by a halberd not three steps away from her.

It is related that the wife of Charles IX., the gentle and pious Elisabeth, awakened by the noise, and advised of what was going on, exclaimed: "Does the King know it?" She was told that it was he who had commanded it. "O my God!" then said the Queen, "I entreat Thee to pardon him, for unless Thou hast pity, I greatly fear this offence will never be forgiven." And bursting into tears, she asked for her book of Hours, and spent all the night in prayers.

While the soul of the good Queen was thus in company with the angels, demons rent the heart of Catherine de' Medici. Tavannes and Villeroy agree in saying that at the last moment she was frightened by her own resolve; that she grew giddy before the abyss; "that she would willingly have recalled it."

Some hours before, Charles IX., hoping to stifle his sinister thoughts by violent exercise, had begun to forge with savage eagerness. When the tocsin sounded, it is said that he, his mother, and his brother, "struck with terror and apprehension of the great disorders about to be committed,"[1] relapsed into hesitation and sent an order to stop the massacre. But it was late. The sun had risen, it lighted up the carnage.

There have been many controversies concerning the quota of responsibility incurred by Charles IX. and his mother. Our own opinion is that a distinction must be made between the King and Catherine. We believe that the monarch should not be accused of premeditation, that "the night, the unexpected situation, the thought of having in the Louvre itself thirty or forty of the most redoubtable Protestants, a Pardaillan, a de Piles, the first swordsmen of France,"[2] all combined to inspire him with a terror which made him suddenly take a resolution.

The reflections made on this subject by M. Merimée in the preface to his *Chronique du temps de Charles IX.* seem to us full of justice. He says: "I cannot admit that the same men could have been able to conceive a crime whose results must be so important, and to execute it so badly. The measures, in fact, were so ill taken that several months after the Saint Bartholomew the war broke out afresh, the

---

[1] Villeroy's Memoirs.   [2] Michelet, *Guerres de religion.*

reformers certainly winning all the glory of it, and retiring from it with new advantages. In fine, is not the assault on Coligny which took place two days before the Saint Bartholomew, sufficient to refute the supposition of a conspiracy? Why kill the chief before the general massacre? Was not this the way to alarm the Huguenots and put them on their guard?" M. Merimée also remarks that the Duke of Guise, threatened by the King and by the Protestants, suddenly sought a support among the people. "He assembles the leaders of the citizen guard, talks to them about a conspiracy of heretics, makes them promise to exterminate them before it breaks out, and the massacre is not thought of until then. As but few hours elapse between the plan and its execution, it is easy to explain the mystery with which the plot was enveloped, and the secret so well guarded by so many men, which would otherwise appear very extraordinary, since confidences fly fast in Paris."

Marguerite's Memoirs, written in simple terms, and with a remarkable accent of impartiality, say explicitly that it was with great difficulty that the Queen-mother extorted the King's authorization of the massacre. "They had a great deal of trouble to make him consent, and if they had not given him to understand that he was about to lose his life and his kingdom he would never have done it. . . . And the Queen, my mother, was never so perplexed as in trying to demonstrate to the said King Charles that this was for the good of his kingdom, on account of the affection he had for M. the Admiral, La Nouë, and Téligny, whose wit and worth he appreciated, being so generous a prince that he never liked any but those in whom he recognized such qualities."

We do not hesitate to think that Catherine was more guilty than Charles IX. She had brought to court, some days before, the widow of Duke Francis of Guise, that woman in whose veins flowed together the blood of Louis XII. and that of the Borgias, and who had declared a *vendetta* against Coligny. The admiral was the Queen-mother's bitterest enemy; and in the view of M. Armand Baschet, whose judgments on this epoch always carry so much weight, it is beyond doubt "that she had meditated and premeditated the death of this redoubtable enemy." Giovanni Michieli, who is usually rather sympathetic than hostile to Catherine, throws the whole responsibility of the crime upon her, attributing to her the attempt on Coligny and the massacre of August 24.

"Your Serenity must know," he says in his relation, "that from beginning to end this whole action has been the Queen's work, arranged, plotted, and directed by her with no aid but that of Mgr. d'Anjou, her son. It is a long time since the Queen conceived this project, as she herself has just reminded her relative, Mgr. Salviati, the present nuncio at court, calling him to witness that she had secretly charged him to acquaint the late Pope, that as soon as possible His Holiness should see what vengeance the King would take on those belonging to the religion.

"According to what she says, this was her only reason for desiring so greatly the marriage between her daughter and the King of Navarre, and thinking lightly of the Portugal marriage, as well as of the other great alliances offered her, because she wished the nuptials to take place at Paris with the intervention of the admiral and the other leaders; she had reflected well, and comprehended that there was no surer way to draw them thither." If the testimony of Giovanni Michieli is of importance, that of the Spanish ambassador is not less interesting. In a despatch of September 6, 1572,[1] Don Diego de Zuniga writes to his government that the admiral's death had been premeditated but that that of the others was sudden. The nuncio, Salviati, who represented the Pope at the French court, affirms in his despatches[2] that if the *archibusiata*, that is, the musket-shot fired at Coligny by Maurevel had succeeded, the Queen-mother would not have resolved on the massacre. He is also of opinion that Charles IX. had not been admitted to the secret of the attempt of August 22. Marguerite of Valois does not hesitate to declare in her Memoirs, that her mother entirely approved of this first attempt at murder, and greatly regretted its failure. The opinion of Brantôme must also be cited, who says in speaking of Catherine: "She has been strongly accused of the Paris massacre. I could

---

[1] Archives of Simancas.
[2] *Annales ecclésiastiques*, by Père Theiner.

name three or four others who were more eager about it than she, and who urged her forcibly, deceiving her with the notion that the threats made on account of the admiral's wound would lead to the slaying of the King, herself, and her children, and the whole court: as to which, it is certain that those of the religion were very wrong to make such threats as they were said to make, for thereby they aggravated the poor admiral's trouble and procured his death. For if they had kept quiet and not said a word, and allowed the admiral to recover, he could afterwards have departed from Paris very comfortably and quite at his ease."

The controversy which now divides historians raged equally among Catherine's contemporaries. "Although there are still those who cannot rid themselves of the notion that this train had been laid long beforehand, and the plot brooded over," Brantôme dismisses the idea of premeditation, so far, at least, as the Saint Bartholomew is concerned. Such also appears to be the opinion of M. Michelet. "Marguerite acquaints us," he says, "that on Sunday, August 24, the Huguenots were to come in a body and denounce Guise formally in presence of the King. Guise, against whom so many proofs could be adduced, neither could nor would deny a stroke which raised him so high in the favor of Catholics; but he would have said that he had done nothing except by order of legitimate authority, that of the Duke of Anjou, lieutenant-general of the realm.

Anjou and Catherine were about to be convicted of having attempted Coligny's murder, because Coligny was urging the King to banish his dangerous heir from France. Anjou might well have perished at the hands of a man so sudden and violent as Charles IX., and Catherine, so often threatened with being sent back to Italy, would probably, on this stroke, have taken the road to Florence." This would explain her desperate effort to induce Charles IX. to give the fatal signal. What does it matter, in any case, whether the catastrophe was one of long or short premeditation? There are deeds for which neither excuses nor attenuating circumstances can be pleaded, and certain rehabilitations can be nothing more than paradoxes.

XIII

ELISABETH OF AUSTRIA AND CHARLES IX.

CATHERINE DE' MEDICI could not wholly forget either the counsels of L'Hôpital, or those of her former confessor, Thomasseau,[1] that tolerant priest whose interesting figure has been already sketched by M. Faugère in his fine *Etude sur le courage civil*. She could not succeed in stifling the voice of conscience. "Although the habit of dissimulation as well as age had formed for her that abbess's mask, wan yet full of depth, which is so remarkable to those who have studied her portrait, the courtiers observed some shadows cross that Florentine mirror."[2] The woman, formerly mild and attractive, who had been hitherto the image of conciliation, now inspired terror.

Charles did not love his mother much, and did not endure patiently the yoke she laid upon him. At this moment the chief object of the King's affection was his mistress, Marie Touchet, only daughter of Jean Touchet, lieutenant of the bailiwick of Orléans.

---

[1] Thomasseau was disgraced at the same time as his friend L'Hôpital, in 1568.

[2] Honoré de Balzac, *Étude sur Catherine de' Medici*.

Little is known of this woman, whose rank was between that of the citizens and the smaller nobility, and who played no part at all in politics. We only know that she was born in 1549, and that she was sixteen when Charles IX. began to love her. She had a son by him who was recognized and wore the royal arms with the title of Count of Auvergne, and afterwards with that of Duke of Angoulême. It is said that when the marriage of the King was about to be concluded, she said, on looking at the portrait of the future Queen: "I am not afraid of this German woman." The young monarch vainly essayed to shake off the trammels of this beauty. He always came back to Marie Touchet. He had given her an estate near the castle of Vincennes where she went in the evening when Charles, after hunting, rested himself in this royal abode.

But neither the love of his mistress, the flattery of his courtiers, the applause of fanatics, nor the dazzling luxury of a court full of amusements, could any longer soothe the melancholy temper of the King. "At this time," says Honoré de Balzac, "he was distinguished by a sombre majesty. The grandeur of his secret thoughts was reflected on his visage, remarkable for the Italian tint that he had inherited from his mother. This ivory pallor, so beautiful by lamplight, so favorable to the expressions of melancholy, set off the brilliancy of his deep-blue eyes." Jealous of his brother, the Duke of Anjou, he was glad to see him start for Poland. But the splendid festivities given on this occasion did not succeed in diverting him. He smiled no more.

Complete light has been thrown on this curious episode of the Duke of Anjou's brief royalty in Poland by a work of great historical value. Its author, the Marquis Emmanuel de Noailles, describes very well the jealousy of the two brothers, the attitude of the Polish nobility, the manœuvres of Catherine and her diplomatic agent, Bishop Montluc, to place a son of France on the ancient throne of the Jagellons. One should read in this fine book the details of the entry of the Polish ambassadors into Paris, and the magnificent entertaiments Catherine offered them at the Tuileries. Then was beheld, says Brantôme, "the most beautiful ballet that ever was, composed of sixteen of the fairest and best-trained ladies and misses, who appeared in a silvered rock where they were seated in niches, shut in on every side. The sixteen ladies represented the sixteen provinces of France. After having made the round of the hall for parade as in a camp, they all descended and ranging themselves in the form of a little and oddly contrived battalion, some thirty violins began a very pleasant war-like air to which they danced their ballet." Then they bore to the kings and queens golden plaques on which were engraved the "fruits and singularities of each province," the wheat of Champagne, the vines of Burgundy, the lemons and oranges of Provence. But none of these allegories had power to amuse Charles IX. any longer, and like the victims of ancient fatality, he had no further acquaintance with joy.

It is curious to observe how exactly the later Valois represented their epoch. Francis I. had personified the Renaissance, Charles IX. sums up in himself all the crises of the religious wars. He is the true type of a morbid and disturbed society where all is violent; where the blood is scorched by the double fevers of pleasure and cruelty; where the human soul, without guide or compass, is tossed amid storms; where fanaticism is joined to debauchery, superstition to incredulity, the culture of intelligence to depravity of heart. This wholly unbalanced character, which plunges from one extreme to the other, which stretches evil to its utmost limits while preserving the vocation to and knowledge of what is good, which mistrusts everybody and yet has, if not the experience, at least the aspiration after friendship and love, is it not the symbol and living image of its time? The account-book of the King during the Saint Bartholomew year indicates the contradictory tendencies of his strange nature. "Here one sees his barbarous instincts manifested in the indemnity he allows to a poor man whose cow he had given to his dogs to eat; here again he buys a mule to be devoured by the lions in the royal menagerie; then, at the side of these bloody caprices, we see him granting assistance to poor students, so that they may continue their studies, or sending a considerable sum to a gentleman of Cyprus, so that he may deliver from the hands of Turkish corsairs his brother and five of his sisters."[1] This monarch, born for enthusiasm, condemns himself to scepticism. Worthy by his instincts to become a great King, he will end by being nothing but a wretched despot, and by showing what an evil education can make of a noble heart and a lofty intelligence.

There was lacking to Charles IX., as well as to Catherine de' Medici, the quality necessary to private persons, and still more necessary to sovereigns: the moral sense. The son has all his mother's defects; but the crafty Florentine, at least, knows how to dissimulate the vices of her soul under a seeming tranquillity: she has the hypocrisy of mildness. Access to her is easy, her conversation is insinuating, her politeness exquisite. Charles, on the contrary, during the two latter years of his life, talks and acts like a madman. His rages border on epilepsy. His countenance, once agreeable, has become savage. "His looks are gloomy, *guardatura malincolica*," says the Venetian ambassador, Sigismond Cavalli. "In his interviews and audiences he never looks those who are speaking to him in the face. He lowers his head, closes his eyes, then opens them suddenly, and as if this movement pained him, he closes them again not less suddenly. It is feared that the spirit of vengeance has taken possession of him. He seeks

---

[1] M. Eudel du Gord, *Recueil de documents historiques sur les derniers Valois.*

fatigue at any cost. He remains on horseback for twelve or fourteen hours together. Thus he goes chasing and running through the woods after the same stag for two or three days, never stopping but to eat, and resting only for a moment at night. Hence his hands are callous, rough, and full of cuts and blisters."[1]

Charles IX., tormented by an unhealthy need of activity, pushes his amusements to convulsive fury. What he calls his pleasures would be cruel sufferings to others. When he winds his horn he blows as if to break his lungs. If he fences, or plays tennis, it is with frenzy. To escape from himself, to tear himself from his gloomy thoughts, he requires incredible fatigues. "This King," says Sigismond Cavalli again, "pushes his search after violent exercise so far as to pound an anvil three or four hours at a time, using an enormous hammer, forging a cuirass, or any other kind of solid armor, and nothing makes him vainer than to tire out his rivals. When one of them gives up the contest, His Majesty derives a marvellous pleasure from it."

This continual over-excitement exhausts the unhappy monarch. Premature wrinkles betray the inward efforts of a tired organization to provide for the labors of intelligence and the violent exertions of the body. At once artist and huntsman, poet and blacksmith, Charles IX., worn out by passion, and

[1] Sigismond Cavalli, *Relazione della Corte di Francia.*

victimized by the flame that devours him, soon becomes a physical and mental wreck. At the hour when his forces betray him he is seized by an invincible sadness. More to be pitied than Tantalus, he sees glory but cannot attain to it. He longs to wrest France from factions, in order to make it enter upon its true destinies, by a noble and valorous spring towards its natural frontiers. He longs to retemper his soul in new emotions; to make the chase give way to war; to hear, not the hunting-horn but the sound of the trumpet in battle. War! war! is thenceforth his fixed idea. One day he calls the men of his suite to show them a black spot he has under his shoulder. "If I die in a battle," he says to them, "this will be a sign by which you can recognize me."— "Sire, do not think of that. Why such a foreboding?"— "Do you think," returns the King, "that I would rather die in my bed than in a battle?"

After fever comes debility, and after exasperation, exhaustion. The frenzied monarch, conquered by bodily and mental torments, became once more good and gentle. The Huguenot nurse who had rocked the infant appeased and consoled the King. There were moments when the tyrant disappeared to give place to a young man who would have desired to revive to hope, love, and life, and who was already growing cold in the shadows of death. Music, that great consoler which gives charm and poetry to sadness, sometimes gave him a moment's respite. Harmony tranquillized him as it did Saul. It is said that in the last days of his existence, so short in time, so long in suffering, he summoned Marie Touchet, who loved in him — or so he believed — the man and not the king. It was time to say farewell. Charles IX. would have liked to live, to be happy, to be just, to be clement, to make himself beloved. At last he understood his mission, his power, and his resources. "But this light was burning in a broken lamp."[1] The moment had come to quit the throne for the tomb. Having been told of an insurrection: "At least," cried the unhappy King, "they might have waited for my death. 'Tis too much to begrudge me that!" Nothing is more melancholy than the end of this prince, upon whom in his death-struggle were heaped all the agonies of his century, the most tragical of all these epochs.

"Ah! my nurse, my own," said he, "how much blood and murder! Ah! what wicked counsels I have followed! O my God, pardon me for them, if it please Thee!" Who would not grow compassionate with Chateaubriand over "this Catholic monarch yielding up his soul amidst remorse, vomiting his blood, sobbing aloud, shedding floods of tears, forsaken by all the world, aided and consoled only by a Huguenot nurse."

The only historian unwilling to believe in the moral tortures of Charles IX. is M. Capefigue, who claims that "the gaiety of this prince never aban-

---

[1] Honoré de Balzac.

doned him for a single instant." The ambassador, Sigismond Cavalli, is not of this opinion. He says that horrible memories disturbed the King to the last extremity and he could find no rest. "*Le congiure sopradette lo cruciavano estremamente, ne mai poteva pigliar requie.*" No, no: do not try to destroy the high morality involved in the spectacle of this great anguish, nor cast a doubt on the testimony of all the contemporaries of a monarch who deserves pity more than hatred. If he is deprived of his sorrows, his tears, his despair, there is nothing left but a monster. Do not seek to rob him of the only thing that can absolve him: his remorse.

The premature death of Charles IX. fulfilled a prophecy already famous. As far back as 1560, the Venetian ambassador, Michieli, had written concerning the death of Francis II. and the malady of the future Henry III.: "This reminds me of a prediction, very popular in France, of the famous astrologer, Nostradamus, which menaces the life of all the princes by saying that the Queen will see all of them on the throne." Catherine had not desired the death of Charles IX. any more than that of Francis II. But by putting blind faith in this prediction of three kings, she expected its fulfilment, and believed it inevitable. Moreover, the dying man had appointed her regent until the arrival of the King of Poland, now King of France. It was a consolation.

Charles IX. was hardly dead before he was forgotten. Yet there was one woman who formed an exception to the general indifference, and who mourned for him from the bottom of her soul: it was his faithful and chaste companion, Elisabeth of Austria. "She loved and honored him extremely," says Brantôme; "although he had mistresses, she never received him ill nor said hard words to him on that account, but patiently endured the wrong he did her." Again Brantôme describes her during her husband's last illness, seated near the dying man, "not close to the head of his bed but at a little distance; as long as she remained there she kept her eyes so fixed upon him that you would have said she was brooding over him in her heart for the love she bore him.... It excited pity in every one to see her so distressed, yet making no display of her sorrow or her love, and without the King's observing it.... She regretted him extremely."[1] For a moment one forgets scenes of horror and carnage to contemplate this sweet German woman, whose gentleness is in such contrast with all her surroundings. Raising her soul to God, she sheds the holy tears which extinguish the fires of hell. Shouts of anger and vengeance no longer re-echo in our ears. We hear nothing but the pious murmur of a voice that prays. We behold a woman who is weeping.

Charles IX. died on Whitsunday, May 30, 1574, in the twenty-fifth year of his age and the fifteenth

---

[1] Brantôme, *Elisabeth d'Autriche.*

of his reign. He left a daughter, Elisabeth of France, born in 1572, who lived only five years and a half. According to Brantôme, she had "the largest heart and mind ever seen in such a little creature. . . . Young as she was, she knew how to preserve her dignity as well as if she had been older. When people went to see her in her chamber and pay her reverence, she would put out her hand to be kissed as prettily as the Queen, her mother, would have done. . . . She shamed the oldest, so much so that people said she had too much intelligence and would not live long." This prediction was soon realized. The widow of Charles IX. had to mourn both her husband and her only daughter. "Ah! Madame," was said to her one day, "what a misfortune that you have no son; your lot would be less pitiful, and you would be Queen-mother and Regent!"—"Alas!" she answered, "do not make such a disagreeable remark. As if France had not afflictions enough without my producing another to complete its ruin. For, if I had a son, there would be more divisions, troubles, and seditions to obtain the administration and guardianship during his infancy and minority, and every one would try to profit himself by despoiling the poor child, as they wanted to do with the late King, my husband." Brantôme, in quoting this touching response, has reason for paying homage to the angelic goodness of a princess whose thoroughly Christian modesty and humility are like an expiation for the pride, ambition, and cruelty of her contemporaries. This holy widow did not remain in France. She returned to Austria, near the Emperor Rudolph, her brother, and erected a convent, the nuns of which she treated as friends. She employed her jointures of Beny, Bourbonnais, Forez, and La Marche, in benefiting those provinces. When her sister-in-law, Marguerite of Valois, fell into disgrace and lost her resources, Elisabeth was the only person who took pity on her; she shared her jointure with her like a true sister. Faithful to the memory of the husband whom she had profoundly loved, and resolved "not to forget him in a second marriage," she refused to ascend the throne of Spain, and died, calm and collected, at the age of thirty-five, having desired no other majesty in her widowhood but the majesty of sorrow.

XIV

LOUISE DE VAUDEMONT AND HENRY III.

CATHERINE DE' MEDICI sent a circular to the governors of the provinces to apprise them of the death of Charles IX. "The loss I have experienced," she said in it, "has so overwhelmed me with grief, that my only desire is to abandon all affairs in order to seek tranquillity of life; nevertheless, yielding to the urgent request he made in his last moments, I have constrained myself to accept the regency he committed to me, and I entreat you to maintain your authority, and prevent all undertakings which might disturb the public peace."

During the three months (May 30–September 5, 1574) in which she held the reins of power, Catherine's chief effort was to maintain the *statu quo*, and to render easy the beginning of the reign of her favorite son, he who was, in the words of a Venetian ambassador, "the right eye and the soul of his mother. *Questo è l' occhio destro e l' anima della madre.*" When there was any negotiating or temporizing to be done, this politic woman felt herself in her element. As Sismondi has well said, "She had arrived at the conviction that she had no equal in craft and subtlety; she practised intrigue like a game wherein her talents shone with the utmost brilliancy and her vanity was flattered by daily successes."

As the times grew more difficult her activity was redoubled. Anxious to see and to do everything herself, incessantly writing to everybody, practising espionage on a grand scale, and always preferring a crooked road to a straight one for arriving at her object, the crafty Florentine, mistress of herself, gracious, obliging, never allowing her sentiments to be divined, "supposing that she still had sentiments," appeared to her contemporaries as the embodiment of address and dissimulation. She was fifty-four years old when Henry III. succeeded to the crown. "If she had had gallantries before this, which is in nowise proved, thenceforward, at all events, her mind was entirely bent on public intrigues: she knew the most secret actions and even the thoughts of those about her court; by means of their rivalries and hatreds she made them equally dependent on her, and prided herself on so using their passions, or vices, as to make them act according to her views."[1]

Notwithstanding the pleasure she took in governing alone, Catherine impatiently awaited Henry III. The King of France and Poland had fled from Cracovia like a robber five days after learning of his brother's death, June 18, 1574. The short stay he had

---

[1] Sismondi, *Histoire de France.*

made in the country demonstrated that he had come there against his will. Among those haughty Sarmatians he had complained like Ovid on the shores of the Euxine Sea. "He wore that crown," says the historian, Pierre Matthieu, "like a rock on his head."[1] He found his greatest diversion in writing to France. He sometimes despatched forty or fifty letters from his own hand by a single courier. "The ladies whom he had not lost sight of had the best part of his labor." He was parading at the time an enthusiastic passion for the wife of the Prince of Condé, Marie of Cleves, daughter of Francis, Duke of Nevers, and Marguerite of Bourbon, a sister of Louis I., Prince of Condé. The young princess, who had only been married two years, shone equally by wit and beauty as by birth and riches. If she had not surrendered to her lover, she had certainly not remained insensible to the homage which so greatly flattered her feminine vanity. It appears that she did not even reject the idea of a divorce, for which her husband's relapse into heresy would have afforded the pretext.

Henry, who gave her hopes of the crown, wrote her the most passionate letters from Cracovia, in blood drawn from his own finger. Souvray, his secretary, opened and closed the puncture whenever it was necessary to refill the pen. His desire to see

---

[1] *Histoire de France*, by Pierre Matthieu, counsellor and historiographer to the King. Paris, 1631.

the princess again was one of the reasons which determined Henry to flee suddenly from Poland. After having retired for the night in presence of his Polish courtiers, he made his escape as soon as he heard them leave his chamber. Accompanied by Miron, his physician, and by Souvray, Larchant, and Du Halde, he noiselessly opened a door of the castle which gave on the open country. He walked a quarter of a league, by a moonless and starless night, until he reached a little chapel where horses were awaiting him. He set spur and galloped twenty leagues. Several Polish gentlemen, who undertook to pursue him, did not catch up with him until he was in Moravia. He tried to excuse his strange departure by means of the advices sent him by his mother. Then, showing the portrait of the Princess of Condé, he added: "It is chiefly love which urges my return to France; I do not know how to love either my friends or my mistress feebly, as you will find on my return to Poland."

Hardly had Henry escaped from his faithful subjects than he experienced a diminution in the love he had alleged as an excuse for his precipitate flight. Instead of returning to France without loss of time, in order to throw himself at the feet of his beloved, he remained eleven days in Austria and two months in Italy. In spite of his recent loss, he went from one festivity to another. Going on board the *Bucentaur* he made a formal entry into Venice. The Papal Nuncio was on the right hand of his throne

and the Doge on the left. Thus he crossed the Grand
Canal, glittering with illuminations, and landed at
the Foscari palace. For several days there was a
constant succession of ovations, banquets, fireworks
on the water, jousts, and rejoicings. These festivities were renewed at Padua, Ferrara, Mantua, and
Turin. The elegantly sensual atmosphere of the
Italian cities charmed the most voluptuous of monarchs. At last, on September 5, he reached the
frontier of his kingdom. Catherine de' Medici received him at Pont-de-Beauvoisin with the greatest
demonstrations of affection, and on the following
day he entered Lyons, where he remained two whole
months. His character soon revealed itself in a most
unfavorable aspect. Allowing none to approach him
but some youthful favorites, he spent his days on
the Saône, in a little painted boat surrounded with
curtains. When he dined, a balustrade placed in
front of his table prevented the courtiers from coming near him. He had the manners of a satrap. At
Lyons he heard of the death of the Princess of Condé,
who expired in giving birth to a daughter, October
30. At first he showed great despair on receiving
this news. Giving to his sorrow the character of
puerility which was always manifest in his tastes
and passions, "he remained for eight days in sighs
and cries," says Pierre Matthieu, "and appeared in
public entirely covered with the insignia and tokens
of death. He wore little death's heads on his shoe
ribbons. He had them on his shoulder knots, and

ordered Souvray to procure him six thousand écus' worth of this kind of trimmings." Shut up day and night in an apartment hung with black, he kissed the portrait of the princess, and a lock of her hair. He called on her with loud cries as if she could respond to his voice. But all these tears and sobs did not witness to a real sorrow. Henry III. knew neither how to love nor how to suffer. At the end of eight days one of his favorites abstracted the portrait, the sight of which nourished his grief. The King was not very urgent in demanding it back again, and after the next day he never again named the poor dead woman.

He quitted Lyons, November 16, and instead of turning towards Paris, he went down the Rhone to visit Avignon. This papal city pleased him greatly. Here he affiliated himself to one of those confraternities of penitents, or flagellants, who were called "the beaten, *les battus*," because they struck their backs and shoulders with whips in penance for their sins. With heads covered by hoods, with no apertures except for the eyes, they went through the streets at night, by torchlight, chanting the *Miserere.* There were three confraternities, the whites, the blacks, and the blues. Following the King's example, the court ladies also enrolled themselves in the congregations. Catherine de' Medici put on sackcloth and publicly received the discipline. Not a soul, even to the Béarnais, the future Henry IV., but figured among the penitents. But Henry III., who found him not altogether apt at this rôle, accused him of not knowing how to wear the hair shirt. The Princess of Condé was a thing of the past, and radically consoled by the sight of the processions of flagellants, the King of France and Poland, delighted to have banished an importunate memory, was now full of thoughts of marriage.

When he had stopped at Vienna for several days on his return from Poland, the Emperor Maximilian II. had secretly proposed to him a union with the widow of Charles IX., Elisabeth of Austria. The King did not reject the proposition; but as his sister-in-law was not much to his taste, he soon forgot the offer that had been made him. A young person whom he had seen some months before at Nancy, Louise, daughter of Nicholas of Lorraine, Count of Vaudémont, had made a lasting impression on him. Born at Noméni, near Metz, in 1553, she lost her mother almost as soon as she was born, but her education had, nevertheless, been carefully attended to.

A character of exquisite sweetness distinguishes her beauty and her piety; her thoroughly Christian modesty and humility are reflected in her countenance. There was nothing brilliant from the pecuniary point of view in the position of her family, and no one could have suspected that the daughter of the Count of Vaudémont would one day become the Queen of France. As she was related by ties of consanguinity to the Guise family, the counsellors of Henry III. sought to deter him from the marriage by representing the dangers that might arise from an inordinate aggrandizement of a house already too powerful. For a moment he seemed shaken in his resolve, even sending Claude Pinart, the Secretary of State, to Stockholm to ask the hand of the sister of the King of Sweden. But Cardinal Lorraine dying while the court was at Avignon, Henry claimed that the Guises had ceased to be formidable, and that nothing now prevented his union with their relative. Claude Pinart was abruptly recalled from Sweden, leaving behind him a sharp resentment in the mind of its sovereign, and Du Guast, Henry's favorite, repaired to Lorraine to ask the Count of Vaudémont whether he would consent to give his daughter to the King of France and Poland.

It is related that Louise was absent when Du Guast arrived. Ever since she was twelve years old, she had gone every week to pray in the chapel of Saint Nicholas, in the neighborhood of Nancy. She always went there on foot, dressed almost as simply as a peasant, and distributed in alms during these days twenty-five écus which her father gave her every month for pocket money.[1] On returning to Nancy she said to her step-mother, who was accustomed to treat her with great severity: "Pardon me, Madame, for not being at your levee this morning." — "It is I who should be at yours," replied the Countess of Vaudémont; "you are Queen of France. I would

---

[1] *Reines et régentes*, by Dreux du Radier.

not let any one else have the joy of telling you this great news; forget, in receiving it, the dissatisfaction I may have given you; and, on the throne where you are to be seated, do not refuse your protection to your brothers, my children, and on their account, to their mother."

Henry III. was crowned at Rheims, February 13, 1575, and married two days afterward. They say the coronation was marked by unlucky omens. The crown did not set well on his forehead and wounded his head. He kept people waiting for hours while the details of his toilet were being perfected, and the coronation Mass was not said until after four o'clock in the afternoon, by torchlight.

In spite of his defects and vices, Henry III. has the merit of making a marriage of inclination with a young girl as amiable as she was worthy of esteem. "This princess deserves great praise," says Brantôme, "for in her marriage she comported herself so wisely, chastely, and loyally with the King, her husband, that the nuptial tie which bound her to him has always remained so firm and indissoluble that it has never been found undone or loosened, even though the King, her husband, sometimes liked and procured a change, according to the custom of the great who keep their own full liberty; moreover, from the very first fine beginnings of their marriage, indeed but ten days after, he deprived her of the chamber-maids and demoiselles who had always been with her and whom she greatly regretted."

Henry III., who was naturally meddlesome and teasing, tormented his wife more than once; but in general he was deferential toward her. He was often seen walking with her in the streets of Paris. He requested the priests of all the churches to expose the tabernacles, which they ornamented with lights and flowers. The King went every day in a coach with the Queen to visit these repositories, and pray and chant litanies before them. On their way back to the Louvre he would stop at the shops and buy birds, monkeys, and little dogs which he tied fast to her belt, or put in a basket which he set on the Queen's lap.

Being very much grieved at having no children, he made novenas and pilgrimages to entreat God not to allow the family of Valois to become extinct. Louise de Vaudémont was equally sorry that their union remained sterile. But this vexation did not alter the sweetness of her character, so different from that of the women of the court. In a society whose very qualities had become defects, where generosity was transformed into mad prodigality, the point of honor into a quarrelsome temper, courage to useless temerity, the taste for art into strange refinements, the women had shared in the general corruption. Their ideas and tastes were as perverted as their morals. Preferring to inspire amazement rather than admiration, they aimed, above all things, at eccentricity. There was always something exaggerated, fictitious about their sentiments, and the gentler emotions no longer sufficed to charm them. Living in a dulled and surfeited epoch, they constantly required unexpected crises, extraordinary incidents, and dramatic situations. They found all passions insipid unless they involved fighting and romantic catastrophes. Whoever aspired to please them must impart a character of oddity, violence, or frenzy to his words and actions. *Billets doux* were written in blood, and ferocity reigned even in pleasure.

The vices of her surroundings throw up into clearer light the virtues of Louise de Vaudémont. Giving umbrage to no one, she yet held aloof from the intrigues and rivalries of which the court was the theatre. All the world respected her. Calumny itself was silent in presence of this good Queen. The agitations around her troubled her not; their noisy tumult did not disturb her prayers. As Saint Augustine says, "The attentive soul makes its own solitude. *Gignit enim sibi ipsa mentis intentio solitudinem.*" The waves of the angry ocean broke at the foot of the altar where the Queen was kneeling. Huguenots and Catholics, leaguers and royalists, united to pay her reverence. They were amazed to see such purity in an atmosphere so corrupt, such gentleness in the midst of a society so violent. Their eyes rested with satisfaction on a countenance whose holy placidity was undisturbed by pride and hatred; and the heroines of the century, wretched in spite of all their amusements and their feverish pursuit of pleasure, made salutary reflections as they contemplated a woman still more highly honored by her virtues than by her crown.

XV

MARGUERITE OF VALOIS AND HENRY OF NAVARRE

THE Queen of France, Louise of Vaudémont, and the Queen of Navarre, Marguerite of Valois, lived at court together. While the one, conducting herself like a saint, was occupied solely in good works and prayers, the other, behaving like a coquette, led a life of pleasures, intrigues, and worldly unrest. The celebrated Queen Margot is a type of the *femme déclassée*. What was lacking to this wonder of wonders? Discretion: that virtue without which all others lose their value. By her faults she wilfully condemned herself to cruel humiliations. She had knowledge, wit, and talent, but no judgment and no wisdom; haughtiness and pride, but no real dignity, no self-respect. Spoiled from her cradle by overstrained flattery, she had lived a wholly factitious life, in an atmosphere of poesy and enchantment. Mobile, impressionable, irritable, capricious, like most over-flattered women, she was constantly seeking diversions and novelties. Dreaming of an impossible felicity, of ideal joys, the glory of a goddess, and the empyrean of a Venus Urania, she would have liked a life of continual enchantments, surprises, and metamorphoses.

The compliments which the courtiers vied with each other in paying her would have turned the head of a more sensible woman. "I remember," says Brantôme, "that a nobleman who had recently arrived at court, and who had never seen the Queen of Navarre, said to me when he caught sight of her: 'I am not surprised, sir, that you all like the court so well; for if you had no other pleasure there than that of daily seeing that beautiful princess, you would have so much that you would be in an earthly paradise.'" The author of the *Dames galantes* records a conversation he had with the poet Ronsard on seeing her enter the grand hall of the Tuileries on the day when Catherine de' Medici gave a supper to the Polish ambassadors: "Tell the truth, sir," he exclaimed (when she made her appearance in a robe of flesh-colored Spanish velvet heavily tinselled, and a bonnet of the same velvet entirely covered with plumes and precious stones), "does it not seem to you that when this beautiful Queen, with her fair face, comes forth in such apparel, she is like Aurora newly born before the day, and that there is much similarity and resemblance in their attire?" M. de Ronsard admitted it, and he made a very fine sonnet on this comparison (which he thought very fine). Marguerite, who was a learned woman, replied in Latin to the address of the Polish ambassadors who, in their enthusiasm, styled her "a second Minerva, or goddess of eloquence." One of them, Leczinski, exclaimed: "No, I wish to see nothing more after such beauty. I would willingly do like the Turkish pilgrims to Mecca, where the tomb of their prophet Mahomet is, who remain so content, so amazed, so enraptured and ravished at beholding so superb a mosque, that they will see nothing else thereafter, and have their eyes burned out with basins of heated brass." Brantôme adds to these ridiculously enthusiastic words: "Truly, if the Poles have been carried away by such admiration, there have been many others like them. I instance Don John of Austria, who, passing through France as secretly as possible, having learned on his arrival at Paris that there was to be a state ball at the Louvre, went thither in disguise, more for the sake of seeing the Queen of Navarre than for anything else; he had opportunity and leisure to watch her dancing, led by the King, her brother; he looked fixedly at her, admired her, and then exalted her above the beauties of Spain and Italy (two regions, nevertheless, which are very fertile in them), and said in Spanish: 'Although the beauty of this Queen may be more divine than human, it is better calculated to ruin and damn men than to save them.'"

In spite of all this éclat, the Queen of Navarre was not happy in her family life. One often sees men married to extraordinary beauties preferring women much less attractive. It was so with the Béarnais. Having espoused against his will a princess who had neither his ideas nor his religion, he esteemed his marriage a weakness on his part. After the Saint Bartholomew his position was both false and precarious. "The Catholic lords and princes treated with contempt this little prisoner of a kinglet whom they constantly hounded with sneers and taunts." Catholic in name, Protestant in heart, and aware of the invectives heaped on his co-religionists, he consoled himself for his humiliations with boisterous pleasures.

Knowing that he might one day be called upon to wear the crown of France, he had defended himself from insults by unalterable indifference. At court he was looked on as a hostage, and, in order to render him an object of suspicion to his former party, he had been obliged to fight in the ranks of the Catholic army at the sieges of Sancerre and La Rochelle. They tried to ruin him at the time of the trial of La Môle and Coconnas, gentlemen of the Duke of Alençon's suite, who were accused of having resorted to sortilege and witchcraft to bring about the death of Charles IX., and who were condemned to death and executed on the Place de Grêve, April 30, 1574. During the trial Henry of Navarre made a deposition drawn up with as much address as dignity, and which he owed to his wife's skilful pen. Marguerite did not love her husband, but she none the less considered herself his ally, from the political point of view, and at grave crises she drew nearer to him. This did not prevent her from betraying him. It seems, even, that she tenderly loved La Môle, and when this gentleman had been decapitated by the executioner, she caused his head to be embalmed, and placed it in a reliquary. The Duchess of Nevers paid the same respect to that of Coconnas.

When Charles IX. died, Henry of Navarre, who was viewed with distrust and hatred by Catherine de' Medici, was reduced to a real captivity. He was not released from it until Henry III. returned to France. He had but one desire when restored to liberty: that of escaping from court, and returning to his former friends. On February 3, 1576, under pretence of a hunting expedition, he drew near to Senlis, crossed the boundaries of the territory to which the court confined him, and, hurriedly crossing the fields, reached the province of Anjou, leaving behind it at Paris, as he said, only the two things he cared least about: his wife and the Mass. Marguerite had not been informed of his departure. Nevertheless she was held responsible for it. Henry III., exasperated, kept her under surveillance. No one dared come to see her. "Adversity is always alone at court," she says in her Memoirs. "The brave Crillon," she adds, "was the only one who, despising prohibitions and all disgraces, came five or six times to my chamber, so astonishing the watch-dogs, they had stationed at my door, that they never dared refuse him admission." Catherine de' Medici, to calm Marguerite, advised her to have patience. She told her that we ought always to behave towards our enemies as though they might one day be our friends, and towards our friends as though they might one day be our enemies.

The princess, ill-used by fortune, entered into a brief period of philosophy and piety. She tells us that she consoled herself by reading and meditation. "Another thing," she says, "which tended toward devotion, was reading in the beautiful book of universal nature the many marvels of its Creator." Apropos of this, Queen Margot indulges in some highly metaphysical considerations: "For every well-nurtured soul," adds she, "becoming aware of a ladder of which God is the last and highest round, rises enraptured to adoration of the marvellous light and splendor of that incomparable essence, and, making a perfect circle, pleases itself no longer with anything but following that Homeric chain, that agreeable encyclopedia which takes its departure from God Himself, the source and end of all things. . . . I received these two boons from my first captivity, to take pleasure in study, and to addict myself to devotion,—boons which I had never before tasted, amid the vanities and splendors of my rightful fortune." So Marguerite had some slight inclinations to religion; but she speedily returned to her worldly passions.

Being much attached to her brother of Alençon, she went to Flanders to further the interests of that prince who aspired to be its sovereign. After paying a visit to Spa, for the sake of her health, she travelled in this country, which Don John of Austria was then ruling in behalf of the King of Spain. There she displayed the greatest luxury. "I went," she says, "in a litter made of double pillows, of pale red velvet, embroidered in gold and emblematically blended silks. This litter was full of windows, each of them emblematic, having either on the inside or outside forty different devices, with Spanish and Italian mottoes about the sun and its effects." A diplomatic and most attractive woman, the Queen of Navarre sought to make friends for her brother in every quarter. She lavished attentions on that Countess of Lalain who suckled her infant in presence of everybody, "which might have been considered an incivility in any one else; but the Countess did it with such grace and naïveté that she received as much praise for it as the company did pleasure." The Queen of Navarre told her how much she regretted not having her for a compatriot. "This country," she replied, "formerly belonged to France, and that is why they plead here still in French, and this natural affection still clings to the greater number of us. . . . Please God to inspire the King of France, your brother, with a desire to regain this country which was his of old."

At Namur, Marguerite saw Don John of Austria, the victor of Lepanto, "who went to meet her in great and superb Spanish magnificence, and received her as if she had been Queen Elisabeth, at the time when she was his queen and Queen of Spain. It was not Don John alone who extolled her, but all those great and brave Spanish captains, even to the renowned soldiers of the old bands, who all went about saying, in their trooper-like refrains, that the conquest of such a beauty would outweigh that of a kingdom, and that happy would be the soldiers who to serve her might die beneath her banner."[1]

On her return from Flanders, Marguerite spent two months in the castle of Fère, in Picardy, with her brother of Alençon. "O my Queen!" said the prince to his beloved sister, "O my Queen, how good it is to be near you!" Fère was an enchanting abode. After describing its charm, Marguerite adds that her brother "would willingly have said, like Saint Peter: 'Let us make here our tabernacles,' if his thoroughly royal courage, and the generosity of his soul, had not called him to greater things." Returning to the Louvre, the Queen of Navarre shared the disgrace of the Duke of Alençon, whom the King held a prisoner in the palace. The Duke succeeded in escaping. By means of a cord he let himself down from his sister's room into the ditch of the Louvre, and fleeing from Paris he retired to Angers.

Some time afterwards, Marguerite was authorized to rejoin her husband in Béarn. Brantôme describes the vexation felt by the courtiers at her departure. "Some said, the court is widowed of its beauty; others, the court is very obscure, it has lost its sun; others, how dark it is at court! there is no torch; others rejoined, we have done finely in allow-

---

[1] Brantôme, *Dames illustres.*

ing Gascony to gasconade us and abduct our beauty, destined to embellish France, the court, the Louvre, Fontainebleau, Saint-Germain, and other fine royal places, in order to lodge her at Pau or Nérac! Still others said, the thing is done, the court and France have lost the fairest flower in their garland."

In his *Causeries d'un Curieux*, always so animated, substantial, and interesting, M. Feuillet de Conches has devoted an excellent chapter to this period of Marguerite's life. Catherine de' Medici herself conducted her daughter back to the King of Navarre. Taking the longest route, she visited Languedoc, Guyenne, and Dauphiny, studying the aims and policy of the Protestant leaders on the spot, and also means whereby to apply the last edict of pacification usefully. Henry of Navarre rejoined his wife at Réole, and thence repaired to Pau, where, as being a Catholic, she was ill received by the fanatical Protestants. The married pair afterwards installed themselves at Nérac, "a place of peace and delights, where the Queen began to enjoy life after the Béarnais fashion. The sweetness of this period of mutual tolerance, which only lasted three years and a half, and to which Marguerite's short memory erroneously ascribes a longer duration, has left its trace in her Memoirs."[1] The Queen thus expresses herself: "Felicity which lasted four or five years while I was in Gascony with him, making our abode for the most

---

[1] M. Feuillet de Conches, *Causeries d'un Curieux*, tome iii.

part at Nérac, where our court was so fine and pleasant that we did not envy that of France, having there Madame, the Princess of Navarre, his sister, who has since married the Duke of Bar, my nephew and myself, with a goodly number of ladies and young girls; and the King, my husband, was attended by a fine troop of lords and gentlemen, as worthy men as the most gallant I have seen at court; there was nothing to be regretted in them except that they were Huguenots. But nothing was ever heard of this diversity of religion, the King, my husband, and Madame, the Princess, his sister, going to the preaching, and I and my train to Mass in a chapel which is in the park." Nothing was talked of in this court of Nérac but love affairs and pleasures. By day they walked and chatted in the beautiful garden "which had long alleys of laurels and cypress." In the evenings "the Queen gave serenades." She danced admirably, and one likes to do what one does well. Sometimes it was the Spanish *pavan*, sometimes the Italian *pazzemeno*, or some other character dance which gave Marguerite an opportunity to display her graceful poses, the suppleness of her figure, the charm of all her movements. But this brilliant existence, which recalled the courts of love of the Middle Ages, did not long remain untroubled.

The dissensions which arose between Henry of Navarre and his wife belong to the annals of scandal rather than to history. We shall not dwell upon them. We shall speak neither of the "belle Fosseuse," "quite childish and quite good," nor of Mademoiselle Rebours, the audacious mistress of the Béarnais. M. Sainte-Beuve has remarked with much justice: "Henry's weaknesses and those of Marguerite mutually accommodated each other without contradiction. Henry soon overstepping limits in his excesses, and she doing likewise on her part, neither was the other's debtor. It does not pertain to us to hold the balance, and enter into details which soon become indelicate and shameful." This situation was soon aggravated in the most unpleasant manner. An incompatibility of temper was evident between the pair, which ended in a definitive broil.

The quarrels, recriminations, and reproaches becoming almost public, the little court of Nérac gave the sorry example of discord and scandal which amused the malignity of the Queen's enemies. Her marvellous beauty had excited too many jealousies for the women who were her rivals not to furiously seek her ruin. Her health was impaired by so many vexations and annoyances. She fell ill in February, 1582, and when she was convalescent she took the unlucky notion of going back to her mother, and thus becoming once more dependent on Henry III., who hated her. Conducted by her husband as far as Saint-Jean-d'Angély, she arrived at Saint-Germain March 18. Suspected by the King and Catherine de' Medici, on ill terms with both Catholics and Protestants, she was about to be dragged into a vortex of intrigues, where her dignity, already so diminished, was to undergo new attacks.

Hardly had she returned to the court of France when Marguerite found herself a prey to a thousand persecutions. She was odious to the King, her brother, on many accounts; her intimacy with the Duke of Guise, her perpetual plottings with the Duke of Anjou (the new title of the Duke of Alençon), her imprudent words, the incisive vigor of her criticisms, her cutting satires on the favorites, had completely alienated Henry III. Through revengeful motives, the King posed as a defender of morality. He who had so many reproaches to make to himself, judged pitilessly the disorders of his sister Marguerite. Marguerite knew that Henry III. wrote frequently to his favorite, the Duke of Joyeuse, who was then residing at Rome, and that she was very badly treated in this correspondence. To obtain proofs of this, she caused masked men to arrest the bearer of the King's despatches. So audacious an act was to put the crowning sheaf on the King's anger. He recapitulated to Marguerite the list of her real or alleged faults, and enjoined her to free the court at once "of her contagious presence." She departed, August 8, 1583, accompanied by two maids of honor and several domestics. At her first station, Bourg-la-Reine, she met the King, who did not stop nor even deign to salute her. A little further on, between Saint-Cler and Palaiseau, Nicolas de l'Archant, Captain of the Guards, followed by sixty archers, rudely stopped her litter, tore off the masks of her maids of honor, loaded them with insult, and led them away prisoners. Such an outrage could not fail to cause a great scandal, and even Marguerite's enemies did not understand why Henry III. was not afraid to insult his own sister so grossly. The King of Navarre immediately assembled his council, and they unanimously decided that he had the right to exact either a formal separation, or the public condemnation of his wife. Meanwhile he refused to receive her.

Henry III. comprehended too late the fault he had committed. As changeable as he was violent, he tried to exculpate himself; and in a long correspondence with his brother-in-law, he attempted to prove that his sole aim had been to withdraw Marguerite from the bad influence of the two maids of honor whom he had caused to be arrested. He added that he recognized the falsity of the reports which impeached the Queen's honor. "Do you not know," he wrote to the Béarnais, "how subject kings are to be deceived, and that the most virtuous princes are frequently not exempt from calumny. Even with respect to the late Queen, your mother, you know what was said about her, and how badly evil-minded persons have always spoken of her." This unseemly allusion to the memory of such a woman as Jeanne d'Albret was hardly calculated to reconcile the brothers-in-law.

Count Hector de La Ferrière[1] has published a letter written to Catherine de' Medici by Marguerite

---

[1] *Deux années de mission à Saint Petersbourg.*

to exculpate herself: "Madame," she writes, "since my unfortunate destiny has brought me to such a wretched state that I do not know whether you can wish for the preservation of my life, at least, Madame, may I hope that you would desire the preservation of my honor, seeing that it is so closely united with yours, and that of all to whom I have the honor of belonging, that I cannot be brought to shame without their participating in it." Catherine de' Medici, on her part, had explosions of grief when she thought of Marguerite's humiliations. She wrote to Villeroy: "I am so much annoyed by letters which make mention of my daughter, that I think I shall die of it, not a single day passing without my receiving some new alarm which afflicts me so greatly that I never experienced such pain. What is considered certain, and she cannot deny it, I have seen the letters she has written to the Duke of Lorraine begging him to receive her in his dominions. These are such severe afflictions that I am almost beside myself."

After a long negotiation, and in view of certain political advantages, Henry of Navarre consented to take back his wife. On her return to Béarn, she found her husband in love with the Countess of Gramont, surnamed the beautiful Corisanda. As she had at first flattered herself that she was about to resume her family life in triumph, she was struck to the heart by this new disgrace, and no longer thought of anything but quitting forever a spouse who was as inconstant as herself. Under pretext of being able to keep Lent better at a distance from a Protestant Prince, she asked permission to repair to Agen, and there attempted to make herself independent with the aid of the League.

Well received at first by the inhabitants of the city, she soon made them discontented by the imposition of exorbitant taxes. They forced her to depart with so much precipitation that she fled on horseback, riding crupperwise with a gentleman named Lignerac, who conducted to the castle of Carlat, "a place smelling more like a den of thieves than the dwelling of a Princess, the daughter, sister, and wife of Kings." Marguerite remained eighteen months in this abode. The Lord of Carlat dying at this time, Lignerac found her another asylum. Hardly was she in safety at Iboy, near Allier, than she was abducted by the Marquis of Canillac, Governor of Auvergne, who interned her in the castle-fortress of Usson. "Poor man!" exclaims Brantôme, "what was he thinking of? To wish to hold captive in his prison her who, with her eyes and her fair face, could bind all the rest of the world like a galley slave in her links and chains." Canillac was Marguerite's dupe. Like the lion in love, he let his claws be cut, and then, one fine day, as he was about to enter the castle, he perceived that the drawbridge was not lowered, and that the Queen, surrounded by soldiers whom the Duke of Guise had sent her from Orleans, was henceforth absolute mistress of the citadel. The poor governor withdrew, very much ashamed of his discomfiture.

Marguerite, in her retreat of Usson, ended, says Mézeray, "by consuming the rest of her youth in adventures more worthy of a woman who had abandoned her husband than of a daughter of France." She was saved from absolute want by the pecuniary aid afforded her by her sister-in-law, Elisabeth of Austria, widow of Charles IX. She had to pawn her jewels and melt down her plate. "I have nothing unpledged," said she; "I fear the worst, I hope little." She remained eighteen consecutive years, from 1587 to 1605, in the castle of Usson. The position of this woman, once surrounded by such homage, had become as false as it was precarious.

Marguerite had the lot of most coquettes; she knew not how to grow old. Unable to accustom herself to the loss of her beauty, she resorted to many artifices for concealing it. Her hair being no longer brown, she made herself ridiculous with blonde wigs. She kept fair-haired footmen who were shorn from time to time for this purpose. Her dress and manners were eccentric. When that moment arrives, glorious to good women, disastrous to vicious ones, when the only surviving beauty is a moral one, only solid qualities can endure. Old age which is majestic in some women is ridiculous in others. The superannuated coquetries of Queen Margot are no longer attractive, their charm has vanished. The raptures had disappeared. The indiscretion still remained. The world nearly always demands an expiation for the successes it has granted. Ruthless satires tread on the heels of fanatical laudations. A contemptuous smile greets these queens of fashion who have not been wise enough to make a timely renunciation of the triumphs which flatter their self-love.

More than once comparison has been attempted between Queen Margot and Mary Stuart. M. Sainte-Beuve very justly remarks that history affords no basis for such a parallel. "Mary Stuart," says the eminent critic, "who possessed much of the wit and grace and manners of the Valois, who as a woman was hardly more moral than Marguerite, had or seemed to have an elevation of heart which was acquired or developed in her long captivity, and which was crowned by her painful death. Of these two destinies, one, in fine, represents a great cause and ends pathetically in the record of victim and martyr; the other is scattered and dispersed in anecdotes and stories, half broad, half devout, with a dash of wit and sarcasm thrown in. Many a tearful tragedy has been based on the death of one; one can make nothing better than a fable (*fabliau*) of the other." But such a fable would be more interesting than many a philosophic study; it would show what it costs even the most brilliant heroines and most striking beauties to stray from good sense and virtue. The story would be licentious in its details and moral in its conclusions.

XVI

CATHERINE DE' MEDICI AND THE DAY OF THE BARRICADES

THE close of stormy careers is nearly always obscured by a veil of sadness, and the nothingness of human grandeur is most felt by those who have possessed it. Such was the sentiment of Catherine de' Medici. The race of Valois was dying out. The crafty Florentine had expended so much trouble, anxiety, and intrigue wholly in vain. The Béarnais was bound to reign. "Deceive not thyself," says Bossuet; "the future has events too strange, and loss and ruin enter by too many gates into man's fortune to be everywhere arrested. Thou dost impede the water on this side: it penetrates the other, it bubbles underneath the ground. You think yourselves well guarded on the environs: the foundation sinks below you, the thunderbolt strikes above. But I shall enjoy the fruits of my labor. What! for ten years of life? But I have regard to my posterity and my name. But perhaps posterity may not enjoy them. Perhaps, also, it may. And such fatigue, such labor, without ever being able to wrest from fortune to which thou dost devote thyself, more than a wretched perhaps!"

Still more preoccupied with the future than with the present, Catherine did not cease to consult the stars. She was always hoping that favorable omens would come to dispel the gloomy presentiments that disturbed her heart. She had erected a column beside her new residence (the Hôtel de Soissons), on the top of which Cosmo Ruggieri conducted his astrological operations. The greatest minds of the sixteenth century lent credence to predictions. "It is probable," said Machiavelli, "that the atmosphere is full of intelligences which announce the future out of commiseration for mortals." The son of the alchemist of the Medici family, Ruggieri, the elder, who had drawn Catherine's horoscope at her birth, and who was a mathematician and a physician as well as an astrologer, Cosmo Ruggieri had acquired a mysterious influence. The Queen-mother spent whole nights in his laboratory. But the stars did not reassure her. It had been predicted to her that three of her sons would wear the crown of France, and yet their dynasty would not be perpetuated. This seemingly improbable prediction had now become a certainty. Francis of Alençon had died in 1584, and Henry III., the sole survivor of Catherine's four sons, had no children. The Florentine's favorite motto, *Prudentia fato major*, was not realized, and destiny was to be stronger than prudence.

No matter whither she turned her eyes, Catherine saw nothing but occasions of uneasiness and sadness. She who had had ten children felt that her race was about to perish. Her daughter, the Queen of Navarre, gave her the keenest pain. Nor was she better satisfied with Henry III. This cherished son, upon whom she placed all her affections, was destined to disillusionize her completely. To frill a lace, to wreathe a velvet cap with pearls, or ornament the sleeve of a doublet with diamonds, such were the favorite occupations of this effeminate prince, in whom maternal blindness had seemed to discover a great man. Catherine, who has been wrongfully accused of the systematic corruption of her sons, was the first to suffer from the puerilities and extravagances of the King. She groaned at the sight of an intelligent mind losing its native qualities one by one, and subsiding into complete abasement. Irritated, as Queen Marguerite says, "by the boundless conceit of the young people" who surrounded Henry III., she quitted the Louvre, and installed herself in the Hôtel de Soissons. Her remonstrances were no longer heeded. Persuaded that if the bark went adrift it was because the great Queen-mother no longer held the helm, she suffered from the kind of disgrace into which she had fallen. The King now obeyed nothing but his whims and caprices. There was no sequence in his policy. After having deceived all parties, he had alienated all of them. The ground was failing under his feet. Things were becoming so bad that Catherine was obliged to abandon her involuntary inaction, and reappear on the scene to try and save her son.

The Catholics had become as dangerous to royalty as were the Protestants themselves. The Duke of Guise had created a state within a state. May 9, 1588, he entered Paris against the orders of his sovereign. His partisans called him the defender of religion, the pillar of the Church, the saviour of his country, the Maccabæus of France, the Just who had come to confound the court of Herod. They kissed his garments. They covered him with flowers. They asked him to touch rosaries. A young girl, emerging from the crowd, threw herself on his neck, crying: "Good Prince, all is saved now, since you are among us!" And yet the Duke of Guise was not without uneasiness. The night before, in passing through Soissons, he had requested the prayers of the Minims, the reformed Franciscans, of the city. Uncertain of the reception he might get from the King, whose orders he had so audaciously braved, he went, immediately on his arrival in Paris, to the hotel of Catherine de' Medici, and asked her to lead him to the Louvre. At this moment Henry III. had passing inclinations to destroy his dangerous rival. "I will strike the shepherd and the sheep will be scattered," said the Abbé d'Elbène in the King's council. "*Percutiam pastorem, et dispergentur oves.*" Catherine feared nothing more than such a resolution. She thought everything might yet be saved by calm and prudence, but that to touch the Duke of Guise, while the anger of the Parisians was so hot, would be to bring on terrible catastrophes. The Queen-mother, anxious to see moderate counsels prevail, got into a sedan chair and was taken to the Louvre. The Duke of Guise followed her on foot, his head bare, and his expression benevolent and firm, and acknowledging by courteous salutes the noisy evidences of popular joy. "Hosanna to the Son of David," shouted the delirious crowd. The approaches of the Louvre were thronged by an immense multitude during the interview between Henry III. and his audacious subject. The Balafré bowed respectfully. "What brings you here?" said the King very sharply. The Duke alleged in answer his desire to dispel the suspicions against him, and to offer his services to the King in quieting the disturbances by which the city appeared to be threatened. "I entreat Your Majesty," he added, "to place confidence in my fidelity and affection, and not to be influenced by the passions and evil reports of those whom he knows not to wish me any good." "Did I not order you," replied Henry III., "not to come here in a time so full of suspicions, but to wait awhile longer?"—"Sire," returned the Duke, "your meaning was not represented to me in such a way as to make me suppose my coming would be disagreeable to you." The dialogue threatened to become venomous. The Balafré, in spite of his coolness, had not seen undisturbed, as he ascended the royal staircase, the hostile faces of the guards drawn up in double lines. He asked himself if he were to go out alive from the Louvre. Catherine then took her son aside, and saying a few words in his ear, conjured him to let the Duke depart. The latter bowed, laying his hand on his heart, and excusing himself on account of his fatigue, slowly withdrew, without being followed or saluted by any one.

Clamorously welcomed by the crowd, who had thought him dead already, the Balafré was conducted in triumph to the Hotel Guise, soon to resemble a citadel. The Queen-mother understood the gravity of the situation better than any one. Making a final effort to avert a conflict, she brought about another interview between Henry III. and the Duke of Guise in the garden of her hotel. This second attempt at reconciliation succeeded no better than the first, and the populace, irritated by the arrival of the Swiss regiments, covered the city with barricades (May 12, 1588). When the news of this popular movement reached the Louvre, the King was at table with the Queen and Catherine de' Medici. "He was entirely unmoved, but the Queens were astonished by it, particularly the Queen-mother, who shed great tears throughout the entire repast."[1] Catherine wept, but she was not discouraged. The Louvre, besieged by fifty thousand rioters, had only four thousand unarmed guards for defenders. The circle of the barricades kept growing narrower, "so that," as said an eyewitness, "unless they could fly in the air like birds, or go underground like rats and mice, it was impossible for the arquebusiers, the Swiss, and the King's officers to get out of this labyrinth."

---

[1] *Récit d'un Bourgeois de Paris.* Manuscript Dupuy.

Henry III. seemed to be ruined. People talked of nothing less than wresting away his crown, tonsuring him, and sending him to end his days in a cloister. Catherine de' Medici, at sight of such a danger, dried her tears, called up all her moral forces, and relying still on her marvellous talent for negotiation, she went to seek the Duke of Guise. The journey across the city was not easy. "The Queen-mother could hardly get through the streets, so thickly sown and narrowed by barricades, that those who guarded them would make no greater opening than was necessary to admit her sedan chair." Nothing can show better than this the prestige which still attached to Catherine's person. It was to her the Duke of Guise had paid his first visit on arriving at Paris, and now, in open riot, all heads were still uncovered in presence of the mother of the King whom the Leaguers were trying to dethrone. The Balafré received her with the utmost respect. They were discussing together, point by point, the details of an arrangement, when a messenger arriving in all haste, announced tidings to the Duke which made him turn pale: Henry III. had just fled from Paris. "I am betrayed," said the Balafré to the Queen-mother. "While Your Majesty is amusing me, the King leaves his palace with the intention of making war on me." Catherine professed to be as much astonished as the Duke by what had just happened. Then she returned tranquilly to her dwelling. During this time, Henry III., who with some fifteen gentlemen had escaped through the fields which were still clear, was flying with all speed, cursing the capital, and swearing that he would only re-enter it through a breach.

Not having even time enough to arrange his spurs: "What does it matter," he exclaimed, "I am not going to my mistress!" Catherine, on her return to the Hôtel de Soissons, congratulated herself on the skill and presence of mind she had just evinced. Once more she had retarded the fall of the house of Valois

XVII

THE DEATH OF CATHERINE DE' MEDICI

DANGER had redoubled the energy and activity of Catherine de' Medici, who remained in Paris seeking to moderate the Duke of Guise and save the crown of Henry III. She had herself carried to the midst of confraternities, and to the armed market-places, in a litter. She said to everybody, that she was trying to establish perfect accord between the League and royalty; that all misunderstandings would be removed, and that the King, full of charity and clemency, would presently return to his good city of Paris.

Convinced that conciliation was the only means of averting the storm, she had never been more amiable toward the Duke of Guise. She overwhelmed him with courteous attentions, and neglected no means of disarming the wrath of the Leaguers. Her address and her skill in negotiation were so consummate, that she induced the Balafré to go with her to the King, who was at Chartres. Accompanied by the Duke, the Cardinals of Bourbon and Guise, the Duchess of Nemours, and the Prince of Joinville, she urgently entreated Henry III. to return to Paris.

It is said that when the monarch declined to grant this request, Catherine began to weep, and said to the King: "My son, what will be thought of me, what conclusion do you want people to come to? Can it be possible that you have changed your disposition, which I have always found so easy to forgive?" Irritated by the applause which everywhere greeted the Duke, Henry III. could hardly conceal his anger. He forbade the officers of his household to visit him. "Several of them, not daring to go thither by day, did so by night, particularly the barrack captains, who offered him guards and assistance in case any attempt were made against him."[1] Catherine was constantly repeating to her son that prudence is the chief quality of a political man, and that difficulties which seem inextricable may be resolved by the aid of quiet procrastination; she told him that as the Duke of Guise was momentarily the stronger, he must employ gentle means with him. Henry III., who was silently preparing his revenge, accepted his mother's advice. The Balafré was appointed Lieutenant-General of the realm. By the edict of union signed at Chartres, July 1, 1588, the King swore not to lay down arms until the heretics were destroyed, ordered his subjects to take a like oath, and gave places of safety to the League. The edict likewise stipulated the perpetual exclusion of heretics from the throne, the admission of Catholics

---

[1] *Histoire manuscrite de la ville de Chartres*, by Canon Souchet.

only to public employments, and a general amnesty for the past, especially for the Day of the Barricades. Finally the States-General were convened at Blois. The Duke of Guise assumed the manners of a master of the palace, and Henry III., concealing his plans of vengeance, affected those of a sluggard King (*un roi fainéant*).

As to Catherine, who had never adopted violent means but once throughout her whole career, and who had regretted that deviation from her customary line of conduct, she sought persistently to deter her son from acting rashly; but the King would not listen to her. Transported by hatred, he had but one desire: to get rid of the Duke of Guise. He did not acquaint his mother with his new resolves. She occupied apartments below his in the castle of Blois; but as he knew very well that she would blame him severely if she knew what he had in mind, he took good care not to tell her. While he was arming the forty-five to strike down the Duke, he warned them to make no noise, because his mother was quietly sleeping on the floor below that on which the murder was brewing.

When the Duke of Guise had given up the ghost, Henry III. hurried down to Catherine's chamber. "Madame," he cried, "now I am the only King; I have no companion any longer, the King of Paris is dead!" — "What! my son," responded the Queen-mother, "you have had the Duke of Guise murdered? Have you foreseen the consequences? God grant you may not be King of nothing at all! You have cut it finely, but I am not so sure you can sew it up again as well." Then she advised her son to write to the cities which sided with the defunct, and to make all speed to acquaint the Papal Legate.

Catherine's political sense divined the storms which so violent a step would bring about the King's head. Gnawed by anxieties and care, ill in soul and body, she was crushed by emotions too strong for her enfeebled nature. Cardinal Bourbon had been arrested at the time when the Duke of Guise was murdered. Catherine, although suffering greatly, had herself carried to the apartment where the prelate was detained, in order to promise him a speedy deliverance. "Ah! Madame," exclaimed the Cardinal on seeing her; "this is some of your work: it is just in your style; you are killing all of us." This accusation, an unjust one, moreover, affected the old Queen deeply. On returning to her chamber she went to bed never to rise again.

Some time previous, as she was recalling the different phases of her troubled and tempestuous career, she had bethought herself of the cloister of the *Murate*, where she had found refuge during the siege of Florence. She expressed her desire to know whether any of the nuns who had seen her as a child were yet living, and sent to request the sisters of the convent to continue praying for her deceased friends: for the late King, her husband, for the two Kings, her dead sons, and for Henry III. and herself, asking, especially, that in their prayers these venerable women should invoke the celestial bounty, "that it might be given her to see France re-established in that prosperity and splendor in which she had found it when she came thither as the betrothed of the Duke of Orleans." This prayer was to remain unanswered. Catherine's dying eyes rested on nothing but subjects of dread and sorrow. She no longer believed in the success of her labors, a thing essentially grievous to political personages. The fruit of her toils was ruined. The house of Valois was about to vanish into the abyss. January 5, 1589, she dictated her will, declaring herself, in the presence of notaries, unable to sign it on account of weakness, "lying ill in bed, but, nevertheless, sound in sense, memory, reason, and understanding, and considering that the days of all human creatures are brief, she is unwilling to pass from this world into the other without making her will, as befits a Christian princess."[1] She expired the next day, fourteen days after the Duke of Guise, and in the same castle. She was sixty-nine years and seven months old.

Her death produced very little impression. No one rejoiced at it, and no one lamented. Her disappearance from the political stage, where for many years she had played so great a part, excited neither emotion nor regret. The great moderatress, *mode-*

---

[1] *Archives de Chenonceaux*, published with an introduction by the Abbé Chevalier.

ratrice degli affari, as a Venetian ambassador styled her, had made no partisans because, instead of espousing the ideas and hatreds of the rival factions, she had tried to manage and conciliate them all. This see-saw system of hers had often succeeded; but the stormy passions of the epoch could not accommodate themselves to it. A burlesque epitaph was composed for her which had great success: —

> "La reine qui ci-gît fut un diable et un ange,
> Toute pleine de blâme et pleine de louange,
> Elle soutint l'État, et l'État mit à bas;
> Elle fit maints accords et pas moins de débats;
> Elle enfanta trois rois et trois guerres civiles,
> Fit bâtir des châteaux et ruiner des villes,
> Fit bien de bonnes lois et de mauvais édits.
> Souhaite-lui, passant, enfer et paradis."[1]

Like all who have played great parts in the destinies of a nation, Catherine de' Medici will long be discussed by historians. She will have apologists and detractors; her name will be in turn the object of exaggerated eulogies and violent invectives. After anathemas written in melodramatic style will come dithyrambs in that of Brantôme, and the paradoxi-

---

[1] The queen who lies here was a devil and an angel,
Loaded with blame and loaded with praise,
She upheld the State and put down the State;
She caused many an agreement and many a dispute;
She produced three kings and three civil wars;
She built castles and destroyed cities,
Made many good laws and bad decrees.
Wish her, passer-by, hell and paradise.

cal rehabilitations which are just now in fashion. Few judges will have the impartiality necessary to apportion the good and evil, to recognize what there was of meanness and what of grandeur in the rôle of the famous Queen-mother, to show forth under its diverse aspects one of the most complex and remarkable characters recorded in history.

XVIII

CONCLUSION

WHILE Catherine de' Medici lay dying in the castle of Blois, two women, the widow and the sister of the Duke of Guise, were stirring up the fire of vengeance in the inhabitants of Paris. Every one flew to arms, the shops were closed, the tocsin sounded, stations established in every quarter. Paris was in a state of siege. More than a hundred thousand persons marched in procession through the streets, blowing out torches and crying: "Thus is becoming extinct the race of Valois!" Nothing could equal the Duchess of Montpensier's hatred for the murderer of her two brothers. Her female vanity united with her family sentiments and ambitious projects to exasperate her against Henry III., who had, it was said, disdained her charms. She limped a little, and she knew that the King had jeered at this slight infirmity. She never forgave such jests. Haughty, violent, vindictive, she had displayed, some months before the Day of the Barricades, a pair of scissors which, she said, would answer to give the monastic tonsure to Henry of Valois.

The mother of the Guises, Anne of Este, whose

first husband had been Francis of Guise, and her second the Duke of Nemours, was not less irritated. She was at Blois when her two sons were murdered, and was at first kept a prisoner by Henry III. A few days afterwards, the King caused the Cardinal of Bourbon, the Prince of Joinville (who had become Duke of Guise on his father's death), the Duke of Elbeuf, and the other captives to embark on different vessels, and went down the Loire himself with this sad company, whom he was about to leave in the castle of Amboise. "O great monarch!" exclaimed the Duchess of Nemours, turning her tearful eyes toward the façade of the castle of Blois, decorated by a statue of Louis XII., her maternal grandfather; "O great monarch! did you build this castle only that the children of your grandchild might be murdered there?" The Duchess of Nemours had been only four days at Amboise when Henry III. set her at liberty. She went to Paris where no one called her anything but the Queen-mother. There she found her daughter, the Duchess of Montpensier, and her daughter-in-law, Catherine of Clèves, widow of the Duke of Guise, who was brought to bed with a posthumous daughter a few days later. The mourning of the Parisians was suspended on account of the birth of this infant, who had the city of Paris for godmother.

They say it was the Duchess of Montpensier who armed the hand of Jacques Clément. Springing forward to meet the messenger who brought her tidings of the murder: "Ah! welcome, friend!" she cried. "But is it true, at least, that this wretch, this traitor is dead? God! how content you make me! There is but one thing I am sorry for, and that is, that he did not know before he died that 'twas I who struck the blow!" Then turning to the women of her suite, and alluding to the threats made by the King: "Well, how does it seem to you? Isn't my head firm? It appears to me it doesn't shake as much as it used to." Then the Duchess hastened to her mother and the pair, intoxicated with joy, entered a carriage, saying to the people who crowded around them: "Good news, friends, good news: there is no Henry of Valois in France any longer!" Followed by an innumerable throng, they reached the church of the Cordeliers and alighted from the carriage. The Duchess of Nemours ascended the steps of the high altar, and harangued the people, who joyfully applauded her.

"Thus sadly terminated by three brothers, like that of the Capets, this most unhappy race of the Valois, a race which would be accursed if the genius of art were not beside it to veil its faults and vices, if the miserable death of its last three kings did not awaken profound sadness and commiseration in the soul."[1] The majority of the women whose portraits we have essayed to sketch were already in their graves. The heroines once so brilliant and so bepraised were scarcely remembered.

---

[1] Lavallée, *Histoire des Français.*

Diana of Poitiers had died, April 22, 1566, forgotten by the court of which she had been the idol. In her will she made particular provision for religious houses to be opened for women of evil lives, as if, in the depths of her conscience, she had recognized the likeness between their destiny and her own.

Two years later, at the end of 1568, the beautiful Elisabeth of France, wife of Philip II., the queen of peace and bounty, Isabel *de paz y de bondad*, as the Spanish called her, had died at the age of twenty-four, after having experienced profound grief and melancholy in the sombre palace of the Escurial, the prison of her youth and beauty.

February 18, 1587, Mary Stuart had laid her head upon the block. "She would not permit the executioner to disrobe her, saying she had not been accustomed to the service of such a gentleman. She took off her robe herself, kneeled down on a square of black velvet, and presented her head to the executioner, who, contrary to the privilege of princes, caused her hands to be held by her valet so that he might strike the blow more securely. Then he showed the severed head to the people, who began to shout: Long live the queen! And, as in this display her head-dress fell to the ground, it was seen that weariness and vexation had, at the age of forty-five, made this poor queen, who had once carried off the prize of beauty from all women in the world, quite white and hoary-headed."[1] Distracted by

---

[1] *Journal-Mémoire* of Pierre de l'Estoile.

political preoccupations, the court of France did not even attempt to avenge the unfortunate victim, and in the following year Henry III. sought the alliance of Queen Elizabeth of England.

Catherine de' Medici herself, Catherine who had made such a grand figure in Christendom, and whose name had been so many times re-echoed, was to be forgotten even more quickly than Mary Stuart. This famous Queen-mother, this celebrated Florentine, "adored and reverenced as the Juno of the court," had no sooner breathed her last sigh than, to use L'Estoile's expression, "they made no more account of her than if she had been a dead she-goat."

The wives of Charles IX. and of Henry III. were still living. One of them retiring to Austria and the other to Chenonceaux, these two widows, who were widows indeed, spent their lives in almsgiving and prayer. From the depths of so much destruction their gentle voices rose to heaven, and implored from God forgiveness for the departed. Elisabeth of Austria died in 1592, mourned by all who had had the happiness to approach her. Louise of Vaudémont lived until 1602, as faithful to the memory of Henry III. as if that prince had been worthy of regrets.

As to Marguerite of Valois, her old age resembled the rest of her existence. In 1590, on the very day when Henry IV. won the battle of Ivry, the Marquis of Curton, who had taken possession of Auvergne for the King, cut in pieces an army corps containing the last defenders of this princess. Marguerite beheld them all perish from the terrace of the castle of Usson. When Henry IV. had made his abjuration, he refused to see her again, and forbade her to call herself the Queen of France. He wished to divorce her; but so long as Gabrielle d'Estrées lived, Marguerite refused this. After the death of the favorite she herself signed a demand of nullity, presented to Pope Clement VIII., based upon the fact that mutual consent had been lacking to the marriage. The Pope delegated certain cardinals and bishops to proceed to an examination of the two spouses. Marguerite expressed her desire, since she must be interrogated, to be so by persons "more private and familiar," her courage being unequal to support such a degradation. "I am afraid," said she, "lest my tears should make the cardinals believe me under some force or constraint, which would be prejudicial to the result the King desires (October, 1599)." Henry IV. showed himself affected by the attitude of his former companion. "I am very well satisfied with the ingenuousness and candor of your procedure," he wrote to her, "and I hope that God will bless the remainder of our days with a fraternal affection, combined with a public felicity, which will render them very happy." Thenceforth he called her his sister.

Returning to Paris in 1605, she ended her days there in that blended piety and coquetry which formed the basis of her character. Always goodnatured and affable, but licentious, extravagant, lacking common-sense, she could not give up gallantries and love. Her desire to appear at the Louvre fêtes made her shut her eyes to the place she occupied there; she was present at the coronation of Maria de' Medici, and took rank there after the King's sister. She lived at Paris, in the Hôtel de Sens, without any title but that of Queen Marguerite. Disgusted with this abode after one of her favorites had been murdered there, she built herself a house in the vicinity of the Pré aux Clercs, and laid the first stone of the Augustinian Convent. Uniting the love for sacred and profane things, which to some women seem not incompatible, she gave much alms and did not pay her debts. Around her figured unworthy favorites, and also an almoner who was to be the hero of charity, St. Vincent de Paul. Marguerite survived Henry IV. and lamented him. She died March 27, 1615, in her sixty-third year. Her last days had been profoundly sad. A prey to fits of discouragement or terror, she shuddered at the approach of death. Having sought for happiness outside the path of duty, she recognized, but too late, that it can only be found in the practice of virtue. With Marguerite disappeared the last heroine of the Valois court.

The most immoral epochs are perhaps those which give rise to the greatest number of salutary reflections. The heroines of the court of the last Valois, if one seriously studies them, and analyzes their sorrows, anxieties, and remorse, afford the moralist precious subjects for meditation. The more pride, ambition, and voluptuousness there is in the career of these women, the better they make us comprehend the poverty and inanity of the passions to which, in their blindness, they surrendered soul and body. On scrutinizing their history, it is very quickly perceived that they never encountered true happiness in the disorders into which they plunged. Ambitious, they saw the scaffolding of their intrigues blown down by the lightest whisper. Proud, they suffered the most cruel humiliations. Voluptuous, they found anguish underlying pleasure. "Of the goods we possess," says Montaigne, "not one is free from some mixture of evil and incommodity.

... *Medio de fonte leporum,*
Surgit amari a liquid, quod in ipsis floribus angit.

Our extremest pleasure has a certain note of groaning and lamentation. Would you say that it is dying of anguish? Even when we conjure up an image of it in its perfection we do so by means of morbid and painful epithets and qualities: languor, softness, feebleness, faintness, *morbidezza,* a great testimony to their consanguinity and consubstantiality." Vice carries its own punishment within itself, and if there is something melancholy even in the midst of its pretended joys, what shall one say of its vexations, its regrets, and its sufferings?

In the sixteenth century as in other epochs, women are not truly great save by the qualities which are the ornament of their sex: the qualities of the heart. Neither the importance of political situations, the éclat of adventures, the prestige of luxury and power, the splendor of youth and beauty, imparts to them the real charm. Their misfortunes are more interesting than their successes. We love Mary Stuart in prison better than Mary Stuart on the throne, and the holy women who, like Elisabeth of Austria and Louise of Vaudémont, keep themselves quietly in the shade, are both more attractive and happier than they who seek the glare of daylight and applause.

During the siege of Florence, when Salvesto Aldobrandini sought to force Catherine de' Médici from the cloister of the *Murate*, which was her asylum, one remembers that Catherine said: "Go, tell my masters that I will become a nun, and spend my whole life near these reverend mothers." Who knows if it would not have been better for the little Florentine if this promise had been kept? Who knows whether the obscure cloister would not have been preferable to the glittering galleries of the Louvre and of Chenonceaux? Perhaps the frieze habit of the nun would have been lighter for Catherine's shoulders than the queenly mantle. She would have been pursued neither by the invectives of her contemporaries nor those of posterity.

Read the depths of the souls of these queens, these favorites, with whom everything seems to succeed.

What miseries do you not find under a brilliant surface, what chagrins, what anxieties beneath the roofs of palaces! Amid the victories of opulence and sensuality, Diana of Poitiers wrote to Madame de Montagu: "When will you come to visit me, Madame, and my good friend, for I am very desirous of a sight of you, which would console me in all my vexations? And look you, they often rise to the utmost pitch, which makes one believe that the abyss is on high!" As she touches the summit of her fortune, the all-powerful mistress experiences that trouble, that disquietude which is the chastisement of satisfied ambition. When she reigns amidst the marvels of Chenonceaux, that "charming castle, flowered, emblazoned, flanked by handsome towers, adorned with caryatides, outlined by balconies with gilded ornaments from top to bottom," there are hours when all these *fleurons*, these arabesques seem tinged with blood, when gloomy thoughts penetrate this "sylvan and luxuriant grove, watered by fountains, verdant as an April field," and when the favorite hears the distant echo of the angry and vengeful cries of the victims of her cupidity.

If a Diana of Poitiers, a Catherine de' Medici, a Mary Stuart, a Marguerite of Valois, could come from their sepulchres to speak to us of life and death, what severe lessons would they not give us! How they would edify us concerning the results of that worldly prudence which the Apostle St. James qualifies as "earthly, sensual, devilish," that prudence by which one thinks to deceive others and deceives himself alone! How they would instruct us as to the true value of human things! How they would say anew to us, concerning riches, grandeur, and glory, the words which a great saint never ceased repeating: "*Quid prodest?* What is the good of it?"

What tears at the bottom of all these histories! Who would not exclaim with L'Estoile, after the story of Mary Stuart's death: "Behold a most tragical life and a true picture of the vanity of worldly grandeur. And then, go and make great account of worldly honors and their felicities!" These two women so much admired, these two queens prouder of their beauty than of their crown, Mary Stuart and Marguerite of Valois, expiated their triumphs, one by execution, the other by the humiliations which certain women find worse than death. How many reflections could not a Bossuet make on the vicissitudes of these fortunes, so fruitful in great lessons! Do not the women of the court of the last Valois say to us, like those of the court of Louis XIV.: "No, according to what we have just seen, health is but a name, life is but a dream, glory but an appearance, graces and pleasures but a dangerous amusement."

Another remark occurs to our mind as we terminate this study: it is that, under the latest Valois, religion is badly understood, badly practised, obscured by fanaticism, disfigured by human passions; and yet that it is still the only light shining in the night, the only power that in presence of pride and debauchery utters the names of humility and chastity, the only force which represents the moral sense and duty. In spite of all their efforts, the persecutors, the torturers, do not succeed in denaturalizing religion. It survives their blasphemies and crimes. The abuses, the excesses committed in its name cannot destroy its beauty. Men wish to convert it into an instrument of perdition, but it remains a cause of salvation. If you could take from these kings the little Christianity remaining to them, they would be monsters of tyranny, Asiatic despots, Nebuchadnezzars, Belshazzars. If you could tear from these favorites, these grand ladies, the faculty of remorse that religion gives them, they would be mere vile courtesans, Messalinas, frenzied pagans. Even Henry III., when he kneels before God, is not so hypocritical as one thinks; he sometimes casts an envious glance toward the obscure destiny of some poor monk, burying his hopes and sorrows in the depths of a cloister. The most depraved natures have their returns toward God when they ask themselves whether, after all, penitence would not be the wisest of schemes. In spite of all the scandals of their careers, the last Valois died good Christians. 'Tis religion which restores the great female sinners of this epoch. 'Tis it which rehabilitates Mary Stuart and gives the head of that unhappy Queen an aureole which will shine throughout the ages. 'Tis it, in fine, which saves a society ploughed up by so many elements of dissolution, so many causes of moral and material ruin, and rescues it from barbarism, from vandalism, and from irretrievable decay. After the storm will come the rainbow. The dynasty of the Valois will become extinct, but France will not perish.

A philosophic, a Christian, sentiment disengages itself from all the crises, adventures, and tragedies of a period so violent and so troubled. What remains of all these agitations, quarrels, intrigues, these ferocious or feverish passions? In thinking of the silence that succeeds so great a tumult, one meditates and communes with himself. From amidst the ruins and the tombs rises the most eloquent of voices. 'Tis the great, the sacred voice of history, which reduces the things of this world to their true proportions, which teaches us, by the spectacle of celebrated misfortunes, to endure the daily miseries of life, and which by evoking the past, diffuses over the present a consoling and instructive charm.

INDEX

Albret, Jeanne d', her birth, 58; forced to marry Duke of Cleves, 59, 60; her marriage annulled, 60; her strong character, 124, 248; marries Antoine of Bourbon, 249; becomes a Calvinist, 249; her harshness and severity, 250; her stern religious attitude, 251; birth of her son Henry, 251; goes to court of France to arrange marriage of her son Henry, 254; her arrival in Paris, 255; shocked by the corruption of Paris, 255, 256; her distrust of the court of France, 256, 257; her attitude towards Catherine de' Medici, 257; her death, 258, 259; her burial, 260.

Albret, Henri d', marries Marguerite of Angoulême, 49, 57; his words at birth of Henry of Navarre, 251, 252.

Alençon, Duke of, marries Marguerite of Angoulême, 13, 19; dies, 28.

Alva, Duke of, espouses Elisabeth of France for Philip II., 188; counsels massacre of Huguenots, 223; unable to influence Catherine de' Medici, 223, 224.

Amboise, executions at, 125, 193, 194.

Anabaptists, The, 52.

Angoulême, Count of. See Charles of Orleans.

Angoulême, Marguerite of. See Marguerite of Angoulême.

Anne of Este. See Nemours, Duchess of.

Anjou, Duke of, afterwards Henry III., persecutes his sister Marguerite, 238, 239; proposes to make an ally of Marguerite, 239, 240; conceives hatred for his sister, 242; his perfidious show of friendship to the Duke of Guise, 243; his hatred for the Guises, 245; allegorical entertainment arranged by, 266, 267; his royalty in Poland, 283. See also Henry III.

Ariosto, verses by, on Catherine de' Medici, 152.

Aubiac, D', 126.

Barricades, the Day of the, 326.
Berquin, Louis de, 48, 49, 50.
Bourbon, Antoine of, 249.
Briçonnet, Guillaume, 47, 48, 85, 86.
Burré, Henry, executed by Henry II., 179.

Canillac, Marquis, abducts Marguerite de Valois, 318.

Carlos, Don, 197; his jealousy of his father's wife, 226, 227; his death and burial, 230, 231.

Catherine de' Medici, gives birth to a son, 90, 174; her cunning, 123, 124; her behavior at the siege of Rouen, 125; a Machiavellian woman, 130; her attendants, 130, 131; misrepresented in romances, 133, 134; her real character, 134; her importance at the court of the Valois, 135; different opinions as to her character and

349

place in history, 135 et seq. ; her character justly estimated, 141 et seq. ; her complex nature, 142 ; new light to be thrown on her career, 147, 148; the childhood of, 149 et seq.; surrounded by dangers, 150, 154; her birth, 150; her family, 150, 151; loss of her parents, 152; verses on, by Ariosto, 152; her life in Florence, 153; taken to the convent of *Santissima Annunziata delle Murate*, 154; transferred to convent of Saint Lucia, 156, 157; visits Rome, 157; her disposition as a child, 158; suitors for her hand, 158; marriage of, to Duke of Orleans, 159; leaves Italy, 159; her reception at Marseilles, 161, 162; her marriage celebrated, 163; her close companionship with Francis I., 164, 165; aristocratic prejudices against, 166; her attitude towards Diana of Poitiers and Duchess d'Étampes, 170, 171; her personal appearance, 171, 172; her fear of divorce, 172, 173; liked by the King and court, 173, 174; her numerous children, 174; crowned at Saint Denis, 178; her behavior towards Diana of Poitiers, 180–182; her care of her children, 181, 182; her thoughtful nature, 183; addresses Parliament, 184; her passion for governing, 184, 219; her rivalry with Mary Stuart, 191; her rule begins, 195; opposes plan to marry Carlos and Mary Stuart, 197; urges Mary Stuart to leave France, 197; her weighty and trying responsibilities, 206, 207; her aim in ruling, 208; her religious attitude, 209 et seq.; a good Frenchwoman, 213; sides with Catholicism, 213–215; her intelligence and constant labor, 216, 217; her calm and easy bearing, 218–221; her vacillating policy toward the Huguenots, 223, 224; her successes, 235; her methods in ruling her family, 237; her attitude toward Jeanne d'Albret, 257; her feeling towards Coligny, 269, 270; her share of responsibility for massacre on Saint Bartholomew's, 275 et seq.; change of her disposition, 281; magnificent entertainments offered by, to Polish ambassadors, 283; her regency after death of Charles IX., 293 et seq.; her study of omens in the stars, 322; her uneasiness, 322, 323; leaves the Louvre, 323; endeavors to prevent conflict between Henry III. and Duke of Guise, 326, 327, 329, 330; accused of killing the Duke of Guise, 332; her last hours, 332, 333; her death and its effect, 333, 334; burlesque epitaph on, 334; soon forgotten, 340.

Catherine of Bourbon, her words concerning Marguerite de Valois, 254.

Cervantes, 9.

Charles III., Duke. See Alençon, Duke of.

Charles V. of Spain, refuses Francis I. an interview, 31; permits Marguerite of Angoulême to visit Francis in prison, 32, 34; meets Marguerite, 36; demands cession of Burgundy, 36, 37; insults Francis I., 88; forms alliance with Pope Clement VII. to subdue Florence, 154, 155; makes an ally of Duchess d'Étampes, 170.

Charles of Orleans, 17.

Charles IX., his words concerning Elisabeth of Austria, 132; his admiration for Mary Stuart, 197; his tour through the southern provinces, 222; forbids Duke of Guise to see Marguerite de Valois, 244; marries Elisabeth of Austria, 245; proposes to marry

INDEX 351

Marguerite to Henry of Navarre, 248, 253; reported dialogue of, with Catherine de' Medici, concerning his interview with Jeanne d'Albret, 255; hastens his sister's marriage, 263; hears of wounding of Admiral Coligny, 268; his hesitating attitude toward Huguenots, 269, 270; his share of responsibility for massacre of Saint Bartholomew's, 275 *et seq.*; his passion for Marie Touchet, 124, 281, 282; his melancholy temper, 282, 283, 284; his strange nature and habits, 284 *et seq.*; his death, 288–291.

Chartres, Edict of, 330.

Châteauneuf, the Demoiselle de, 126.

Claude of France, 5.

Clement VII., Pope, allies himself with Charles V., 154; besieges Florence, 155; summons Catherine de' Medici to Rome, 157; accepts overtures for Catherine's hand for Henry, Duke of Orleans, 158; enters Marseilles to meet Francis I., 161, 162; celebrates marriage of Catherine de' Medici, 163; supposed to have deceived Francis I. in his alliance, 166.

Cleves, Duke of, marries Jeanne d'Albret, 59, 60.

Coche, the, poem by Marguerite of Angoulême, 78.

Coligny, Admiral, his delight at reception at Paris, 261, 262; wounded by a musket shot, 268.

Condé, Princess of, the passion of Henry III. for, 295; her death, 297.

Delaroche, Paul, 133.

Diana of Poitiers, her beauty, 124; the passion of the Duke of Orleans for, 167–169; her bitter rivalry with Duchess d'Étampes, 169, 170; her influence over Henry II., 175 *et seq.*; created Duchess of Valentinois, 176; her care of herself, 179, 180; her attitude toward Catherine de' Medici, 180–182; forced to return her jewels, 190; her influence at an end, 190; her death, 339.

Diplomatie vénitienne, la, 147.

Dolet, his Latin ode to Marguerite of Angoulême, 12.

Don John of Austria, his admiration for Marguerite de Valois, 306; meets Marguerite de Valois, 310.

Eleanor, sister of Charles V., 37, 41, 169.

Elisabeth of Austria, 132; her marriage to Charles IX., 245; crowned Queen of France, 246; her Christian character, 246, 247; her words on hearing of the massacre of Huguenots, 274; her fidelity to Charles IX., 290; her last years and death, 292, 340.

Elisabeth, daughter of Charles IX., 291.

Elisabeth of France, joins Charles IX. at Bayonne, 222, 224, 225; her birth and marriage, 225, 226; devotion of her subjects, 227, 228, 234; her affection for France, 228, 229; a tragic legend concerning, 229, 233; her death, 231, 232, 339; her lovely character, 233.

Erasmus, his letter to Marguerite of Angoulême, 11; his letter to Francis I., 48.

Étampes, Duchess d', 27; her bitter rivalry with Diana of Poitiers, 169, 170; vanquished by Diana of Poitiers, 176; sued by her husband for the salary of the government of Brittany, 177.

Étaples, Lefèvre d', 46–49.

Ferrière, Count Hector de la, his collection of the letters of Catherine de' Medici, 147.

352 INDEX

Flagellants, the, at Avignon, 298.
Florence, revolution in, 153; besieged, 155; capitulates, 157.
Francis I, his remark concerning a court without women, 3; his place in history, 7; his nature, 7 *et seq.*; Henri Martin's estimate of, 8; imprisons the daughter of Marguerite of Angoulême, 14; admiration of his mother for, 18; appears at court of Louis XII., 18; run away with by a horse, 19; his character according to Henri Martin, 20; acquires glory by the battle of Marignan, 20, 21; magnificent opening of his reign, 21; loses battle of Pavia and made prisoner, 26; his religious feeling, 26; his devotion to Mademoiselle d'Heilly, 27; composes poetry in captivity, 27; patriotic letter to the parliaments of France, 27, 28; devotion of France to, 28; transferred to Spain, 29, 30; received by Spaniards with respect, 30; refused interview with Charles V., 31; imprisoned at Madrid, 31; his humiliation, 31, 32; asks for his sister, 32; very ill, 34, 35; visited by his sister, 34, 35; convalescing, 36; abdicates the throne in favor of the Dauphin, 37, 38; his conditions of captivity improved, 41; returns to France in exchange for two of his sons, 42, 43; his sense of obligation to his sister, 43; his attitude towards the Reformation, 48-50; defied by the reformers, 52; resolves to treat heresy with severity, 52; burns six victims, 53; addresses the court, parliament, and ambassadors, 53; orders suppression of printing, 54; faithful in his attachment to his sister, 54, 55; determined to prevent marriage of Jeanne d'Albret with son of Charles V., 58, 59; marries Jeanne d'Albret to Duke of Cleves, 59, 60; his health declining, 62, 63; his death, 64; his taste and talent for poetry, 76, 77; receives Pope Clement VII. at Marseilles, 162, 163; his gallantry, 163; his knowledge and good judgment, 164; his passion for hunting, 164; constantly changing his abode, 165.

Francis II., his passion for Mary Stuart, 192; his early death predicted, 193; his death, 195.

Gaurico, Luke, his prediction concerning death of Henry II., 189.
Guise, Duchess of, 125.
Guise, Charles de, Archbishop of Rheims, 175, 176.
Guise, the house of, favored by Henry II., 175.
Guise, Henri de, his appearance and manners, 243; the love of Marguerite de Valois for, 242, 243; marries the Princess of Porcian, 244; accused of wounding Admiral Coligny, 268; enters Paris against orders of Henry III., 324; a dangerous rival to Henry III., 324, 327; murdered by Henry III., 331.

Heilly, Mademoiselle d'. See Duchess d'Étampes.
Henry II., the influence of Diana of Poitiers over, 175 *et seq.*; causes Catherine de' Medici to be crowned, 178; his execution of heretics, 178, 179; his verses to Diana of Poitiers, 180; the end of his reign, 184; his weakness and follies, 187; opposed by Parliament, 188; killed by Montgomery, 189. See also Orleans, Henry, Duke of.
Henry III. flees from Poland, 294, 296; his life in Poland, 295; his

INDEX 353

passion for the Princess of Condé, 295; his stay in Austria and Italy, 296, 297; mourning the death of the Princess of Condé, 297, 298; joins the Flagellants at Avignon, 298; his fancy for Louise of Vaudémont, 299; his coronation and marriage, 301; torments his wife, 302; forces Marguerite de Valois to leave the court of France, 315; excuses himself to Henry of Navarre, 316; his effeminacy, 323; his crown threatened, 324–327; flees from Paris, 327, 328; his hatred of Duke of Guise, 330, 331; murders Duke of Guise, 331; his death, 338. See also Anjou, Duke of.

Henry of Navarre, his birth, 251; his early bringing up, 252, 253; presented to Henry II., 253; receives news of his mother's death, 261; his arrival at Paris, 261; his lack of sympathy for his betrothed, 262, 263; his marriage ceremony and festivities, 263–267; his position at court after Saint Bartholomew's, 307; leaves court of France, 308; his weaknesses and excesses, 314; refuses to receive his wife after she is driven from court of France, 316; is prevailed upon to take back his wife, 317.

Heptameron, the, as a literary work, 92, 93, 94; the scene of, 95; the synopsis of, 95 *et seq.*; the serious element in, 102; philosophical reflections in, 103, 104; vindication of rights of women in, 104, 105; the types of character in, 105, 106; freedom of speech in, 106, 107; the literary style of, 110.

Huguenots, the, threaten vengeance for the wounding of Coligny, 269; hesitating attitude of Charles IX. toward, 269, 270;

massacre of, on Saint Bartholomew's, 273 *et seq.*

La Bruyère, his verdict on Rabelais, 4, 5.

Leonardo da Vinci, 21.

Lorenzo the Magnificent, 151.

Lorenzo II., the marriage of, 151; his death, 152.

Lorraine, Cardinal, 197, 198, 300.

Louise de Vaudémont, Henry III. conceives affection for, 299; her character, 299–303; her betrothal to Henry III., 300; her marriage, 301; faithful to her husband's memory, 340.

Louise of Savoy, 17; her description of her son's dangerous adventure with a horse, 19; her devotion to her son, 18, 19; extract from her journal concerning her son's victory over the Swiss, 20, 21.

Louvre, the, besieged, 326.

Luther, 45.

Machiavelli quoted, 129, 130, 141.

Marck, William de la, Duke of Cleves. See Cleves.

Margot, Queen, nickname for Marguerite de Valois, 124.

Marguerite of Angoulême, estimate of her character, 5–7, 10–16; M. Luro's words concerning, 10, 11; Sainte-Beuve's estimate of, 11; Erasmus's letter to, 11; Dolet's Latin ode to, 12; Brantôme's estimate of, 12; her marriage to the Duke of Alençon, 13, 19; her daughter imprisoned by Francis I., 14; her sad life, 14–16; her birth and parentage, 17; her remarkable talents, 17, 18; appears at court of Louis XII., 18; devoted to her brother, 19; the most brilliant woman at the court of Francis I., 23; her lofty character, 24, 25; her letter to her imprisoned brother, 27; letter to Marshal de Montmorency, 28; loses her husband, 28; letter to her brother when he was transferred to Spain, 29, 30; visits her brother in prison at Madrid, 32, 34, 35; verses written during her journey to Madrid, 33, 34; prays at her brother's bedside, 35; meets Charles V. for negotiation, 36, 37; favorably impresses the Council of Spain, 36; arouses interest of Eleanor, sister of Charles V., 37; returns to France, 38, 39; extracts from letters of, to Francis I., 40, 41; her religious faith, 44 *et seq.;* her religious correspondence with Guillaume Briçonnet, 47, 85, 86; marries Henri d'Albret, 49, 57; attacked by religious enemies, 50, 51, 54; her religious poem, *Miroir de l'âme pécheresse*, 51, 52, 78; her fidelity to Catholicism, 55, 56; poverty the result of her second marriage, 58; issue of her second marriage, 58; her life during her last years, 60–63; her grief at her brother's death, 65, 66; her poems mourning her brother, 66–68; her religious life after her brother's death, 68, 69; her death, 70; mourned by her subjects, 70; poem dedicated to her by Ronsard, 71, 72; Nisard's graceful tribute to, 73; her literary work, 74 *et seq.;* her literary talents compared with her brother's, 78; her volume of poems, 78 *et seq.;* her devotion to her brother, 62–66, 77, 78, 84, 87–89; her correspondence, 84 *et seq.;* her letter on the birth of a son to Catherine de' Medici, 90; her wit and wisdom displayed in the *Heptameron*, 98 *et seq.;* her vindication of the rights of women in the *Heptameron*, 104; her truth to life in the *Heptameron*, 92, 106; her character and her place in history, 108–110, 113; her literary ability, 110–112; misrepresented in novels, 111, 112; her noble nature, 113 *et seq.;* her sad career, 113, 114; universally respected, 116; her exquisite sensibility, 118, 119.

Marguerite de Valois, her beauty, 124, 131, 237, 238, 305, 306; her marriage, 125; d'Aubiac's words concerning, 126; her birth, 237; persecuted by her brother, Duke of Anjou, 238, 239; promises her brother her assistance, 241; her feelings for her mother, 242; her affection for the Duke of Guise, 242, 243; slanderous stories concerning her relations with the Duke of Guise, 244; her marriage with Henry of Navarre arranged, 253, 254; her marriage ceremony and festivities, 263–267; uneasiness of, the night preceding Saint Bartholomew's, 272, 273; her character, 304; her marriage unhappy, 306, 307; her love for La Môle, 307; her reading and meditation, 309; visits Flanders, 309, 310; meets Don John of Austria, 310; visits her brother, Duke of Alençon, 311; joins her husband, 311, 312; her life at the court of Nérac, 313; her disagreements with her husband, 313, 314; returns to the court of France, 314; forced to leave the court of France, 315; returns to her husband, 317; at Carlat and Usson, 318, 319; compared with Mary Stuart, 320; her old age, 340; her last days, 341, 342.

Marguerites, Les, de la Marguerite des Princesses, a volume of poems by Marguerite of Angoulême, 78.

Mary Stuart, her influence at the French court, 123, 124; brought

INDEX 355

up by Catherine de' Medici, 182, 183; her marriage, 184, 186; her beauty, 191, 192; the passion of Francis II. for, 192; retires to the convent of Saint Peter, 195; verses written during her grief, 195; her farewell to France, 198–200; her arrival in Scotland, 200; her sad fate, 201, 202; the sympathy of posterity for, 202–205; her death, 339.

Marot, Clément, 48, 49, 74.

Medici, Catherine de'. See Catherine de' Medici.

Medici, the, family, 150, 151.

Mendoza, Cardinal, his harsh words to Elisabeth of France, 225.

Mérimée, his words concerning massacre of Saint Bartholomew's, 275, 276.

Meyerbeer, 127.

Michael Angelo, 22.

Miroir de l'âme pécheresse, poem by Marguerite of Angoulême, 51, 52, 78.

Montmorency, Marshal de, 28, 32, 54, 235.

Montpensier, Duchess de, 124, 126; her hatred for Henry III., 336; her joy at his death, 338.

Navarre, Henry of. See Henry of Navarre.

Navarre, Marguerite of. See Marguerite of Angoulême.

Nemours, Duchess of, 337.

Nérac, the court at, 313, 314.

Noirmoutiers, Marquise de, 126.

Orleans, Charles of, 17.

Orleans, Henry, Duke of, afterwards Henry II., marries Catherine de' Medici, 159; becomes the Dauphin, 167; his passion for Diana of Poitiers, 167–169. See also Henry II.

Paris, barricaded by the Leaguers, 326; in a state of siege, 336.

Philip II. wishes to marry his son Carlos to Mary Stuart, 197; weds Elisabeth of France, 225, 226; suspected of poisoning his wife, 229, 230; his pitiless nature, 233, 234.

Poems of Marguerite of Angoulême, 33, 61, 66–68, 80–83.

Poems of Francis I., 77.

Protestantism, in France, the development of, 210, 211.

Rabelais, 4, 8, 11.

Raphael, 22.

Reformation, the beginnings of, 44 *et seq.*

Reumont, Alfred de, his work on the youth of Catherine de' Medici, 149.

Rheims, Archbishop of. See Charles de Guise.

Rome taken by assault, 153.

Roussel, Gérard, 52.

Saint Bartholomew's, 125, 126, 273 *et seq.*

Sainte-Beuve, his estimate of Marguerite de Valois, 11.

Saint-Germain, the edict of, 235, 236.

Satyres et des Nymphes de Diane, poem by Margaret of Angoulême, 78.

Scott, Walter, 133, 202.

Sixteenth century, society in the, 3–5, 8–10, 11, 127 *et seq.*; immorality of, 128–130; new discoveries in the history of, 133; its appeal to the imagination, 133.

Stile de la reine Jehanne, the, 254.

Touchet, Marie, passion of Charles IX. for, 124, 281, 282.

Tournon, Cardinal de, 238.

Valois, Marguerite de. See Marguerite de Valois.
Valois, the heroines of the court of, 342–348.
Vaudémont, Louise de. See Louise de Vaudémont.

Women of the sixteenth century, 3 *et seq.*; their influence under reigns of the Valois, 123 *et seq.*; the nature of, 125–128; **their immorality**, 128–132.

FAMOUS WOMEN OF THE FRENCH COURT

FORMER series of M. Imbert de Saint-Amand's historical works have depicted the great French historical epochs of modern times. The stirring events of the Revolution, of the Consulate and Empire, and of the Restoration period, ending with the July revolution of 1830 and the accession of Louis Philippe, are grouped around the attractive personalities of Marie Antoinette, the Empresses Josephine and Marie Louise, and the Duchesses of Angoulême and of Berry. The remarkable and uniform success of these works has induced the publishers to undertake the translation and publication of a previous series of M. de Saint-Amand's volumes which deal with epochs more remote, but not for that reason less important, interesting, or instructive. The distinction of the cycle now begun with the "Women of the Valois Court" and ending with "The Last Years of Louis XV.," is that, whereas in former series several volumes have been devoted to the historical events associated with each of the titular personalities to which they were closely related, in the present instance a more condensed method is followed. The color of the present series is more personal, and therefore more romantic, as is to be expected in the annals of a period during which the famous women of the French Court were not only more numerous but more influential than their successors of later times. The dawn of the modern era, chronicled in M. de Saint-Amand's "Marie Antoinette and the End of the Old Régime" was the beginning of the extinction of the feminine influence that flourished vigorously in affairs of state from Marguerite of Angoulême to Madame Dubarry. It is the history of this influence that the author has graphically written in the four volumes now announced — "Women of the Valois Court," "The Court of Louis XIV.," and "The Court of Louis XV.," and "The Last Years of Louis XV."

FAMOUS WOMEN OF THE FRENCH COURT

The first volume is devoted to Marguerite of Angoulême and Catherine de' Medici and their contemporaries at the French court during the days of the last of the Valois — the most romantic period of royalty probably in all history. The two principal figures are depicted with striking vividness, — the half Catholic, half Protestant sister of Francis I., the grandmother of Henry IV., the author of the famous "Heptameron," and one of the most admirable historical figures of any epoch; and the diplomatic, ambitious, unscrupulous but extremely human Catherine, universally held responsible for the awful Massacre of Saint Bartholomew. But the subordinate though scarcely less famous women who adorned the Valois Court — Diane de Poitiers, the Duchess d'Étampes, Marguerite of Valois, Marie Stuart, and others — are described with an equally brilliant and illuminating touch.

The volumes on the women of the great Bourbon epoch, the epoch of Louis XIV. and Louis XV., when the Bourbon star was in the zenith, contain a great deal of intimate history as well as setting in relief the interesting personalities of the famous La Vallière and Montespan and that perennial historical enigma, Madame de Maintenon, in the volume devoted to the court of the "Sun King," and those of Madame de Pompadour, Madame Dubarry, Queen Marie Leczinski, and other celebrities who made Versailles what it was during the long and varied reign of Louis XV. The study of Madame de Maintenon is a real contribution to history, and the pictures of the clever and dazzling beauties who controlled so long the destinies not only of France but measurably of Europe itself from the accession of "le Grand Monarque" to the first threatenings of the Revolution "deluge" are extremely lifelike and skilfully executed. The historical chronicle of the time is by no means lost sight of by the author, but in this series even more than in his works heretofore published in English he appears not only as an interesting and impartial historian, but as a brilliant historical portraitist.

FOUR NEW VOLUMES.
WOMEN OF THE VALOIS AND VERSAILLES COURTS.

Each with Portraits, $1.25. Price per set, in box, cloth, $5.00; half calf, $10.00.

WOMEN OF THE VALOIS COURT.	
THE COURT OF LOUIS XIV.	*In press.*
THE COURT OF LOUIS XV.	*In press.*
THE LAST YEARS OF LOUIS XV.	*In press.*

FAMOUS WOMEN OF THE FRENCH COURT

VOLUMES PREVIOUSLY ISSUED.

THREE VOLUMES ON MARIE ANTOINETTE.

Each with Portrait, $1.25. *Price per set, in box, cloth*, $3.75; *half calf*, $7.50.

MARIE ANTOINETTE AND THE END OF THE OLD RÉGIME.
MARIE ANTOINETTE AT THE TUILERIES.
MARIE ANTOINETTE AND THE DOWNFALL OF ROYALTY.

In this series is unfolded the tremendous panorama of political events in which the unfortunate Queen had so influential a share, beginning with the days immediately preceding the Revolution, when court life at Versailles was so gay and unsuspecting, continuing with the enforced journey of the royal family to Paris, and the agitating months passed in the Tuileries, and concluding with the abolition of royalty, the proclamation of the Republic, and the imprisonment of the royal family, — the initial stage of their progress to the guillotine.

THREE VOLUMES ON THE EMPRESS JOSEPHINE.

Each with Portrait, $1.25. *Price per set, in box, cloth*, $3.75; *half calf*, $7.50.

CITIZENESS BONAPARTE.
THE WIFE OF THE FIRST CONSUL.
THE COURT OF THE EMPRESS JOSEPHINE.

The romantic and eventful period beginning with Josephine's marriage, comprises the astonishing Italian campaign, the Egyptian expedition, the *coup d'état* of Brumaire, and is described in the first of the above volumes; while the second treats of the brilliant society which issued from the chaos of the Revolution, and over which Madame Bonaparte presided so charmingly; and the third, of the events between the assumption of the imperial title by Napoleon and the end of 1807, including, of course, the Austerlitz campaign.

FOUR VOLUMES ON THE EMPRESS MARIE LOUISE.

Each with Portrait, $1.25. *Price per set, in box, cloth*, $5.00; *half calf*, $10.00.

THE HAPPY DAYS OF MARIE LOUISE.
MARIE LOUISE AND THE DECADENCE OF THE EMPIRE.
MARIE LOUISE AND THE INVASION OF 1814.
MARIE LOUISE, THE RETURN FROM ELBA, AND THE HUNDRED DAYS.

The auspicious marriage of the Archduchess Marie Louise to the master of Europe; the Russian invasion, with its disastrous conclusion a few years later; the Dresden and Leipsic campaign; the invasion of France by the Allies, and the marvellous military strategy of Napoleon in 1814, ending only with his defeat and exile to Elba; his life in his little principality; his romantic escape and dramatic return to France; the preparations of the Hundred Days; Waterloo and the definitive restoration of Louis XVIII. closing the era begun in 1789, with "The End of the Old Régime," — are the subjects of the four volumes grouped around the personality of Marie Louise.

FAMOUS WOMEN OF THE FRENCH COURT

TWO VOLUMES ON THE DUCHESS OF ANGOULÊME.

Each with Portrait, $1.25. *Price per set, in box, cloth*, $2.50; *half calf*, $5.00.

THE YOUTH OF THE DUCHESS OF ANGOULÊME.
THE DUCHESS OF ANGOULÊME AND THE TWO RESTORATIONS.

The period covered in this first of these volumes begins with the life of the daughter of Louis XVI. and Marie Antoinette imprisoned in the Temple after the execution of her parents, and ends with the accession of Louis XVIII. after the abdication of Napoleon at Fontainebleau. The first Restoration, its illusions, the characters of Louis XVIII., of his brother, afterwards Charles X., of the Dukes of Angoulême and Berry, sons of the latter, the life of the Court, the feeling of the city, Napoleon's sudden return from Elba, the Hundred Days from the Royalist side, the second Restoration, and the vengeance taken by the new government on the Imperialists, form the subject-matter of the second volume.

THREE VOLUMES ON THE DUCHESS OF BERRY.

Each with Portrait, $1.25. *Price per set, in box, cloth*, $3.75; *half calf*, $7.50.

THE DUCHESS OF BERRY AND THE COURT OF LOUIS XVIII.
THE DUCHESS OF BERRY AND THE COURT OF CHARLES X.
THE DUCHESS OF BERRY AND THE REVOLUTION OF JULY, 1830.

The Princess Marie Caroline, of Naples, became, upon her marriage with the Duke of Berry, the central figure of the French Court during the reigns of both Louis XVIII. and Charles X. The former of these was rendered eventful by the assassination of her husband and the birth of her son, the Count of Chambord, and the latter was from the first marked by those reactionary tendencies which resulted in the dethronement and exile of the Bourbons. The dramatic Revolution which brought about the July monarchy of Louis Philippe, has never been more vividly and intelligently described than in the last volume devoted to the Duchess of Berry.

"*In these translations of this interesting series of sketches, we have found an unexpected amount of pleasure and profit. The author cites for us passages from forgotten diaries, hitherto unearthed letters, extracts from public proceedings, and the like, and contrives to combine and arrange his material so as to make a great many very vivid and pleasing pictures. Nor is this all. The material he lays before us is of real value, and much, if not most of it, must be unknown save to the special students of the period. We can, therefore, cordially commend these books to the attention of our readers. They will find them attractive in their arrangement, never dull, with much variety of scene and incident, and admirably translated.*" — THE NATION, *of December 19, 1890.*

Milton Keynes UK
Ingram Content Group UK Ltd.
UKHW040715141024
449705UK00001B/88